Advances of Research on Teacher Thinking

Edited by

M. Ben-Peretz, R. Bromme and R. Halkes

SWETS NORTH AMERICA INC. / BERWYN
SWETS & ZEITLINGER B.V. / LISSE
1986

LIBRARY OF CONGRESS CATALOGING-IN-PUBLICATION DATA

Advances of research on teacher thinking.

   Bibliography: p.
   1. Teachers--Psychology.   2. Thought and thinking.
I. Ben-Peretz, Miriam. II. Bromme, Rainer, 1951-
III. Halkes, R.
LB2840.A35 1986   371.1'001'9   86-23116
ISBN 90-265-0774-7

CIP-GEGEVENS KONINKLIJKE BIBLIOTHEEK, DEN HAAG

Advances

Advances of research on teacher thinking / ed. by M.
Ben-Peretz, R. Bromme and R. Halkes. - Lisse :
Swets & Zeitlinger
Met lit. opg.
ISBN 90-265-0774-7
SISO 454 UDC 371.32
Trefw.: didactiek.

Cover design H. Veltman
Printed by Offsetdrukkerij Kanters B.V., Alblasserdam
Copyright 1986 ISATT and Swets & Zeitlinger B.V., Lisse

ISBN 90 265 0774 7

CONTENTS

ADVANCES OF RESEARCH ON TEACHER THINKING: INTRODUCTION

M. Ben-Peretz
University of Haifa
Israel

R. Bromme
Universität Bielefeld
Fed. Rep. of Germany

R. Halkes
Tilburg University
The Netherlands

The number of studies of teachers' thought processes has increased since the beginning of the seventies. How important teachers' and students'views are for what is actually going on in classrooms may have been evident to practitioners before. Certain practical problems, however, had to arise before researchers became aware of the importance of teachers' cognitions for processes in school.

Among these practical problems were the difficulties encountered by attempts to change the curriculum and to improve teaching which were due to the ignorance of teachers minds and interpretations. (Olson, 1982). Other practical problems arose from the phenomenon that theories once learnt during teacher education seemed to evaporate from the teachers' knowledge. Prospective teachers are taught theories concerning pedagogy, psychology and subject matter areas, but experienced teachers claim that it was necessary for them to forget all theories from university and to learn the real "practice" in the classroom instead. But were did the theories once learnt go, and what are their actual uses? On the other hand, it has become just as evident in recent years that teacher education focussing on the behavioral aspect while neglecting the teachers' knowledge and views will fail, as has been shown by the development of microteaching towards an ever more cognitive education of teachers to be. (Macleod and McIntyre, 1977)

Of course, the practical problems of teacher education and school reform are not the only causes for the expansion of research into teachers'thinking. Developments in psychology and in sociology have laid the foundation for this growth as well. Contributions came in particular from the cognitive orientation in psychology, the interpretative paradigms in sociology, the wider acceptance of methods collecting verbal data and the study of information processing in other practical fields (such as medical doctors' diagnoses). These developments in the basic research of psychology and other disciplines, as well as changing perspectives in

1

educational research (cfr. Allender, 1986) have provided both theoretical and methodological impulses to study teachers' cognitions.
Besides practical problems and theoretical developments in related fields, the study of teaching and learning in school itself has raised several questions about teachers' cognitions. Teacher effectiveness research, for instance, has made clear in recent years that a teacher's effectiveness depends on his/her ability to orchestrate appropriate methods and to adapt the content and method of his/her teaching to the situation at hand. Hence the cognitive prerequisites for and the thinking processes of teachers have to be analyzed in order to explain why some are successful and some are not. Curriculum research has shown that the teacher's interpretation of the curriculum is crucial for what is taught in school. Many processes of teaching and learning cannot be understood and explained when the views and the knowledge of the individuals involved are not considered.

These challenges were met by establishing research groups, centers and associations. The 1974 Conference of the US National Institute of Education on "Teaching as clinical information processing" provided an important impulse (NIE 1975) for the US and Canada. Another decisive step to foster communication between those already active in the field was the founding of the AERA Special Interest Group "Teacher and Student Cognitions" which created a common basis for researchers on the North American continent in 1983. Simultaneously, researchers in the new field met for conferences on a national level in several European countries. A European initiative of 1983 led to founding the "International Study Association on Teacher Thinking (ISATT)" which intends to promote a worldwide exchange of ideas and experience in the field of teacher cognitions. It has since received growing interest on the part of educational researchers with various concerns. In October 1983, ISATT held its first symposium to launch the association, publishing the proceedings in a volume edited by Halkes and Olson (1984).

The second conference took place at Tilburg University (The Netherlands) in May 1985, gathering researchers from 12 countries. The present volume is based on papers presented at this conference; it is, however, no account of the proceedings. It is structured around three areas of research which, in our opinion, are of particular importance for the further development of the field.

The first topic concerns the leading metaphors (e.g. teachers as decision makers, as scientists, etc.) for the subject under study, the second refers to the content and process of thinking concerning specific tasks and the third covers the methods of data collecting and analysis.

These topics deal with paradigmatic or underlying assumptions being the foundation of all research activities in the field. These however, are by no means uniformly conceptualized between researchers. It is necessary to create awareness of these more implicit assumptions. Everybody working in this field uses a "leading metaphor" with regard to teachers and prefers certain methods which presuppose, for instance, a certain view of the accessibility of teachers' cognitions.

We selected papers which may contribute towards making these assumptions more clear and which are in our opinion, good examples of how fundamental issues have been addressed.

The first topic of "leading metaphors" for the subject under study was extensively discussed at both ISATT's conferences. The leading metaphor delineates what is understood by the notion of thinking within "teacher thinking". In the present volume Clark reflects on the development of these conceptions in the US and Canada. While the teacher has formerly been treated as a decision maker, such as a physician making clinical decisions, he/she is now being conceptualized as a "professional who constructs meaning", who develops and tests his/her personal theories about the world around him/her. In Europe, the emphasis has been on the constructivist aspect and personal theories from the very beginning. This is why the metaphor of the teacher as a subjective theorist, which stresses this very aspect of subjective reconstruction of meaning, has become widely accepted (see, e.g., Huber and Mandl 1984, and critically Bromme 1984). However, a thorough review of the European developments is lacking and we would like to urge for this.

It may be appropriate to abandon a too narrow concept of teachers' cognitive processes in favor of the wide range of experience, beliefs, and knowledge which is pertinent beyond decisions. However, psychological concepts are needed for the cognitive processes that are relevant for teaching. Hence, one function of the leading metaphor is to make explicit the types of structures and processes within the teacher's mind as assumed by the researcher. The second function of the leading metaphor pertains to the relation between cognitions and teaching behaviour.

It is self-evident that research into teachers' thinking runs the risk of excessive "cognitivism". We are witnissing an extension of what is meant by "teachers' thinking". Almost all factors influencing teacher activity are subsumed under this notion. This has led to an over-emphasis on internal and mental control of activity. Both the teacher's task proper and his/her working context influence his/her activities and they need not pass through the teacher's mind in every instance to exert an influence (take for instance factors like the temporal frame of schooling or the architecture of the school building). A metaphor for the teacher is required in order to become aware of what is subsumed under "cognition" and which other factors are relevant for the teacher's activities, but are not "cognitive".

The leading metaphors' third function concerns the teacher's task on which the researcher's interest is focussed. E.g., the metaphor of the teacher as decision maker was more or less fitted to the task of assessing students, for instance in the context of giving marks or making predictions. This metaphor however, does not fit as well to the task of presenting new knowledge contained in subject matter during the lessons. The metaphor the researcher uses leads him to consider specific tasks more than others, thereby obstruing the view on other tasks.

In our view it is essential to consider the nature of the teacher's task, i.e. the fact that this nature has a specific effect on the demand this task places on the teacher's thinking. Hence the metaphors of the teacher as a decision maker or as a subjective theorist may one day be replaced by that of:" a teacher is a teacher is a teacher..." which would reflect the fact that there are specific characteristics of the task demand teachers have to cope with and master.

The task demands however do not present themselves as clear as one would wish they would. Dilemmas emerge in teaching, situations in which the teacher is confronted or believes to be confronted with alternatives for action perceived as both worthwhile or threatening or situations with goals evaluated as incompatible such as fostering individual students versus whole class instruction, or still otherwise, with negative side effects of prefered actions.
This phenomenon of dilemmas relates to the leading metaphor of the study at hand as well as to the nature of the task: dilemmas could be interpreted as caused by conflicts in teachers'minds and/or as contradictory aspects of the actual task.

The book's second part is intended to make the features of teachers'tasks and of task-related thinking more clear.
There are tendencies in the field to take into account the specificity of the teacher's task and its effect on the shape and content of teacher's thinking, and this volume provides examples for this. It includes studies of teachers' task related thinking concerning their knowledge about the students, a new subject like computer literacy and teaching itself.

All the studies in this part of the book, however, deal with topics which may be important for teachers'everyday teaching.
The assessment studies focus on the daily judgement of students which is necessary to enable teachers to adapt to the knowledge and abilities of students. The studies about the thinking of a new curriculum may contribute towards filling in the now widely acknowledge gap concerning teachers' subject matter related thinking, while the studies of teachers' teaching criteria and their perception of the job itself may render insight into the aspects of teaching that they themselves see as conditions for doing a better job.

The book's methodological section illustrates the relation between the researcher's choice of his/her leading metaphor and his/her methods of data collection, providing examples for methods not widely known, but meriting wider use. The topic behind the methodological contribution is how to make sure that the researcher's cognitive entities are not confused with those of the teachers. This is pertinent problem both for strict approaches (using, for instance, judgment scales for data collection) and for so-called weak approaches (using, for instance, semi-standardized interviews). The question as to the meaning of teachers'terms which are interpreted as verbal data remains open. If practical knowledge is of a shape different of that of everyday knowledge and of theoretical knowledge, these differences may be situated in the different semantic fields of the terms used by teachers and researchers. Some studies indicate that this may well be the case; this is an important field for future research.

So much to learn, the contributions to this volume do not provide answers to all questions raised. They show however, how far we have come and how we intend to proceed.

Bielefeld, Haifa, Tilburg, June 1986.

REFERENCES

Allender, J.S., (1986). Educational Research: A personal and social Process. *Review of Educational Research,*56, 2, 173-196.
Bromme, R. (1984). On the limitations of the theory metaphor for the study of teachers' expert knowledge. In : Halkes,R. and Olson, J.K., (eds), *Teacher thinking: a new perspective on persisting problems in education.*Lisse: Swets and Zeitlinger, 43-58.
Halkes, R. and Olson, J.K. (eds).(1984). *Teacher Thinking: a new perspective on persisting problems in education.*Proceedings of the first symposium of the International Study Association on Teacher Thinking, Tilburg, October 1983. Lisse: Swets and Zeitlinger.
Huber G.L. and Mandl,H.,(1984). Access to teacher cognitions: problems of assessment and analysis. In: Halkes,R. and Olson, J.K. (1984),*Teacher Thinking: a new perspective on persisting problems in education.* Lisse: Swets and Zeitlinger, 58-73.
MacLeod, G. and McIntyre,D. (1977). Towards a model for micro-teaching. *British Journal of Teacher Education,* 3, 111-120.
NIE, National Institute of Education, (1975). *Theory Development* (Report of Panel 10, National Conference on Studies in Teaching). Washington D.C.: National Institute of Education.
Olson, J.K. (1982). Classroom knowledge and curriculum Change. In: Olson, J.K. (ed). *Innovation in the Science Curriculum.* London: Croom Helm.

TEN YEARS OF CONCEPTUAL DEVELOPMENT IN RESEARCH ON TEACHER THINKING

Christopher M. Clark
College of Education
Michigan State University
United States of America

SUMMARY

This paper describes conceptions of the teacher, of students, of
subject matter, of context, and of the research process that characterized the field of research on teaching in 1975 and contrasts these
with contemporary views. Concerns are raised about the meaning of
these conceptual developments with regard to multi-disciplinarity,
competition for research funding, absence of attention to populations
of teachers and students who are most at risk, focus on thinking
processes to the exclusion of content, and insufficient attention to
unintended side effects of research on teacher thinking.

INTRODUCTION

In the last decade many researchers have become active in research on
teacher thinking. We have done tens of studies, invented new methods
and designs, formed special interest groups and organizations (like
ISATT), and published books, journal articles, monographs, and
reviews. Now the time has come to ask ourselves what we have accomplished in the service of teachers and students--what does this work
add up to and in what directions should we proceed?
      This is a critical paper. It is critical because I care deeply
about education and I care deeply about researchers on teacher
thinking and the work that we do. The work, research on teacher
thinking, is exciting and important. And I believe that today we
have reached a crucial decision point ourselves--a choice between
continuing to be merely curious about teachers' thought and action,
or to also do good for teachers, students, communities and for ourselves. I hope to influence that choice and to suggest ways in which
to act on it in the years to come.
      I have organized this paper into two major sections. The first
and longer part traces the development of conceptions that have influenced research on teacher thinking during the past ten years. In
that section, I contrast views of the teacher, of students, of subject matter, of context, and of research that characterized our field
ten . years ago with contemporary views. In part two of the paper, I
raise some nasty and unsettling questions about what the last ten

years of conceptual development in our field imply. Part one cele-
brates how far we have come. Part two calls us to reflect and (perhaps) to repent.

1. CELEBRATION OF CONCEPTUAL PROGRESS

Conceptions of the teacher

How did the founders of research on teacher thinking think about the
teacher? Who was this person in 1975? What roles did teachers play
and what tasks were they expected to perform? And what was the status
of teachers' knowledge at that time? My reading of the report of
Panel 6 of the National Institute of Education Conference on Studies
in Teaching (NIE, 1975) offers the following portrait: The teacher
is a decision-maker. The teacher is in a clinical relationship with
students. A major role of the teacher is to diagnose needs and
learning problems of students and to wisely prescribe effective and
appropriate instructional treatments. The metaphor of teacher as
physician was alive and well in 1975, and many of the methods of
inquiry proposed for use in the study of teacher thinking were first
developed to study the clinical decisions of medical doctors. In
1975, the teacher was also portrayed as a kind of business executive
who operated in a "boundedly rational" world by defining a problem
space in an infinitely complex task environment and by seeking merely
satisfactory solutions to problems and dilemmas rather than working
toward optimal solutions (Simon, 1957).

This, then, is our composite portrait of the teacher in 1975.
Perhaps it tells us as much about the scholars who wrote the Panel 6
Report as it does about teachers ten years ago. The medical metaphor
certainly reflects the fact that Shulman and Elstein (1975) spent
many more hours working with physicians than listening to teachers in
the years immediately preceeding the NIE conference. This image of
the teacher also reflects our tendency to borrow theory and method
from psychology, in this case, cognitive psychology with a heavy
overlay of information processing theory. The heroes of the day were
Simon, Brunswick, Hammond, and Kleinmuntz.

In the past ten years, the image of the teacher implicit or
explicit in research on teacher thinking has evolved. Decision-
making has been replaced with "sense-making" as the central cognitive
activity of teachers. (This is not to say that teachers do not make
decisions, but rather that teachers' decision-making is now seen as
one among several activities in the service of making meaning for
themselves and their students.) The metaphor of teacher as physician
is giving way to the image of teacher as reflective professional
(Schon, 1983). In a sense, this change represents a move toward a
more abstract conception of teacher and teacher's role. Medicine is
a profession, and so are architecture, law, business, and the military.
We have moved away from the primarily diagnostic-prescriptive way of
thinking about the mental life of teachers toward a more general view
of teaching as a profession that calls for extensive knowledge of the
content to be taught and of the psychologies of learning and of
students, all of which must be interpreted, adapted, and artfully
applied to particular situations by the reflectively professional

teacher. This view of the teacher supplements or subsumes role definitions that emphasize the technical skills of instructing as the defining characteristics of effective teaching.

The teacher of 1985 is a constructivist who continually builds, elaborates, and tests his or her personal theory of the world. The notions of bounded rationality, task environment, and problem space are still invoked, but with some important developments. First, we are coming to recognize that it is unfair and incomplete to impute all of the responsibility for defining a problem space to the teacher. Powerful influences outside the control of individual teachers play parts in defining the problem space. A classroom with fifty hot and hungry children of poverty calls forth a rather different problem space than does a class of twenty compliant and comfortable children of the middle class. A further twist on the notion of bounded rationality in teachers is the realization that teachers, like their students and other human beings, can and often do hold multiple conflicting theories and explanations about the world and its phenomena (Roth, 1984). Teachers (and researchers) tend to switch back and forth among these inconsistent and incompatible ways of thinking and explaining. And the amazing thing is that this kind of inconsistent, imperfect, and incomplete way of thinking works rather well in the complex and practical world of the classroom. Teachers accept merely satisfactory solutions to problems not because they are lazy or ignorant, but because many of the problems that they face are genuine dilemmas (Berlak & Berlak, 1981; Lampert, 1985; Wagner, 1984) that have no optimal solutions. In short, we have begun to move away from the cybernetically elegant, internally consistent, but mechanical metaphors that guided our earlier work.

Conceptions of Students

Ten years ago, the image of students held by the founders of research on teacher thinking had to be inferred, because little direct attention was paid to writing about the image of the student. My inferences are that students were seen as puzzles to be solved or as patients to be diagnosed. While a great deal of attention was paid to the teacher as an active processor of information, students were still seen as relatively passive and manipulable recipients of information. Early research on teacher thinking was justified by claiming that teacher thinking controlled teacher behavior and that teacher behavior was what produced student learning. Students, by implication, were objects to be acted upon by teachers with more or less thoughtful technical skill. Students were also seen as the source of cues that teachers might notice and decide to use as a basis for adjusting their own teaching behavior (NIE, 1975; Marx, 1978; Cone, 1978; Shavelson, Cadwell, and Isu, 1977; Peterson & Clark, 1978).

In the past ten years, our way of thinking about students has also evolved. There is some recognition that, like teachers, students are thinkers, planners, and decision makers themselves (Wittrock, 1986). Students are now seen as transformers of knowledge--active learners who enter the classroom with robust preconceptions about the world and how it operates (Posner, Strike, Hewson & Gertzog, 1982; Roth, 1984). Students are now called "novices" who have responsibilities for

cooperating in their own learning. The metaphor of the individual
medical patient to be diagnosed is giving way to a more dynamic and
social view of students who learn from one another, who build on and
draw from what they already know and believe, and who necessarily make
a somewhat different sense of what teachers teach them than the sense
that the teacher intended to communicate. In short, students are
constructivists also, and our research has just begun to explore what
happens when two sets of constructivists, differing in knowledge,
experience, motivation, and authority, put their heads together.
Shulman and Carey (1984) have recently suggested that the educational
research community has evolved in its thinking toward a view of humans
as collectively rational. This view acknowledges the importance of
attending to how teachers and students exercise their abilities "...to
participate intelligently and reasonably in groups, to pursue multiple,
mutually shared goals through the exercise of reason jointly produced
and collaboratively exercised" (Shulman & Carey, 1984, p. 517).

Conceptions of Curriculum

At the beginning of this era of research on teacher thinking, mention
of curriculum was noticeably absent from our literature and our delib-
erations. The psychologists were in charge and our focus was on how
teachers dealt with the "givens" of schooling. Subject matter was
seen as one of these givens--a condition or set of variables to be
described or controlled. Research by DeGroot on chess masters was
cited in this early literature (Shulman and Elstein, 1975), but the
way in which that work was cited did not include much attention to the
content and organization of subject matter knowledge in the minds of
either chess masters or, by extension, school teachers.

Two lines of research in the past decade have done much to enrich
our sense of the role that curriculum and subject matter knowledge
play in understanding teaching generally and teacher thinking in particular. The first of these lines of research is that on distinctions
between the knowledge and performance of novices and experts. Research in this area by Greeno (Greeno, Glaser, & Newell, 1983),
Leinhardt (Leinhardt, 1983; Leinhardt, Weidman, & Hammond, 1984),
Larkin (Larkin, McDermott, Simon & Simon, 1980) and others demon-
strates that the amount of knowledge and also the ways in which experts
organize their knowledge in a richly interconnected conceptual network is rather different from the amount and organization of knowledge
in the minds of novices. These differences have profound implications
for the ease with which experts approach and solve both familiar and
novel problems, including problems of pedagogy. We have come to believe that there are qualitative differences in the ways in which
experts and novices know and think about what they know.

A second line of research that bears on teachers' subject matter
knowledge is that on teacher planning (see Clark and Peterson, 1986,
for a detailed review). It was a surprise to me in 1978 that my own
research on teacher planning, which I thought of as primarily psychological, aroused so much interest among curriculum theorists. As I
began to correspond with curricularists and to publish in their journals, I came to see that teacher planning is a means for organizing
and transforming subject matter knowledge and curriculum into peda-
gogically useful forms and routines. I came to understand teacher

10

planning as a link between thought and action that, in many respects, defines and sometimes distorts the content to be taught. I came to see a connection between what process-product researchers call "opportunity to learn" and the dynamics of teacher planning that shape opportunity to learn.

Both the research on novice-expert contrasts and that on teacher planning support the idea that teachers' knowledge of content to be taught and the ways in which that knowledge is organized are crucial influences on teacher thinking and action. More recently, ethnographers and philosophers have shed even more light on the importance of what teachers know and how they hold and use their knowledge. Here, I think of the important work on personal practical knowledge done at the Ontario Institute for Studies in Education (Elbaz, 1983; Connelly and Clandinin, 1984; Clandinin, 1985; Kroma, 1983), of Lampert's analysis of the nature of teachers' knowledge and needs (Lampert, 1985), and philosophical analyses of conceptions of knowledge and education by Buchmann and her colleagues at Michigan State University (Buchmann, 1984; Buchmann and Schwille, 1983). Along with the phrase "subject matter knowledge" the word "epistomology" has become much more common in the literature of research on teacher thinking. That is, we have come to appreciate that analysis of teachers' mastery of the facts and procedures of the disciplines they teach is insufficient. We must also come to understand teachers' ways of knowing and their beliefs about the nature of knowledge itself before we can begin to understand the role of knowledge and curriculum in teacher thinking and in education more generally (Floden, 1983).

One intriguing hypothesis about the way in which teachers' knowledge is organized is that it takes the form of cases (Shulman, 1986). This line of thinking helps us to distinguish between knowledge of a discipline in the forms commonly represented in textbooks (i.e., abstract principles, general laws, fundamental ideas, and puzzle forms) and replaces it with images of cases, vivid experiences, and good examples. This line of thought also suggests that there may be important differences between the ways in which, say, scientists or mathematicians hold and express their knowledge and the ways in which teachers of science or mathematics hold and express their knowledge of the same phenomena. Perhaps the distinction between disciplinary knowledge and pedagogical knowledge is overdrawn, but I think that it holds some promise. In part of my own work of the next several years, I intend to pursue a program of research on the psychology, epistemology, and pedagogy of good examples in teaching. I think we need to know more about what makes a good example good, how teachers learn to create, recognize, and use good examples, when good examples can get us into trouble (conceptually speaking), and how students' understandings of and memory for what they are taught are affected by the quality of the examples used in teaching.

Conceptions of Context

Perhaps the most dramatic set of conceptual developments in research on teacher thinking relate to the changes in how we have come to think of the context of teaching. My impression of our 1975 image of context is that the school classroom was seen as the unit of analysis: a clearly bounded yet complex task environment, the major purpose of which was to produce or foster student learning. This is essentially the same image of the context of schooling found in the process-product and teacher effectiveness literature. Phillip Jackson (1968) alerted us to some of the invisible complexities of the classroom almost 20 years ago. But, as researchers on teaching, we tended to believe strongly in the power of the classroom walls as boundaries for the physical, social, and psychological context of education.

The active presence of anthropologists of education in our field during the past 8 years has done a great deal to broaden and enrich our conceptions of context. We have moved away from a rather impoverished and fragmented notion of context as an aggregation of "background variables" to a richer, more dynamic, collectively defined and negotiated understanding of context (Shultz, Florio, and Erickson, 1982; Erickson, 1986). But most of the anthropological and multi-disciplinary studies of teaching in our literature illuminate the internal dynamics of classroom context. We have learned how class-room rules and routines are negotiated, discovered, and enforced. Field workers and socio-linguists have shown us how cultural differences and similarities between teacher and students can impede or enable teaching and learning (Phillips, 1972). But with all this progress in our thinking about context, I believe we have a need for more conceptual development in this area. My developing view is that the school and classroom are rather more permeable settings for teaching and learning than our literature and our thinking suggest. Schools and classrooms are the locus of social, psychological, physical, political, and metaphysical action, embedded in the world and affected by it. The purposes of schooling and of classrooms are many and varied, and only occasionally is student learning the first and over-riding priority. Context is not a "variable" or a collection of more or less mechanical components, any more than a river or the temperate zone of the northern hemisphere are aggregations of variables. I believe that we must think more synthetically and holistically about context if we are to continue to make progress in understanding teacher and student thinking and their ramifications.

Conceptions of Research

My conception of research on teacher thinking has certainly developed in surprising ways during the past ten years. I would like to sum-marize these conceptual developments under four headings: a) Methods of Inquiry; b) Concepts and Models; c) Aims and Products of Research; and d) The Relationship of Research to the Practice of Teaching.

In the past ten years I believe we have moved from a dependence on methods of the psychology laboratory to a dependence on methods of field work. The psychology laboratory contributed techniques such as stimulated recall interviewing, clinical interviews of various sorts, experimental designs for policy capturing studies, and think-aloud and protocol analysis methods. Use of these methods has sparked interesting and important debates about their validity and reliability, and raised fundamental questions about the limits of what can be learned from introspection, recollection, and self-reports of cogni-tive processes (Nisbett and Wilson, 1977; Eriksson and Simon, 1980; Yinger and Clark, 1982; Huber and Mandl, 1984). While this debate is certainly not yet settled, our approach to the study of teacher thinking has tended to move from relatively well-controlled and researcher-defined conditions and settings to the more representatively complex teacher- and school- defined world of real classrooms. Anthropological description and field work analysis methods have been added to evolved versions of laboratory methods. The emphasis has moved from hypothesis testing about cognitive processes to what Erickson (1986) calls interpretive analyses, in which we become more explicit about the role of the investigator in making sense of his or her experience. Thick description, triangulation, and collaborative interpretation of descriptive research have become more common (Erickson, 1986). We have begun to adopt the canon of "disciplined subjectivity" in place of the myth of "scientific objectivity."

Ten years ago the majority of our concepts used to frame questions and describe teachers' thinking came from psychology, and our models for describing processes had a decidedly cybernetic quality (e.g., Peterson and Clark, 1978; Shavelson and Stern, 1981). In the ensuing years, the limitations of these primarily psychological concepts and cybernetic models have become more apparent. Perc Marland has written a nice analysis of the relative strengths and limitations of models of teachers' interactive thinking (Marland, 1983), and Clark and Peterson (1986) discuss the shortcomings of both their own and Shavelson and Stern's (1981) models of teacher thinking during instruction. Similarly, the once-unquestioned rational planning model has been challenged by empiricists and theorists such as Robert Yinger (1977). I agree thoroughly with Yinger's more recent exortations that we should put energy into developing and discovering what he calls "the language of practice" (Yinger, 1985), by which he means a language using concepts and terms that mirror and express life in classrooms as teachers and students see and experience it, rather than as visiting social scientists see it. As a field, we have become somewhat more sensitive to the dangers of reification of our own invented concepts and models, but there is still abundant need for caution. We must remind ourselves that it is possible for many false and even dangerous models to "fit" the intrinsically partial data that we have about teachers' thought processes.

Ten years ago, researchers on teacher thinking were primarily concerned with increasing the depth of our understanding of the mental lives of teachers in order to be able to a) explain why teaching operates as it does, and b) to improve the practice of teaching both by direct training interventions and more indirectly by organizing schools, curriculum, policies, etc. to fit more smoothly with the operations and limitations of the mental lives of teachers. In short, the early promise of this work was to produce fundamental psychological knowledge that had immediate implications for practice. Recently, I closed an extensive review of research on teacher thinking with the assessment that "A decade of research on teachers' thought processes has taught us as much about how to think about teaching as it has about teachers' thinking" (Clark and Peterson, 1986). I still believe that this is so; that is, that the psychological processes that we have learned somewhat more about are not unique to teachers but are generally human qualities, strengths, and limitations. But we have gained a new and more detailed appreciation for teaching in all of its complexity; of this there can be no doubt. And beyond this appreciation, I believe the field has begun to adopt the aim of empowerment of individual teachers. That is, the aim of providing the reflectively professional teacher with tools and encouragement to frame and solve his or her own unique professional challenges in much the way that other professionals do. We are now on a mission of advocacy and service to teachers rather than on a quest of discovery in a strange and unfamiliar land.

Finally, we take up a continuing and troublesome issue: that of the relationship between research and the practice of teaching. The early literature of our field is rather silent on this topic, except for the ever-present analogy to the study of medical decision-making. However, it has rarely been the case that researchers on teacher thinking actually see themselves in the same kind of power and respect relationship to school teachers as they do to physicians. The implied relationship to teaching practice was essentially explanatory and prescriptive. The implication was that effective planning and decision-making would be discovered, described, modelled, and taught to less experienced and less effective teachers. Hand-in-glove with this implication was the idea that successful research will make the effective practice of teaching easier.

Today, I think we are in a different, though still incomplete relationship to practice of teaching. I have advocated thinking about research on teaching as providing service to the practice of teaching (Clark, 1984). My work with Susan Florio-Ruane in the MSU Written Literacy Forum (Clark & Florio, 1983) is one example of an ambitious, expensive, and rewarding way to work out and discover appropriately helpful relationships between research and practice; between researchers and practitioners. Others, particularly in science education (e.g., Posner, Strike, Hewson & Gertzog, 1982; Roth, 1984), have attempted to improve the practice of teaching by designing curriculum materials and teacher's guides that are intended to make use of what we have learned about students' preconceptions and about teachers' planning and subject matter knowledge. Teacher education programs at Michigan State University have been reorganized to reflect new discoveries about the formerly invisible domain of teacher thinking and to incorporate and draw implications from contemporary views of knowledge and knowledge change (Confrey, 1982). And, perhaps most importantly, I see changes in the relationships between teachers and researchers. Teachers' knowledge is now more respected by researchers than was the case in 1975 (Clark and Lampert, 1985). Teachers have begun to come more active as full partners in the research process (Burton, 1985; Florio and Walsh, 1981), and a few courageous researchers have spent a year or more shouldering the responsibilities, demands, and rewards of classroom teaching themselves. All this has led to a constructive turning away from the goal of "making good teaching easier" to that of portraying and understanding good teaching in all of its irreducible complexity and difficulty. Quality portraiture may be of more practical and inspirational value than reductionistic analysis and technical prescriptiveness.

14

2. REFLECTIONS AND IMPLICATIONS

What do these conceptual developments of a decade of research on teacher thinking mean, and where do they lead? First, I believe that they reflect progress, in the best sense of that word: Gains in what we know about teachers and the tasks they face, improvements in our methods of studying and describing thought and action, more effective ways of teaching some subject matters, and more complete preparation of prospective teachers. Ten years of research on teacher thinking have made possible a constructive combination of research on instruction with research on curriculum. Practicing teachers have been brought more fully into the important enterprise of understanding, describing, and improving teaching and learning.

But there are also less positive and more worrisome ways to interpret these conceptual developments of the last ten years, and I raise these now--because it is time to ask big questions; to take a larger perspective on our work; to ask what we have really accomplished, and at what costs. We have a rare opportunity to confront these larger questions, to think and reflect together, and possibly, to chart a new course for research on teacher thinking. To do so, I believe that we should examine the darker side of progress in research on teacher thinking. Please consider these hypotheses about what my list of conceptual developments in research on teacher thinking could imply:

First, these conceptual and methodological developments could reflect merely application of the theories and methods of more and more academic disciplines. Multi-disciplinary research was called for early in the life of our field. This was because the early writers realized that the complexities of schooling would not yield to the point of view of a single discipline. Psychology was followed by anthropology, sociology, economics, and philosophy. To these were added the practical wisdom of experienced teachers. But, at some point, multi-disciplinarity may have become an end in itself. Borrowing more and more heavily from other disciplines will certainly add to the variety of concepts and tools for inquiry at our disposal. But we should ask, does this variety represent progress, or merely proliferation?

A second possible explanation for our conceptual progress is that of competition between paradigms, people, and institutions. Competition for research funding (at least in North America) is vigorous. And one of the principal grounds on which research proposals are judged is originality. Thus, there seems to be more of a premium placed on making our research distinct from that of our predecessors than there is on synthesis, replication, and conceptual coherence. This pressure for originality and distinctiveness may have been self-imposed. It also may have produced a richer variety of approaches and tools for inquiry than would have otherwise developed in ten years. But now may be the time to reject originality and distinctiveness, return to our fundamental research questions, and proceed to answer those questions by using the small number of research designs and methods of inquiry that seem to have served us well.

A third implication of our short history is most unsettling. As I have reviewed the literature of research on teaching, I have developed the conviction that this work represents a failure of moral courage on our part. In my judgment, none of the research on teacher thinking has directly addressed serious and difficult problems and crises in education. For example, the work on teacher planning and decision making has been done almost exclusively in nice, well-organized, upper middle class suburban elementary school classrooms. We have omitted any attention to all to more volatile and challenging problem areas in our education systems including poverty, nationalism, cultural conflict, racism, sexism, discrimination, and massive failure to learn in certain quarters of our educational systems. Have we doomed ourselves to triviality by our lack of moral courage? Are we satisfied with serving our own intellectual curiosities while teachers of the poor and the handicapped struggle without help? Or have we just reached the point at which our own understandings of teacher thinking permit us to sail in more troubled waters?

A fourth possible reading of our recent history is that we continue to prize process over the content and substance of instruction. We have described and come to better understandings of various planning, decision-making, and reflective processes used by teachers. But there is considerably less attention in our work to the quality and organization of what is being taught. Even the curricularists among us seem more caught up in a focus on process than on the content of teaching. To the extent that this is so, we are no different and no better than the process-product researchers who can tell us how to increase time on task, but who have nothing to say about the quality and worth of the tasks themselves.

Fifth, I am concerned that our research reflects a narrow parochialism, in which we stare so intently at the teacher as the source, linchpin, and dynamo of education that we have become insensitive to the other very powerful forces and constraints that shape and influence schooling. Like solar astronomers, we have become partially blind by staring too long at the sun. Where are the students, the curriculum, the community, and a dynamic theory of their interactions? The teacher is certainly an important and central agent in education. But let us not lose all sense of proportion as we frame and interpret our research.

A sixth interpretation of our work is that, unconsciously, we have promoted an insidious form of eleitism. We have elevated and lionized those few school teachers who are most like ourselves (reflective, analytic, verbally articulate, sophisticated in their knowledge, liberal and worldly in their values). These are the teachers whose planning, thinking, and decision-making we study and, unreflectively, portray as ideals for all other teachers, experienced and novice alike. While our rhetoric sounds a call for "power to all teachers", our research is cast in such a way that only those few teachers who are already most like us can identify with it. In what ways does this work serve those who need our support most? (A related point made recently by Roger Simon of OISE is that our advocacy of reflection, self-examination, and attention to private and individual cognitive activity of teachers may have an unintended and paradoxically conservative effect. For by urging teachers to focus mainly on their inner lives, we draw their attention away from the larger, collective, external forces and entities that may be manipulating and controlling them and the entire system of education.)

Seventh, and finally, our research on teacher thinking may entail the assumption that the end justifies the means. That is, that we need not examine the moral, social, and psychological costs of a method of instruction (e.g., direct instruction for children of the poor; conceptual change teaching of science) if that method leads to higher achievement test scores or "more correct" conceptual organization of ideas. If we are on a mission of discovery, we have responsibility to discover and count the costs of unintended and unexamined side effects of our suggestions and prescriptions, as well as documenting the ways in which our discoveries have solved old problems.

3. CONCLUSION

I could have pointed to many promising, exciting, and praiseworthy implications of our ten years of research on teacher thinking. I have done so in other places, at other times (e.g., Clark and Peterson, 1986). But my purpose here is to set a self-critical tone for researchers on teacher thinking. As you reflect on your own research, read the reports of colleagues, and plan future studies I urge you to ask yourselves and your colleagues:

> What are the social and personal dangers in pursuing this line of inquiry?

> How should your ways of working be changed to better serve the interests of all educators, school children and the world community?

> How does knowledge about teacher thinking fit into larger, more dynamic, and more complete conceptions of education?

In my judgment, we need to put at least as much as energy and creativity into answering the question "How shall we do good?" as we have into inventing methods for probing and describing the hidden world of teacher thinking.

REFERENCES

Berlak, A. & Berlak, H. (1981). *Dilemmas of schooling: Teaching and social change.* London: METHUEN.

Buchmann, M. (1984). The use of research knowledge in teacher education and teaching. *American Journal of Education, 92*(4), 421-439.

Buchmann, M. & Schwille, J. (1983). Education: The overcoming of experience. *American Journal of Education, 92*(1), 30-51.

Burton, F. (1985, January). *Off the bench and into the game: A classroom teacher's conception of doing action research.* Paper presented at the Meadow Brook Research Symposium on Collaborative Action Research in Education. Oakland University, Rochester, MI.

Clandinin, D.J. (1985). Personal practical knowledge: A study of teachers' classroom images. *Curriculum Inquiry, 15*(4), 361-385.

Clark, C.M. (1984, June). *Research in the service of teaching.* Paper presented to the Contexts of Literacy Conference, Snowbird, Utah.

Clark, C.M. & Florio, S. (1983). The Written Literacy Forum: Combining research and practice. *Teacher Education Quarterly, 10*(3).

Clark, C.M. & Lampert, M. (1985). *What knowledge is of most worth to teachers? Insights from studies of teacher thinking.* (Occasional Paper No. 86). East Lansing, MI: Michigan State University. Institute for Research on Teaching.

Clark, C.M. & Peterson, P.L. (1986). Teachers' thought processes. In M. Wittrock (Ed.), *Handbook of Research on Teaching,* Third Edition. (pp. 255-295). New York: Mcmillan.

Cone, R. (1978, March). *Teachers' decisions in managing student behavior: A laboratory simulation of interactive decision-making by teachers.* Paper presented at the annual meeting of the American Educational Research Association, Toronto, Canada.

Confrey, J. (1982). Content and pedagogy in secondary schools. *Journal of Teacher Education, 33*(1), 13-16.

Connelly, F.M. & Clandinin, D.J. (1984). Teachers' personal practical knowledge. In R. Halkes & J. Olson (Eds.), *Teacher thinking: A new perspective on persisting problems in education.* Heirewig, Holland: Swets.

Elbaz, F. (1983). *Teacher thinking: A study of practical knowledge.* New York: Nichols Publishing.

Erickson, F. (1986). Qualitative methods in research on teaching. In M. Wittrock (Ed.), *Handbook of Research on Teaching,* Third Edition. (pp. 119-161). New York: Mcmillan.

Eriksson, K.A. & Simon, H.A. (1980). Verbal reports as data. *Psychological Review, 87,* 215-251.

Floden, R.E. (1983, February). *Actively learning to be expert: A new view of learning.* Paper presented at the Annual Meeting of the American Association of Colleges for Teacher Education, Detroit.

Florio, S. & Walsh, M. (1981). The teacher as colleague in classroom research. In H.T. Trueba, G.P. Guthrie, H.H.P. Au (Eds.), *Culture and the bilingual classroom: Studies in classroom ethnography.* Rowley, MA: Newbury.

Greeno, J. Glaser, R. & Newell, A. (1983, April). *Summary: Research on cognition and behavior relevant to education in mathematics, science, and technology.*

Research paper submitted to the Ntional Science Board Commission on Precollege Education in Mathematics, Science and Technology by the Federation of Behavioral Psychological and Cognitive Sciences.

Huber, G. & Mandl, H.(1984). Access to teacher cognitions: Problems of assessment and analysis. In R. Halkes & J.K. Olson (Eds.), *Teacher thinking: A new perspective on persisting problems in education.* (pp. 58-72), LISSE: Swets & Zeitlinger.

Jackson, P.W. (1968). *Life in classrooms.* New York: Holt, Rinehart and Winston.

Kroma, S. (1983). *Personal practical knowledge of language in teaching: An ethnographic study.* Unpublished doctoral dissertation University of Toronto.

Lampert, M. (1985). How do teachers manage to teach? Perspectives on problems in practice. *Harvard Educational Review, 55,* 178-194.

Larkin, J.H., McDermott, J. , Simon, D.P. & Simon, H.A. (1980). Models of competence in solving physics problems. *Cognitive Science, 4,* 317-345.

Leinhardt, G. (1983, April). *Routines in expert math teachers' thoughts and actions.* Paper presented at the annual meeting of the American Educational Research Association, Montreal.

Leinhardt, G., Weidman, C. & Hammond, K.M. (1984, April). *Introduction and integration of classroom routines by expert teachers.* Paper presented at the annual meeting of the American Educational Research Association, New Orleans.

Marland, P.W. (1983). *Models of teachers' interactive thinking.* Unpublished paper, James Cook University, Townsville, Australia.

Marx, R.W. (1978)*Teacher judgments of students' cognitive and affective outcomes.* Unpublished doctoral dissertation, Stanford University.

National Institute of Education (1975). *Teaching as clinical information processing* (Report of Panel 6, National Conference on Studies in Teaching). Washington D.C. : National Institute of Education.

Nisbett, R.E. & Wilson, T.D. (1977). Telling more than we can know: Verbal reports on mental processes. *Psychological Review, 84,* 231-259.

Peterson, P.L. & Clark, C.M. (1978). Teachers' report of their cognitive processes during teaching. *American Educational Research Journal, 15,* 555-565.

Philips, S.U. (1972). *The invisible culture: Communication in classroom and community on the Warm Springs Indian Reservation.* New York: Longman.

Posner, G., Strike, K. Hewson, P. & Gertzog, W. (1982). Accomodation of a scientific conception: Toward a theory of conceptual change. *Science Education, 66*(2), 211-227.

Roth, K. (1984). Using classroom observations to improve science teaching and curriculum materials. In C.W. Anderson (Ed.), *Observing science classrooms: Perspectives from research and practice.* 1984 Yearbook of the Association for the Education of of Teachers in Science. Columbus, OH: ERIC Center for Science, Mathematics, and Environmental Education.

Schon, D. (1983). *The reflective practitioner: How professionals think in action.* New York: Basic Books.

Shavelson, R. Cadwell, J. & Izu, T. (1977). Teachers' sensitivity to the reliability of information in making pedagogical decisions. *American Educational Research Journal, 14,* 83-97.

Shavelson, R.J. & Stern, P. (1981). Research on teachers' pedagogical thoughts, judgments, decisions, and behavior.*Review of Educational Research, 51,* 455-498.

Shulman, L.S. (1986). Those who understand: Knowledge growth in teaching. *Educational Researcher, 15*(2), 4-14.

Shulman, L.S. & Carey, N.B. (1984). Psychology and the limitations of individual rationality: Implications for the study of reasoning and civility. *Review of Educational Research, 54,* 501-524.

Shulman, L.S. & Elstein, A.S. (1975). Studies of problem solving, judgment, and decision making: Implications for educational research. In F.N. Kerlinger (Ed.), *Review of Research in Education, 3,* 5-42.

Shultz, J.J., Florio, S. & Erickson, F. (1982). Where's the floor? Aspects of the cultural organization of social relationships in communication at home and at school. In P. Gilmore and A.A. Glatthorn (Eds.), *Children in and out of School: Ethnography and education.*Washington, D.C.: Center for Applied Linguistics.

Simon, H.A. (1957). *Models of man.*New York: Wiley.

Wagner, A.C. (1984). Conflicts in consciousness: Imperative cognitions can lead to knots in thinking. In R. Halkes & J.K. Olson (Eds.), *Teacher thinking: A new perspective on persistent problems in education.* (pp. 163-175) Lisse: Swets & Zeitlinger.

Wittrock, M.C. (1986). Students' thought processes. In M.C. Wittrock (Ed.), *Handbook of Research on Teaching,* Third Edition, (pp. 297-314). New York: Mcmillan.

Yinger, R.J. (1977). *A study of teacher planning: Description and theory development using ethnographic and information processing methods.*Unpublished doctoral dissertation, Michigan State University, East Lansing.

Yinger, R.J. (1985, December). *Learning the language of practice.* Paper presented at the Symposium on Classroom Studies of Teachers' Personal Knowledge. Ontario Institute for Studies in Education, Toronto.

Yinger, R.J. & Clark, C.M. (1982). *Understanding teachers' judgments about instruction: The task, the method, and the meaning,* (Research Series No. 121). East Lansing, MI: Michigan State University, Institute for Research on Teaching.

WHAT IS "PERSONAL" IN STUDIES OF THE PERSONAL

D. Jean Clandinin and F. Michael Connelly
The University of Calgary and
The Ontario Institute for Studies in Education

SUMMARY

The chapter presents an analysis and interpretation of studies of "teachers' theories and beliefs," which focus on individual teachers' thoughts and actions and which are called by us "studies of the personal." The analysis is presented in terms of "what is asserted," i.e., the key terms, stipulated definitions and origin of ideas and "what is done," i.e., the problem, method and outcome of each of the studies. While there is wide diversity in key terms and stipulated definitions, there is an underlying commonality in problems undertaken and in resulting outcomes. The second part of the article interprets the analytic descriptions of the studies by examining two relationships of importance in understanding the personal: the relationship of personal evidence to personal experience and the relationship of the personal to practical action. These relationships are based on a conception of the composition of teacher thought composed of prior experience (biography), ongoing action (practice) and thinking in isolation of these two. The interpretation suggests that most of the studies assume, but do not inquire into, an explanatory relationship between prior experience and the way teachers think. However, several assume a dialectical relationship and one assumes a problematic relationship between knowledge and action. Most studies operationally define teacher thinking independent of prior experience or action although some studies use complex combinations in their collection of data and in their resulting conceptions of thinking. This context of possible relations is the basis for a discussion of a variety of generic possibilities for research.

INTRODUCTION

Recent reviews (Feiman-Nemser and Floden, 1984; Clark and Peterson, 1984) of teacher thinking and teacher knowledge have drawn attention to a small set of interesting studies named by the reviewers "teacher theories and beliefs." What is especially interesting about these studies is that, one way or another, they purport to study the personal, that is, the what, why and wherefore of individual pedagogical action. As Clark and Peterson (1984) say, the purpose of this cluster of studies is "to make explicit and visible the frames of reference through which individual teachers perceive and process information" (p. 19); and Feiman-Nemser and Floden (1984) say the intent of these studies is to "get inside teachers' heads to describe their knowledge, attitudes, beliefs and values" (p. 4-5). Thus, in contrast to studies focussed on group action, and to others focussed on generalized patterns of behavior in populations, this research, if the reviewers' assessment is correct, is focussed on individuals' thought.

But what is the personal and how is it related to pedagogical action? The first clue to this question is given by the reviewers' descriptive language. Their key terms are "frames of reference," "knowledge," "attitudes," "beliefs," and "values,"; terms presumably derived from the substance of the studies. The conceptual scope implied by these terms is considerable and we must turn to the studies themselves to assess the meaning specific researchers make of the idea of "studies of the personal."

Here, the scope remains wide with a somewhat bewildering array of terms naming the research. For studies noted by Clark and Peterson, there are "teachers' conceptions" (Duffy, 1977), "teacher perspectives" (Janesick, 1982), "teachers' understandings" (Bussis, Chittenden, & Amarel, 1976), "teacher constructs" (Olson, 1981), "teacher principles of practice" (Marland, 1977), "teacher beliefs and principles" (Munby, 1983) and "teacher practical knowledge" (Elbaz, 1981). When we examine the Feiman-Nemser and Floden review, and add relevant research reported at the ISATT meeting (Halkes & Olson, 1984), we have the personal additionally defined in terms of "teacher conceptions" (Larsson, 1984), "teachers' thinking criteria" (Halkes & Deijkers, 1984), "personal constructs" (Pope & Scott, 1984), "personal knowledge" (Lampert, 1985) and "teachers' personal practical knowledge" (Connelly & Clandinin, 1984).

To the extent that key terms are telling of how the personal is conceptualized in inquiry, this list suggests little commonality among researchers. Matters often thought to be different in principle are treated by different researchers, for example, "conceptions," "perspectives," "criteria," "beliefs" and "knowledge." Still, it is possible that because this small sub-field is relatively new, these various terms, for example, "personal knowledge," "personal constructs" and "conceptions," are simply different words naming the same thing.

The task of resolving these questions and of assessing the implied concept of the personal at work in specific inquiries consists, for our purposes, of two different tasks, the analysis and description of the set of inquiries and, subsequently, an interpretation of the description in terms appropriate to the personal. We show that there is a degree of commonality in how researchers conceive of the personal in inquiry and we set forth a possible conceptual structure of inquiry in this field based on a commonplace notion of thinking and on different conceptions of teacher thinking evident in the research.

DESCRIBING STUDIES OF THE PERSONAL

1. Method of Analysis

The first task results in a description of what is asserted (Table 1:
Part 1) and of what is done (Table 1: Part 2) in inquiry. Our
underlying assumption is an operational one to the effect that what
one does in inquiry defines the phenomena and resulting knowledge
claims. Thus, what a researcher does reveals his/her meaning.
Perhaps because this set of studies on the "personal" has only a small
tradition on which to draw, there is a fairly rich content of
conceptually-asserted material in each paper as each author explains
his/her work. We have already noted that each author specifies a key
term by which the work is identified and, presumably, which names the
phenomena under inquiry. These terms are conceptualized and defined
in each of the papers and conceptual origins are noted. For instance,
Halkes and Deijkers' key term is "teachers' teaching criteria" which
they define as "personal subjective values a person tries to pursue or
keep constant while teaching." Conceptually their work originates, in
part, in the curriculum implementation literature. These matters are
summarized in Table 1: Description of Studies of the Personal - Part
1: "What is Asserted" in three columns titled, "key term,"
"stipulated definition" and "origin of ideas."
   Table 1 - Part 2 : "What is done" presents a description of the
"pattern of inquiry" used in each study, structured according to
"problem", "method" and "outcome." Halkes and Deijkers, for example,
define their problem as one of identifying teacher criteria used in
solving classroom disturbances. Their method is to analyze the
relevant literature; identify seven criteria; convert them to
sixty-five operational statements presented in a Likert-scaled survey
instrument; and have teachers respond. Their claims, relative to the
problem of determining teacher criteria, constitute a set of summary
statistics, and discussion of them, based on the survey.

2. Commonalities among the Inquiries

2.1 What is Asserted: With respect to what the authors assert they
are doing (Table 1: Part 1), we have already noted in our opening
remarks that a wide diversity of key terms, and definitions of them,
is offered. There is somewhat less diversity in the asserted origins
of the work due to the fact that three of the studies claim to use
Kelly construct theory. (It is interesting to notice the differences
in language that emerge from Kelly's work for these three authors. In
a relatively new and fluid field such as this, even elementary
terminology is apparently subject to re-naming.) Overall, it is
apparent that a flood of different theoretical resources are entering
this field from general curriculum studies, psychology, philosophy of
various persuasions, and empirically-based typologies.

2.2 What is Done: Turning from what is asserted to what is done we
find that similarity begins to overshadow difference. The patterns of
inquiry for the studies in question (Table 1: Part 2) reveal more
commonality in this research than is implied both in the reviews
(Clark & Peterson, 1984; Feiman-Nemser & Floden, 1984) and in our
observations of "what is asserted" by the researchers.

Table 1: Description of Studies of the Personal
Part 1: What is asserted

Authors	Key Term	Stipulated Definition	Origin of Ideas
Halkes & Deijkers	Teachers' teaching criteria	Personal subjective values a person tries to pursue or keep constant while teaching.	Literature on innovation and curriculum implementation; teacher thought, judgments, decisions and behavior; and attitudes to education
Marland	Principles of practice	Principles that guide a teacher's interactive teaching behavior and that can be used to explain teacher interactive behavior.	Not stated
Pope & Scott	Personal constructs/theories/ epistemologies/	Teachers' view of knowledge and of pedagogic practice.	Kelly's personal construct theory
Olson	Construct	An underlying theory that teachers use in thinking about, evaluating, and classifying teacher and student behavior.	Kelly's personal construct theory
Munby	Beliefs and principles (implicit theory)	Coherent structures that underlie a teacher's practices.	Kelly's personal construct theory
Bussis/ Chittenden/ Amarel	Teachers' understanding	Teachers' beliefs about curriculum and students in terms of classroom activities (surface content) and teachers' learning priorities for children (organizing content) and the connections between the two.	Phenomenological inquiry
Janesick	Perspective	A reflective, socially-derived interpretation of experience that serves as a basis for subsequent action. Combines beliefs, intentions, interpretations, and behavior. A frame of reference within which the teacher makes sense of and interprets experience rationally.	Symbolic interaction
Larsson	Teachers' conceptions	A conception describes the way teachers conceive of some phenomena. The conceptions are basic elements in the understanding of teachers' ways of looking at their work and in some cases, of understanding their acts.	Phenomenography
Duffy	Teachers' conceptions of reading	A conception of reading is the approach to reading which the teacher believes is most like him or herself.	Research-based typology of approaches to teaching reading.
Lampert	Personal knowledge	Personal knowledge is knowledge of who a teacher is and what he/she cares about and knowledge of students beyond paper & pencil tests that is used by a teacher in accomplishing what she/he cares about, what students want and what curriculum requires.	Not supplied
Elbaz	Practical knowledge	A complex practically-oriented set of understandings which teachers actively use to shape and direct the work of teaching.	Phenomenology (particularly Schutz and Luckmann)
Connelly/ Clandinin	Personal practical knowledge	Knowledge which is experiential, embodied, and reconstructed out of the narratives of a teacher's life.	Experiential philosophy

24

Table 1: Description of Studies of the Personal
Part 2: What is done

Authors	Problem	Method	Outcome
Halkes & Deijkers	To identify teacher criteria used in solving class disturbances.	Analyze literature to develop seven categories of teaching criteria; convert to sixty-five operational statements presented in a Likert-scaled instrument; have teachers respond.	A set of summary statistics of the teaching criteria used by teachers.
Marland	To identify teacher thoughts that guide teaching behavior and can explain teaching behavior.	Videotape teaching events; conduct stimulated recall interview describing "thoughts" while teaching; sort individual statements from interview into categories of statements called principles.	Five principles of practice that guide teaching behavior.
Pope & Scott	To explore pre- and in-service teachers' epistemologies; their views on teaching and learning and what interactions, if any, there are among these interactions with implications for teacher education.	Identified four theoretically-derived epistemologies; conducted interviews and observations of pre- and in-service teachers in which teachers reflected on own views of knowledge and practice; researchers derived teacher's personal theory or epistemology. Administered REP test; personal constructs derived from teacher's response to Repertory Grid test; sorted data from REP tests and interviews and observations from individual teachers into four theoretically-derived categories.	Concludes that student teachers can become aware of their initial epistemologies.
Olson	Problem of implementing a new science curriculum; how teachers deal with new curriculum.	Identified different science teaching methods; prepared and presented statements of 20 science teaching events to 8 teachers; teachers sorted events; discussed and located basis of grouping; labelled basis of grouping.	Identified underlying constructs in implicit theories of teaching; identified main feature of new science curriculum; identified ways teachers changed curriculum project to make it compatible with personal constructs.
Munby	Problem of explaining how and why a nominally common curriculum is interpreted and implemented differently by each teacher.	14 teachers each generated 20 descriptive statements (elements) of what a visitor to his/her class would see; teachers sorted elements and discussed basis of grouping; terms and phrases used became constructs within teacher's implicit theory; constructs further analyzed through interviews which led to labels for groups and for their relationships; produced statements called teachers' beliefs and principles.	Illustrated wide individual differences in beliefs and principles of teachers working at same school and within same subject matter specialization.
Bussis/ Chittenden/ Amarel	To investigate the understandings and constructs of teachers implementing open or informal teaching.	Clinical interviews with teachers implementing open or informal teaching. Analyzed data to identify orientations for aspects of teachers' belief systems.	Identified four contrasting orientations for each of four aspects of teachers' belief systems: curriculum priorities; role of children's needs and feelings; children's interests and freedom of choice; importance of social interaction among children.
Janesick	To describe and explain the classroom perspective of a teacher.	Participant observer with teacher; interviews with teacher, other school staff and students; analyzed data base to offer interpretation of teacher's perspective.	Identified the teacher's classroom perspective and offered an account of how the teacher gave meaning to the day-to-day events in classroom and how he constructed curriculum.

25

Table 1: Description of Studies of the Personal
Part 2: What is done (continued)

Authors	Problem	Method	Outcome
Larsson	To describe teachers' assumptions about phenomena in their professional world.	Semi-structured interviews with 29 adult educators on phenomena of learning and knowledge in order to gain insight into conceptions of teachers. Analyzed data in order to identify conceptions and restrictions of teaching.	Identified two restrictions and two conceptions of teaching (two qualitatively different ways of conceptualizing what teaching ought to be).
Duffy	To describe the distribution of conceptions of the teaching of reading among teachers.	Identified five conceptions or contrasting reading approaches from the literature; added a sixth conception (confused/frustrated); six propositional statements derived from each approach.	Summary statistics on reading approaches used by teachers.
Lampert	To examine teachers' thinking about the problems of practice.	Teacher-researchers gathered weekly over a two-year period to discuss everyday work dilemmas; during these discussions they were observed and interviewed. Conversations/discussions considered as "text" to be interpreted and understood as an expression of the way they think about work dilemmas. "Text" analysed to produce comparisons.	Noted comparisons among theories of teaching constructed by scholars, theories constructed by teachers themselves and teachers' concrete reflections on practical problems that arise daily in their classrooms.
Elbaz	To offer a conceptualization of the kind of knowledge teachers hold and use.	A series of semi-structured interviews with one teacher; analysis of transcript data base; researcher interpretation of teacher's practical knowledge.	Identified five content areas of practical knowledge; five orientations of practical knowledge; three ways in which practical knowledge is held.
Connelly & Clandinin	To understand the kind of knowledge teachers hold and use; how to talk about personal knowledge.	Participant observation of practices of several teachers over several years; semi-structured interviews with participants; researcher participant mutual construction of teacher's narratives; development of theory of personal practical knowledge.	A theory of personal practical knowledge as made up of participants' rhythms, images, personal philosophy and as based on narrative unities in participants' experience.

Problem: To begin, there is an underlying commonality in problems undertaken. Several focus directly on teacher thought by "identifying (Halkes & Deijkers; Marland), "exploring" (Pope & Scott; Bussis, Chittenden & Amarel), "describing" (Larsson and Duffy), and "examining" (Lampert) some particular content aspect of knowledge. Two others (Olson and Munby) specify their problem as one of accounting for action in terms of teacher thought, specifically, of determining why curricula are differentially implemented by teachers. In inquiry, however, the difference in problem between Munby and Olson, and the others, mostly disappears when their method is reviewed. Both adopt a version of Kelly construct theory methodology and have teachers generate constructs (terms and statements) which, in effect, constitute the content of teachers' thinking, something that marks the nature of the problem for the others. Implementation per se is not subjected to inquiry in either Olson's or Munby's work. The three remaining studies (Janesick, Elbaz, Connelly & Clandinin) also focus directly on teachers' thoughts. The difference between the problem in these studies and in others is that these three studies are only indirectly concerned with the content of teacher thought. Their problem is one of re-imagining its form and composition. Elbaz is interested in the structure of teacher thought; Janesick is interested in the overarching features which shape the specific bits and pieces of a teacher's knowledge; and Connelly and Clandinin are concerned with the language for thinking about teachers' knowledge. Accordingly, a review of the problems in the twelve studies shows that nine are aimed at discovering the content of teacher thought, and three, while also concerned with content, are primarily focussed on the form of and/or the language of discourse about, personal knowledge.

<u>Method</u>: As might be expected, there is somewhat more diversity in method than there is in problem. But, because different methods are often used in aid of a common kind of problem, diversity in method is not the best indicator of the degree to which studies differ.

Two used formal teacher response instruments (Halkes & Deijkers, Duffy); one used stimulated recall (Marland); three used versions of Kelly construct-based statement sorting techniques (Pope & Scott, Olson, Munby); four used versions of interview techniques (Bussis, Chittenden, & Amarel, Larsson, Lampert, Elbaz) and two used participant-observation (Janesick, Connelly & Clandinin). There are, of course, variations in detail within each of these methods, especially, the interview method for which there are clinical, semi-structured, and conversational approaches in the listed studies.

<u>Outcome</u>: The resulting interpretations using these various methods are formed by the more common underlying problems. For instance, Halkes' and Deijkers' instrumentation leads to particular statements about the content of teachers' thought just as does Munby's more elaborate teacher statement-sorting process. In the end, the question of what is in the teacher's mind is answered by seven of the researchers with quite similar kinds of statements. From the point of view of what it is we learn of teachers' personal knowledge, "principles," "constructs," "criteria," and "conceptions" seem to name the same kind of thing. The terms and methodology differ but the problem and conclusions arising from the inquiry are remarkably similar in kind. None of the five remaining studies use specific words (e.g., to name a construct), phrases (e.g., to name a belief), or short descriptions (e.g., to describe assumptions) to account for teacher thought. Their interpretations consist of longer, more complex, less precise, and more context dependent accounts. Accordingly, while there is some similarity in the problem, both method and outcome are different. There is a sense, then, that these five studies yield understandings different in kind from the other seven.

INTERPRETING DESCRIPTIONS OF STUDIES OF THE PERSONAL

The second task of assessing the implied concept of the personal at work in specific inquiries consists of an interpretation (Table 2) of the studies described in Table 1. This interpretation has been structured by a commonplace conception of what it is that composes teacher thought. This commonplace conception is outlined below as a preamble to the interpretation.

1. The Composition of Teacher Thought

Table 2 is designed on the assumption that one useful way of thinking about teachers' practical thought is to conceive of it as composed of ongoing action and prior personal experience. To state this is virtually to state a commonplace. When we teach, we think about our teaching and this thinking is composed in part of all the various things we do in our teaching. Schön (1983) names this aspect of practical thought "reflection in action." Furthermore, it is impossible, when a person thinks, to do so without reference to themselves as people. All the things one knows, has studied, and has done are in one way or another present in one's thoughts. This aspect of thinking is explicitly addressed in biographical and autobiographical studies. Thus, both action and prior experience compose our practical thinking.

Now, while the distinction between ongoing pedagogical action and past experience as elements composing thought may be commonplace, there are uncommon consequences of this view for our understanding of what is done, and of what might be done, in inquiry into teacher thinking. The functional separation in this body of literature between thought and action (Clark & Peterson, 1984), is, clearly, one of the possible directions for inquiry given this commonplace conception. When thought and action are imagined to be separate each may be studied in isolation. Classroom interaction studies, especially popular a few years ago, are illustrative of the latter. Currently, as our interpretation below shows, the former is occurring, where thought is studied directly outside the context of a classroom or other practice setting. Those who study either thought or action might, of course, argue that the other was assumed within the work. For example, those who pursue classroom interaction studies might claim that they assume that people are thinking when they interact; and those pursuing thinking studies might claim that they assume that actions flow from thought. The point we are making, however, is that in these studies the two are not simultaneously subjected to inquiry. Rather, the study of one <u>assumes</u> something about the other. There is a difference between inquiries which assume a relationship and those where the relationship is subjected to inquiry. Accordingly, the commonplace conception permits the identification of studies which define different relations of thought and action in inquiry.

Furthermore, the assumptions at work encourage different ways of imagining the uses of research results. Specifically, when thought is assumed to direct action, descriptions of thought stand to be taken as more or less abstract shorthand accounts of the rules governing practice. Given these rules, methods of intervention, which the philosopher McKeon has labelled "logistic," may be imagined. "Logistic" methods of relating theory and practice are ones where practice is treated as being under the control of theory via strategic means. However, the commonplace conception of thinking makes it easy to imagine still other thought-practice relations; ones, for example, where practice directs thought or, possibly, interacts with thought. In McKeon's terms, studies embodying such relationships might be called "problematic" or "dialectical" in their working relations of theory and practice.

If we extrapolate these commonplace notions of thought and action to encompass prior experience, as well as future action, a complex array of possibilities for inquiry are imaginable.

2. Interpretations

Returning to the studies, the most telling point of departure for an interpretation, in terms of prior experience and ongoing action, is the particular act and/or kind of thought which serves as evidential of the personal in inquiry. Whatever it is that passes as fact may be said to be as experientially close as one will get in the inquiry to touching whatever it is that is "personal" in the phenomena of the inquiry. For instance, for Halkes and Deijkers, what is personally evidential is the teacher's self ratings on the Likert scales eventually summarized in tabular format; for Olson, what is personally evidential is individual teacher names for teacher-sorted categories of teaching events; and for Elbaz, what is personally evidential is informal teacher interview statements describing and reflecting upon the teacher's experience.

Following our remarks on the composition of teacher thought, whatever is taken to be personally evidential in the research potentially exhibits two relationships of importance in understanding the personal: the relationship of personal evidence to personal experience and the relationship of the personal to practical action. Table 2: Interpreting Descriptions of Studies of the Personal is, accordingly, presented in three columns, "what is evidential of the personal," "relationship of personal evidence to past experience" and "relationship of knowledge to action."

2.1 What is Evidential: In our discussion of Table 1, we noted that most of the studies reviewed focus on the content of teacher thought. These studies use as evidence of content, specific teacher statements about themselves (Table 2, column 1). For instance, Duffy's teachers rate themselves on a prepared instrument, Munby's teachers effectively generate their own instrument by the use of describing and categorizing procedures, and there are variations in-between such as Olson's, where teachers are given a list and asked to sub-divide it into categories and to name each. The principle difference in the evidential basis within this set of studies is that, in some, the descriptive terminology is supplied by the researchers (e.g., Halkes & Deijkers, Duffy) and, in others, it is supplied by the participating teachers (e.g., Marland, Pope & Scott). But in both kinds of study it is the teacher who eventually lays claim to the content description of his/her thought.

Three of these studies (Janesick, Elbaz, Connelly & Clandinin) while sharing the teacher-determined evidential base of the other eight studies use qualitatively different evidence. Two of the studies (Janesick and Connelly & Clandinin) use teaching practice, as well as teachers' statements about themselves, evidentially. Given the interpretive direction in these studies, practice precedes teacher assertions and is ultimately considered more telling in the accounts of teacher knowledge offered. Given this dual evidential base, and relative significance of each basis in understanding thinking, these studies effectively define personal knowledge in terms of both of

Table 2: Interpreting Descriptions of Studies of the Personal

Authors	What is evidential of the personal	Relationship of personal evidence to past experience *	Relationship of knowledge to action **
Halkes & Deijkers	A teacher's self-rating on prepared statements	By implication: Assumption that teachers' rating of statements correspond to teaching practice	Logistic
Marland	A teacher's statement of guides to his/her interactive teaching behavior collected in stimulated recall interview	By implication: An implied explanatory relationship between principle given and teaching acts	Logistic
Olson	A teacher's grouping and labels for predescribed teaching events (How a teacher sorted 20 statements and named the sort)	By implication: Assumption that description of pre-set teaching events corresponds to teaching practice	Logistic
Munby	A teacher's generation of statements describing his/her class; grouping and labels for groupings of statements; researcher selected labels and phrases from teacher's discussion of basis of groupings	By implication: Assumption that a teacher-generated description corresponds to a teacher's practice. Implied relationship between term and experience through descriptions of teaching and explanatory reason for grouping	Logistic
Janesick	A teacher's practices and interview responses	Practices and interview responses based on teacher's interpretation of his own experience	Dialectic
Larsson	A teacher's responses in a semi-structured interview	By implication: Interview responses assumed to be based upon teacher's experience	Logistic
Pope & Scott	In-service and pre-service teachers' descriptions of their practices, and researcher observation of teachers' practices	By implication: Interview responses and descriptions assumed to be based on teacher's experience	Logistic
Bussis/ Chittenden/ Amarel	A teacher's descriptions of his/her planning and teaching	By implication: Interview responses assumed to be based on teacher's experience	Logistic
Duffy	A teacher's self-rating on prepared statements	By implication: Assumption that rating of statements of teaching approaches corresponds to teaching practice	Logistic
Lampert	A teacher's interview description of practice and conversations between a group of teachers	By implication: Assumption that teacher interview responses and contributions to conversations based on teacher's experience	Problematic
Elbaz	A teacher's description of her practice and of how she feels about it	Teacher interview responses based responses based on teacher's professional experience in school where she worked.	Dialectic
Connelly/ Clandinin	Biographical detail, emotionality, morality, aesthetic, based on narrative of experience	Narrative accounts based on mutual reconstruction of experience as expressed in practices in interview and in classroom	Dialectic

* By implied, we mean situations where experience is used as a way of explaining the personal evidence but where the relationship is not under study in the research.

** Following McKeon, as described in text.

"thought" and action. Their claims about teacher thinking are, equally, claims about action and cognition. Elbaz and Connelly and Clandinin go one step further and include biographical teacher statements as part of their evidential base.

2.2 Knowledge to Action: From these interpretations of the evidential basis of each study, it is clear that different relations of thinking to practice are operationally at work in the research. Those studies (Janesick, Connelly & Clandinin) that use action evidentially adopt a reflexive "dialectical" relationship between thought and action. In Janesick's study, for instance, particular classroom actions bring forth, and are seen to be part of, the teacher's perspective. Elbaz also appears to hold an assumption of the dialectical relationship of thought and action although this relationship is not subjected to inquiry in her work. Lampert appears to imagine the relationship as "problematic" - one in which teachers face, and work through, certain classroom dilemmas. In the remaining studies, thought as described in the studies is assumed to direct action. This "logistic" assumption is most clearly in evidence in the Munby and Olson studies, where it is assumed that the descriptions of different knowledge contents for different teachers accounts for differential implementation of curriculum materials. Accordingly, such studies tend to have a more practical, useful flavor about them.

2.3 Personal Evidence to Prior Experience: With respect to prior experience, most studies appear to assume that prior experience "explains" why teachers think the way each study describes they do. This assumption is mostly of little influence on the actual conduct of various inquiries although it presents research possibilities in some. Munby, for example, assumes his claims about teachers' knowledge will be more valid if teachers generate descriptions of teaching based on their experience. Contrast this use of prior experience, for example, with Olson's, whose descriptions of teaching are prepared from the research literature. Elbaz goes further and focusses her interviews on her participating teacher's teaching history. In both Munby and Elbaz's case, however, this experiential history is eventually submerged in the way results are presented, rather than being treated as components of teacher thought.

2.4 Cognitive and Affective Evidence and Knowledge: Our examination of what is personally evidential in these studies is revealing in yet another important respect. Most of the studies admit as evidence material which, for our purposes might be called "cognitive" aspects of teacher thinking. Marland, for example, has statements of principle: the three Kelly construct studies use statements which may be called "constructs;" and so forth. Ultimately, this research leads to an account of the cognitive functioning of teachers on such matters as values and beliefs held, principles adopted, constructs formed, and knowledge of subject matter, classrooms and teaching. Four studies (Janesick, Lampert, Elbaz, and Connelly & Clandinin) additionally admit as evidence "affective" states of mind of the teacher. Elbaz's teacher, Sarah, for example, describes how she was unhappy in certain teaching situations and of how she created others in which she felt better about herself and her teaching. In the end, for Elbaz, this affective evidence tended to be utilized to produce claims on the cognitive state of the teacher's mind, for example, that practical knowledge is oriented to social situations. This use also characterizes Lampert's work. Janesick and Connelly and Clandinin, however, create statements of teacher knowledge which combine affective and cognitive evidence. Janesick's teacher's group "perspective," for example, is one laden with value. This use of value is not only cognitive, as it would be if one were to study the teacher and the teacher were to assert (or the researcher to assert on the teacher's behalf) that one of the teacher's values was group action. Instead, Janesick's claim is that the teacher holds a perspective and that this perspective is, in part, composed of a structure of, and belief in, group action and also a feeling of a certain intensity, altered by circumstance, of the worth of particular group teaching situations. Her term "perspective," and Connelly and Clandinin's term "image," are terms which refer to the emotional quality of personal knowledge.

CONCLUSIONS

The analysis presented in this paper may be summarized in three points. The first refers to the theoretical and linguistic diversity in the field and the remaining two provide answers to the question of the paper, "What is personal about studies of the personal?"

First, there is more commonality in the patterns of inquiry into the personal than is apparent in the authors' language and stated intentions. People using different terms such as "construct," "criteria," "beliefs and principles," appear in fact, to often mean much the same thing. To the extent that this commonality holds, we may imagine some positive evolution in our understanding of the nature of the personal as it applies to teacher thinking in the years to come. Furthermore, the variety of theoretical resources should enrich inquiry in the field. We do think, however, that the theoretically-borrowed language, and the various theoretical origins of the asserted ideas, may also have a tendency to inhibit understanding among researchers. The differences in theoretical origin and corresponding differences in theoretical language tend, we think, to divide the field, making researchers skeptical of using and cross-referencing one anothers' ideas. Diversity of thought is a mixed blessing.

The second point is that there are significant differences in how we may imagine the composition of teacher thought. The three general components suggested in this review are practical actions, biographical history, and thoughts in isolation of these two. Most research reviewed above focusses on the third. Various combinations not now treated as part of the literature in reviews of this topic are possible as seen, for example, in biographical studies (Pinar, 1981; Grumet, 1978; Darroch-Lozowski, 1982); in experientially based studies of thinking (Hunt, 1976); and in narratively oriented studies of all three components in combination (Connelly & Clandinin).

The third point, also a matter of the composition of teacher thought, is that most studies conceive of teacher thought in cognitive terms. But it is possible, following experiential epistemologists, such as Lakoff and Johnson (1980), and experiential ethicists, such as

McIntyre (1981), to imagine thinking simultaneously in cognitive and affective terms. To claim that knowing something means having aesthetic, moral and emotional states of mind about that thing has a limited tradition in the pages of philosophy and in education, where affect is often treated as an impurity in reason. Our view is that a cognitive and affective understanding of the personal practical knowledge of teachers will help produce more living, viable understandings of what it means to educate and to be educated (Clandinin, 1985; Connelly & Clandinin, 1985, in press).

Finally, we should like to note that the latter two points create a variety of generic possibilities for research. A cognitive approach to biography, for example, might yield a kind of positivistic study of personal biographic origins much, in the same way, as a psychoanalyst might discover certain features in one's background that explain in some causal sense one's current state of mind. A narratively-oriented study emphasizing cognitive and affective aspects of action, thought and biography would, of course, require different methods and would yield different outcomes. A narrative approach to thought and biography, for example, might yield stories linking, as it does in Schafer's (1981) psychotherapy, thought and biography, not as cause and effect, but as one among several possible explanatory narratives. Accordingly, one might undertake research which combined a narrative interpretation of biography, thought, and action in experiential terms and which joined cognitive and affective matters in the narrative. Readers will be able to imagine other possibilities of interest.

REFERENCES

Bussis, A. Chittenden, E. & Amarel, M. (1976). *Beyond surface
curriculum*. Boulder, Co.: Westview Press.
Clandinin, J. (1985). Personal practical knowledge: A study of
teachers' classroom images. *Curriculum Inquiry, 15* (4), 361-385.
Clark, C. & Peterson, P. (1984). *Teachers' thought processes*
(Occasional Paper No. 72.). East Lansing, Michigan: Michigan
State University, The Institute for Research on Teaching.
Connelly, M. & Clandinin, J. (in press), On narrative method,
personal philosophy and narrative unities in the study of
teaching. *Journal of Research in Science Teaching*.
Connelly, M., & Clandinin, J. (1985). Personal practical knowledge
and the modes of knowing: Relevance for teaching and learning.
NSSE Yearbook, 84(2), 174-198.
Connelly, M. & Clandinin, J. (1984). Personal practical knowledge at
Bay Street School: Ritual, personal philosophy and image. In R.
Halkes & J.K. Olson (Eds.), *Teacher thinking : A new perspective
on persisting problems in education* (pp. 134-148). Lisse: Swets
and Zeitlinger B.V.
Darroch-Lozowski, V. (1982). Biographical narrative as the expression
of existence. In V. Darroch & R.J. Silvers (Eds.), *Interpretive
human studies* (pp. 215-227). Washington D.C.: University Press
of America, Inc.
Duffy, G. (1977). *A study of teacher conceptions of reading.* Paper
presented at the National Reading Conference, New Orleans.
Elbaz, F. (1981). The teacher's "pratical knowledge": Report of a
case study. *Curriculum Inquiry, 11*(1), 43-71.
Feiman-Nemser, S. & Floden, R. (1984). *The cultures of teaching*
(Occasional Paper No. 74); East Lansing, Michigan: Michigan
State University, The Institute for Research on Teaching.
Grumet, M. (1978). Supervision and situation: A methodology of
self-report for teacher education. *Journal of Curriculum
Theorizing, 1* (1), 191-257.
Halkes, R., & Deijkers, R. (1984). Teachers' teaching criteria. In
R. Halkes & J.K. Olson (Eds.), *Teacher thinking: A new perspective
on persisting problems in education* (pp. 149-162). Lisse: Swets
& Zeitlinger B.V.
Halkes, R. & Olson, J.K. (Eds.). (1984). *Teacher thinking: A new
perspective on persisting problems in education*. Lisse: Swets &
Zeitlinger B.V.
Hunt, D. (1976). Teachers are psychologists, too: On the application
of psychology to education. *Canadian Psychological Review, 17*(3),
210-218.
Janesick, V. (1982). Of snakes and circles: Making sense of classroom
group processes through a case study. *Curriculum Inquiry, 12*(2),
161-189.
Lakoff, G., & Johnson, M. (1980). *Metaphors we live by*. Chicago: The
University of Chicago Press.
Lampert, M. (1985). How do teachers manage to teach: Perspectives on
problems in practice. *Harvard Educational Review 55*(2), 178-194.

Larsson, S. (1984). Describing teachers' conceptions of their
professional world. In R. Halkes & j.K. Olson (Eds.) *Teacher
thinking : A new perspective on persisting problems in education*
(pp. 123-133). Lisse: Swets & Zeitlinger B.v.

Marland, P. (1977). *A study of teachers' interactive thoughts*.
Unpublished doctoral dissertation, The University of Alberta,
Edmonton.

McIntyre, A. (1981). *After virtue: A study in moral theory.* Notre
Dame: University of Notre Dame Press.

McKeon, R. (1952). Philosophy and action. *Ethics, 62*(2), 79-100.

Munby, H. (1983, April). *A qualitative study of teachers' beliefs and
principles*. Paper presented at the annual meeting of the American
Educational Research Association, Montreal, Canada.

Olson, J. (1981). Teacher influence in the classroom. *Instructional
Science, 10*, 259-275.

Pinar, W. (1981). Life history and educational experience. *Journal of
Curriculum Theorizing, 3*(1), 259-286.

Pope, M. & Scott, E. (1984). Teachers' epistemology and practice. In
R. Halkes & J.K. Olson (Eds.), *Teacher thinking: A new perspective
on persisting problems in education* (pp. 112-122).
Lisse: Swets & Zeitlinger B.V.

Schafer, R. (1981). Narration in the psychoanalytic dialogue. In
W.J.T. Mitchell (Ed.), *On narrative* (pp. 25-49). Chicago: The
University of Chicago Press.

Schön, D. (1983). *The reflective practitioner: How professionals think
in action*. New York: Basic Books, Inc.

HOW DO TEACHERS THINK ABOUT THEIR CRAFT?

Sally Brown
Department of Education
University of Stirling
Scotland

Donald McIntyre
Department of Educational Studies
University of Oxford
England

SUMMARY

Research is described which attempts to explore the integrated knowing, thinking and action which are assumed to characterise teachers' professional craft knowledge. Its approach gives priority to: (i) investigating how teachers think about what they do well in the classroom, (ii) letting those in the classroom (i.e. teachers and pupils) decide what is done well, (iii) using pupils' judgments about teachers to decide with whom the research is done and (iv) persuading teachers to articulate what they do well and how they do it. As a research strategy it fits into the heterogeneous grouping known as "case-studies", but it also has a primary concern with the development of generalisations across teachers. An account is offered of the research approach, collection of data and some preliminary steps in the generation of a conceptual framework to reflect the ways in which experienced teachers think about the strengths of their own teaching.

AN INVESTIGATION OF TEACHERS' PROFESSIONAL CRAFT KNOWLEDGE

Our interest is in the practical part of experienced teachers' professional knowledge which we refer to as professional craft knowledge (PCK). By that we mean the knowledge which is:

(i)   embedded in, and tacitly guiding, teachers' everyday actions in the classroom;

(ii)   derived from practical experience rather than formal training;

(iii)   seldom made explicit;

(iv)   related to the intuitive, spontaneous and routine aspects of teaching rather than to the more reflective and thoughtful activities in which teachers may engage at other times;

(v)   reflected in the "core professionalism" of teachers and their "theories in use" rather than their "extended professionalism" and "espoused theories".

The plans for our research have drawn on the ideas of Deforges and McNamara (Deforges and McNamara, 1977 and 1979; McNamara and Deforges, 1978), and our aim is to generate theory which is grounded in the practice of classroom teaching. Our starting point is to assume that most experienced teachers already use a wide range of sophisticated skills about which it would be most valuable for us to learn. It is their strenghts and not their deficiences in which we are interested. This approach has implications for the use which might later be made of our findings for in-service staff development or the design of more appropriate educational innovation. At present, staff development and innovation tend to operate in our country to a deficit model: problems or omissions are identified and the gaps are plugged. Our research implies a different model in which those developments and innovations would be built on existing strengths. Furthermore, an understanding of what experienced teachers do well would have clear benefits for pre-service teacher education.

RESEARCH APPROACH

Decisions about which of the many aspects of teachers' PCK the research will be concerned with, are made by those inside the class-room: pupils' statements about their teachers' strengths determine which teachers we approach with an invitation to become involved (we look for high levels of agreement among pupils about specific teacher characteristics and for a variety of characteristics among teachers); and teachers' perceptions of their own strengths determine the particular aspects of their teaching to which we pay attention. Our concern is with what teachers see as necessary and desirable to do in their classroom circumstances, with understanding how teachers construe their own teaching, and not at all with evaluating that teaching. Every effort has to be made to minimise the influence on our data collection and analysis from the well-known models of teaching and teachers generated by 'outsiders' (e.g. process-product or teacher as decision-maker, classroom manager, information processor, facilitator, dilemma-resolver).

The context in which we have chosen to work is primarily that of teaching in the early years of secondary school (with pupils aged 12 to 14) and, to a lesser extent, in the later years of primary (with pupils aged 10 to 12). All the classes we work with are mixed ability within comprehensive schools. Sixteen teachers have been involved: in secondary, the twelve teachers come from art, computing, English (2 teachers), French, geography, history, mathematics, physical education, outdoor education and science (2 teachers); and the four primary teachers have responsibilities across the curriculum. No assumptions can be made about the validity of the findings for other contexts (e.g. for the teaching of other age groups).

The research has to find ways of stimulating teachers to articulate and elaborate aspects of their tacit professional craft knowledge. How that will be done will depend on the nature (presently unknown) of that knowledge. The investigation has been planned, therefore, in two stages. First, we are attempting a straightforward exploration of the ways in which teachers construe those features of

their existing patterns of classroom teaching which give them satisfaction. These patterns are highly adapted to the circumstances in
which they find themselves and the purposes to which they find they
have to give priority. The second stage will use the findings of the
first to help to decide a strategy for persuading teachers to
elucidate as fully as possible how they do the things which they do
well. It is the first of these stages which is reported here.

The demands that our research makes on teachers are substantially less than, for example, those which action research would
call for. We do not ask them to become researchers but rather to
talk about their classroom practice; the responsibility for the
theorising remains with us. Nevertheless, our anxiety at the start
of this empirical research was high. We were to be concerned with an
exploration of: the complexities and uncertainties of teachers'
professional craft knowledge and practical expertise; their intuitive
performances (which some believe are not open to explicit description
and must remain implicit in their actions); the plethora of
decisions, judgments, interactions and behaviours of which experienced
teachers may be unaware and which they carry out more or less
spontaneously; and the ways in which they make use of their previous
experiences in dealing with new and, strictly speaking, unique situations which they encounter in the classroom. Although we started
from the assumption that there is such a thing as teachers'
professional craft knowledge, we knew that for the most part this
knowledge is not articulated. Was it sensible, therefore, to plan to
undertake an investigation of what pupils and teachers construed as
good teaching?

We knew that pupils could talk in general terms about what their
teachers do well; the data collected in our preliminary work had
satisfied us of this. Whether pupils would be willing and able to
identify specific instances of the qualities displayed by teachers in
particular lessons remained to be seen. We knew from previous
experience that teachers would be able to talk about their teaching,
but we could not predict whether they would do so only in terms of
their formal teaching knowledge (e.g. as formulated in most teacher
education courses), how talking about their teaching might affect
their classroom performance (e.g. increasing self-consciousness or
engendering paralysis) or if our probing would stimulate post hoc
rationalisations of a kind in which we were not interested.

THE COLLECTION OF DATA

Before the teachers finally agreed to work with us we showed them
summaries of the statements made about them by pupils. However, we
requested that prior to seeing this summary each teacher should give
us a brief account of what they saw themselves as doing well in their
teaching. This they all agreed to do and so provided us with a
preliminary set of data to help us formulate comparisons between
teachers' and pupils' constructs of the teaching.

Some aspects of our approach have been common across all the
teachers with whom we have worked. We have endeavoured to retain a
pattern of observing and recording two to four hours of teaching for
each teacher; each teacher has made the choice of the unit of work to

be observed; we asked each teacher to tell us in writing what aspects of their teaching they were particularly pleased with (i) at the end of the first observed part of the unit and (ii) as they reflected on the whole unit of work at the end; we interviewed each teacher after the second and any subsequent observed lessons; we asked pupils at the end of each observed lesson and at the end of the unit of work to tell us (in writing) about what their teachers did well; we gave the teachers copies of the audio tapes of the lessons; and in the light of them having had an opportunity to listen to the tapes, we carried out two further and longer interviews some two weeks after the end of the unit of work.

There were differences, however, among the different cases. In the primary schools we usually observed two full mornings with a variety of different aspects of the curriculum intertwined. In the secondary school, timetabling and time allocation differed among subjects: 'two to four hours of teaching' in English and French was a week's work including several double periods; in art it was two weeks of single periods; in physical education there were two double periods of basketball over two weeks; in outdoor education we had a whole day expedition; and in computing there were five weeks of single periods. This has consequences not only for practical arrangements but also for the unity in a 'unit of work', for how pupils and teachers construe the lessons as having continuity and for organisation, tactics and strategies which teachers use to provide introductions to, and linkages between, the classroom work of different lessons.

We are not yet at the point where we can offer an account of our "results". All we can do is to give some tentative impressions of what appears to be emerging from the analysis of our data.

ANALYSIS OF THE DATA

Data From Pupils

Some general ideas about the teachers we worked with can be gleaned from the pupils' statements. These were of two kinds: first, some pupils (about 350) were asked to comment on general qualities which they admired in their teachers; and secondly, others (about 400) were asked to comment on what they thought was good about the teaching in a particular lesson. In relation to the first of these, we can say that with very few exceptions the statements we collected were sensible, positive and useful. Qualities of teachers which were cited included the ability to create a relaxed and enjoyable atmosphere, classroom control, presentation of work so that it is interesting and understandable, clarity of explanations and instructions, helping with difficulties, treating pupils as mature individuals and encouraging pupils to raise expectations of them-selves. An exploratory study with fifty-seven teachers reassured us that their categorisation of pupils' statements agreed with our own. It was these statements that were used to select the teachers, and so our sample is biased towards those teachers who have good relation-ships with their pupils.

Our collection of comments from pupils about what had gone well

in each lesson or selection of work was quite productive. They
almost always commented on how these teachers explained clearly so
everyone understood and knew what to do, the ways in which they were
ready to help pupils when they were stuck and the classroom control
that ensured the work would be carried out in a relaxed and
industrious atmosphere. Beyond this, the statements reflected the
diversity of the qualities displayed by the different teachers such as
an individual's use of humour to sustain an enjoyable atmosphere, a
readiness to take account of pupils' opinions, a supportive way of
dealing with pupils' public errors, efforts to involve everyone in the
activities and to develop self-confidence, kindness and warmth,
effective demonstrations, specific subject related qualities, taking
the trouble to provide background information and choice of helpful
and enjoyable lesson content or activities.

We became aware, however, of some of the limitations of this
approach. We are convinced that we should not use it with pupils
younger than our youngest group (age 10). The texture detail and
elaboration provided in the written responses becomes very thin at
this stage, and the approach which at all stages is biased towards the
views of the competent writers becomes even more suspect with younger
pupils. It also seems that pupils have a low tolerance for repeating
the same task at the end of each lesson.

Data From Teachers

The data we have collected from the classrooms and subsequent interviews with teachers is astonishingly varied and enormously rich. The
accounts they give of what they themselves do well are striking in
their individuality but demonstrate high levels of internal
consistency. In one sense, the diversity of the coherent "stories"
of good teaching is unnerving when we face the prospect of trying to
reach widely generalisable constructions of teachers' craft knowledge.
Nevertheless, we are currently stimulated by what the different
teachers say about such things as:

- the ways in which they manage information about, and
  introductions to, the work of the lesson;

- their approaches to taking account of differences among
  their pupils;

- the ways in which they deal with the errors which pupils
  make;

- their attempts to build up confidence and trust with pupils;

- their distinctive concerns for the characteristics of
  individual pupils;

- their strategies for diffusing potential discipline problems
  and for making sure that recalcitrant pupils do not become
  alienated from the work or the experiences;

- the nature and purpose of their 'discussions' with pupils;

- their efforts to ensure that everyone is involved in the work and all achievements are recognised;

- their ways of managing group activities;

- how they change tack when pupils' interest or attention may be flagging;

- how they endeavour to ensure that pupils' creative efforts will not be hindered by technical expertise that is lacking;

- the ways in which they create a relaxed and enjoyable but, nevertheless, disciplined atmosphere.

Towards Generalisations: A Framework of Concepts

Since our approach uses sixteen case studies, one of our concerns must be to understand how each teacher, as an individual, evaluates and talks about his or her own teaching. However, if our aim is to understand, communicate and ultimately to use those aspects of PCK that we are investigating, then we have to formulate our findings in ways that are potentially generalisable across teachers. This implies an attempt to establish generalisations and economical concepts across the individual cases. Such generalisations will not be of the probabilistic kind which arise from the application of statistics to large data sets in, for example, survey research or experimental studies. Our generalisations are better described as naturalistic, and as forming hypotheses to be carried from one case to the next rather than as general laws applying across a population. Together, the generalisations make up a provisional theoretical framework which is intended to expose and make explicit some aspects of the tacit knowledge of expert experienced teachers (who may well manage and teach their classes in such taken-for-granted and routinised ways that they are unconscious of the craft knowledge embedded in their actions).

We have used a careful step-by-step, case-by-case, iterative, inductive process to identify a set of concepts which appear to be generalisable among the criteria which teachers use in evaluating their own teaching as satisfactory. Outsiders' concepts (such as "objectives" or "decision-points") have been eschewed unless they arise directly from the teachers' accounts. Ideally, the generalisations formulated should: be directly supported by evidence; be falsifiable; not discount any of the teachers' accounts; go beyond evidence from one individual or one occasion; demonstrate fully the logic and rationality of the teachers' actions; and be recognisable and acceptable to the teachers.

At the time of writing we have carried out a detailed analysis of at least one interview with each of the sixteen teachers. Using the data from the secondary teachers we have inductively generated a tentative framework of concepts which appears to encompass and reflect the ways in which these teachers talk about the strengths of their classroom teaching. Only a tiny proportion of their statements cannot be so accommodated. The data from the primary teachers are also fully accounted for within the framework, but these were not used in the inductive framework-building process. (The sample of primary teachers is too small to predict whether the same framework would emerge if we had started with a consideration of their data.)

The framework is still in its infancy, but we are finding it useful to organise our ideas about the ways in which teachers perceive their own teaching. The rest of this paper outlines some of the central concepts which seem to be helpful in characterising teachers' thinking and are sufficiently simple to reflect the immediacy and spontaneity of classroom actions.

In the first place, it seems that most teachers evaluate their lessons in terms of what we have called normal desirable states of pupil activity (NDS). A lesson is deemed satisfactory so long as pupils continue to act in these ways which are seen as routinely desirable. Different teachers may have different criteria for what counts as an NDS. For example, they may expect pupils to be (i) interested, involved and asking questions, or (ii) working independently, using worksheets and doing everything pretty much on their own, or (iii) thinking about what they are doing. These NDSs may vary according to the phase of the lesson or the particular pupils being taught.

In addition to (and occasionally instead of) criteria of NDS of pupil activity, some teachers evaluate their lessons in terms of concepts of progress. The concepts of progress which are used fall into three broad categories: development of pupils' attributes (e.g. knowledge, confidence); progress through the work (e.g. the syllabus, the teacher's plan for the day); and the production of something (e.g. an artifact, a performance).

The concepts of NDS and progress are distinguished by the former involving a pattern of activity being maintained without change over a period (albeit sometimes a short period) of time, and the latter introducing a development aspect in contrast with the steady state of the former. For example, where a teacher talks about "pupils understanding" we would categorise a reference to "pupils under-standing what is going on in the classroom or what the teacher is saying" as NDS; if the emphasis is on "pupils developing an under-standing of something", then this would be seen as an example of progress. Unambiguous categorisation, however, is not always possible: where teachers talk about "pupils picking things up" (in the sense of understanding), we have some difficulty in deciding how this should be classified. This is no great problem since the framework of concepts is intended to communicate ideas about teaching and not to enable every statement to be reliably coded.

It will be necessary to examine more closely than we have been able to do so far the relationship between the concepts of NDS and progress for individual teachers. A cursory look suggests that sometimes an NDS and an example of progress may simply be different ways of looking at the same thing; or the progress may be a necessary development prior to the establishment of an NDS; or the NDS may provide the necessary conditions for making the progress.

The third set of generalisable concepts relates to the standards which teachers apply to their criteria for the first two kinds of concepts (NDS and progress). These standards depend on the conditions which impinge on the teaching. It seems that there are several sub-sets of concepts here which refer to conditions of time (usually a constraint and includes timetabling factors), material conditions (space, equipment, class size, weather), pupils (enduring characteristics or behaviour on the day), and teachers (personal characteristics or feelings/behaviour on the day). We have yet to unpack this complex of concepts, but we are aware that conditions of one kind can affect conditions of other kinds. For example, a constraint of time may result in pupils, or teachers feeling under pressure; in that event, time may be the basic cause of, say, a disruption in the NDS of pupil activity, but the immediate causal factor may be seen as some aspect of the pupils' or teacher's behaviour.

A fourth set of concepts is concerned with the teachers' evaluations of their own activities. These evaluations appear to have two facets: first, the extent to which their actions maintain their NDS; and secondly, the extent to which their actions promote progress. In addition, it appears that the conditions (time, material conditions, pupils, teachers), which influenced the standards applied to NDS or progress, are also seen to impinge on and lead to variation in the teachers' actions.

At the moment, therefore, our emerging conceptual framework for teachers' thinking about their classroom teaching has to take account of our evidence that:

> The criteria and goals teachers use for evaluating their teaching are concerned with: first, maintaining some normal desirable state of pupil activity, and secondly, promoting some kind of progress. The teachers evaluate all their own actions in relation to these purposes. The standards they apply to achieving these goals in practice, and the single-mindedness of their own actions, are influenced by various conditions which impinge on the teaching.

It is also of interest to note some of the things which do not characterise our teachers' evaluations of their classroom teaching. For example, the words "learning", "objectives", "aims" and "decisions" are rarely used and, as yet, we have not identified examples of teachers evaluating any aspect of their teaching as inherently desirable, as characteristic of good teaching, or indeed in any other terms than as instrumental towards some kind of NDS of pupil activity or some kind of progress. However, we would emphasise that these are not conclusions, only ideas which we are exploring.

Our next step is to see whether our tentative generalisations hold up when we analyse the rest of our data. And then the crucial questions for the teachers: Are the abstractions we have made from their accounts intelligible to them? Do they distort what the teachers are telling us? Do they capture the major emphases of the ways they think about their classroom teaching?

ACKNOWLEDGEMENT

We gratefully acknowledge a research grant from the Scottish Education Department (SED) for this research.   The views expressed in this paper, however, are those of the authors and are not necessarily shared by the SED.

REFERENCES

Deforges, C. & McNamara, D. (1977). One man's heuristic is another man's blindfold: some comments on applying social science to educational practice. *British Journal of Teacher Education*, 3, 1, 27-39.

Deforges, C. & McNamara, D. (1979). Theory and practice: methodological procedures for the objectification of craft knowledge. *British Journal of Teacher Education*, 5, 2, 145-152.

McNamara, D. & Deforges, C. (1978). The social sciences, teacher education and the objectification of craft knowledge. *British Journal of Teacher Education*, 4, 1, 17-36.

THE USE OF CONCEPT MAPPING IN THE STUDY OF TEACHERS' KNOWLEDGE STRUCTURES

F. Elbaz, R. Hoz, Y. Tomer, R. Chayot, S. Mahler
and N. Yeheskel
Department of Education
Ben-Gurion University of the Negev
Beer-Sheva 84105 ISRAEL

SUMMARY

In this paper the development of teacher thinking is conceived in terms
of knowledge structures, and declarative and procedural knowledge. A
framework is set that comprises three interacting factors: the kind of
knowledge, the location in which it develops, and the role assumed by
the teacher (or student). This framework was used to identify transition points within each factor, at which changes in knowledge structures are expected to occur. Representations of knowledge structures
are obtained by using a general analysis scheme for cognitive maps
which are constructed by individual students from a set of domain-
related concepts. This procedure is exemplified by the application of
the above scheme to the maps of one biology student teacher, which
resulted in the specification of both his knowledge structures and
their development over a short period of time.

1. INTRODUCTION

A substantial number of studies on teacher thinking to date involves
either experienced or beginning teachers. This paper is concerned with
the development of teacher knowledge from the onset of formal training
i.e., during preservice education. We propose to study this development using a conceptual framework drawn largely from cognitive psychology. Within this framework we will speak of the knowledge structures
(or cognitive structures) of human beings as the organized body of
knowledge which is stored in long term memory in the form of concept
hierarchies, schemas, propositional networks and production systems
(Ausubel, Novak, and Hanesian, 1978; Schallert, 1982; Anderson, 1985).
In particular, we will use the distinction between declarative and
procedural knowledge. *Declarative knowledge* refers to the internal
representation in the form of propositional (semantic) networks containing concepts and their relations. It is an essential component
of expertise in a variety of domains, teaching included (e.g., Chi,
Glaser, and Rees, 1982; Lesgold, 1983; Leinhardt and Smith, 1984), and
may also take the form of scripts (Schank and Abelson, 1977) plans
(e.g., Hayes-Roth and Hayes-Roth, 1978), and images (Elbaz, 1983;
Clandinin and Connelly, 1984) which guide both covert (conceptual) and

overt behaviors. *Procedural knowledge* refers to the operations that can be performed on the declarative knowledge by the application of cognitive skills. Anderson's (1982) theory suggests that declarative knowledge is the origin and source from which procedural knowledge is developed by practice; on the other hand, work on teachers' personal practical knowledge suggests that the opposite relationship also holds following teachers' reflection on their classroom practices.

The study of the development of teachers' knowledge structures in the course of preservice programs and afterwards must take into account these important issues:
1) The interaction of three major factors: (a) the kind of knowledge acquired by prospective teachers, (b) the locations where training and instruction take place (university and school), and (c) the various roles of persons involved in training (university teachers, school teachers, student teacher, beginning teacher, school pupils).
2) The difficult transitions between the categories within each factor which must be made (a) from theory (declarative knowledge) to practical classroom skills (procedural knowledge), (b) from the university to the school, and (c) from student to teacher.

We will first discuss the factors involved in the development of teachers' knowledge structures, and this will be followed by description of the methods by which cognitive maps are obtained and analysed to represent knowledge structures, and detect changes in them.

2. FACTORS INVOLVED IN DEVELOPMENT OF TEACHER KNOWLEDGE STRUCTURES

The development of teachers' knowledge structures is a complex process in which several factors interact, in particular 1) the *kinds* of knowledge acquired, 2) the *location* where training and instruction take place, and 3) the roles assumed by *participants* in the training program. (The factor "role" is nested within the factor "location", and these factors are crossed with the factor "kinds of knowledge".)
A. In studying the knowledge structures of prospective teachers we will look at two main aspects: content and use. By "content" we mean that knowledge which is represented in memory mainly as *declarative*, but in the disciplinary domain it also includes *procedural* knowledge, e.g., inquiry skills and techniques. By "knowledge-in-use" we mean the operations, both conceptual and physical, that teachers carry out in the course of their work, e.g., planning instructional sequences, managing class activities. The nature of, and relationship between the substantive knowledge, or content, and the knowledge-in-use of teachers is difficult to specify at this stage in research on teachers' thinking.
1. The content knowledge to be acquired by the prospective teacher will be classified, for convenience, into three domains (some overlap between these domains may exist); Disciplinary knowledge--subject matter knowledge which is to be taught in the classroom; pedagogical knowledge--knowledge of principles involved in teaching the subject matter; and contextual knowledge--knowledge both explicit and tacit which orients the prospective teacher in the school setting.

Within each of the domains obstacles exist in the provision and acquisition of pertinent and usable content knowledge. For disciplinary knowledge the student will be called upon to make a transition from using the criteria of valid knowledge which he was taught as an undergraduate, to using criteria appropriate to teaching the subject matter. Furthermore, while disciplinary knowledge is usually taught and learned by direct instruction, and is mostly declarative it may include procedural components that are taught and learned by indirect (as well as direct) means, e.g., knowledge of inquiry or problem-solving skills in the discipline. The prospective teacher must not only acquire these components but translate them into a form appropriate for students.

Pedagogical knowledge is a major component of any teacher training program but few training programs have solved the problem of how to provide theoretical pedagogical knowledge which will both engage the student intellectually and be amenable to eventual transformation into knowledge-in-use, which is strictly procedural. Prospective teachers are still lectured on the discovery method, and conversely we find an emphasis on competencies, without provision of tools to reflect on one's teaching and adapt it to varied situations. Contextual knowledge is subject to similar problems of transition. Prospective teachers may acquire formal knowledge of the school system, for example, but the encounter with reality is usually a shock nevertheless, and it is rare for prospective teachers to be given help in articulating their own understanding of the school system on the basis of their experience.

2. With respect to "knowledge-in-use", both declarative and procedural knowledge are involved, with complex causative relationships. Student teachers come into training with a stock of knowledge-in-use developed from their previous experience as students and from the variety of informal teaching situations which abound in everyday life. This knowledge-in-use sometimes interferes with the different knowledge-in-use to be acquired in the program. This phenomenon is in line with other findings that knowledge structures are stable (e.g., Preece, 1976, 1978; Champagne, Hoz, and Klopfer, 1984), and student misconceptions are highly resistant to modification (e.g., McKlosky, Caramazza, and Green 1980; Novak, 1982).

B. The location is a central factor in the development of teachers' knowledge. In one location, viz. teacher education institution, certain types of knowledge are acquired by prospective teachers for use in the other one, viz. school, where professional operation takes place. We expect changes to occur in the nature of this knowledge with changes in location. For instance, pedagogic knowledge which was acquired as declarative knowledge should be transformed into procedural knowledge in order to be used by the same person who is now a school teacher in the other location. Further, the location would seem to affect the manner in which knowledge can be conveyed and acquired in the first place: universities impose certain styles of teaching and learning, whereas on-site training in the school invites other kinds of instruction. The fact that universities and school are cut off from one another within the larger society further complicates the transition.

C. The change in role from student to teacher is a complex one, involving many factors: there is a cognitive change from the acquisi-

tion of pre-structured content to the shaping of content for students,
a change in level of activity from (relatively) passive to active; a
change in degree and scope of responsibility, a change in social
status, and a personal change in how one views oneself as a result.
The change in role from student to teacher is likely to be significant
as far as the nature of knowledge is concerned. For example, the same
subject matter may be viewed differently by the prospective teacher in
the program and after graduation, during school teaching. Likewise
the pedagogical and contextual knowledge which is available to the
teacher is different from that to which he had access as a student.
The prospective teacher does not really learn how to talk to parents
until he or she sits behind the desk as the one who will decide on the
fate of their child.

We have sketched the major factors involved in the development of
teachers' knowledge and have indicated some of the transition points
at which changes should take place in the knowledge of the prospective
teacher if he or she is to function effectively in the classroom. In
the rest of this paper we focus on a particular, limited aspect:
teachers' knowledge structures in one discipline.

3. CONCEPT MAPPING AS A PROBE OF KNOWLEDGE

Knowledge structures can be abstracted from cognitive maps which are
obtained from our revised ConSAT (Concept Structuring Analysis Task,
Champagne and Klopfer, 1981; Hoz et al., 1984) interview. ConSAT was
developed from Novak's (1980) concept mapping technique, originally
designed to help depict the hierarchical organization of concepts in a
text, in order to better understand the text and to learn it meaningfully (Novak, 1980). Several probes of knowledge structure have been
developed (see Champagne et al., 1984, for comprehensive discussion
and comparison). These probes are characterized by (i) producing
representations in the form of a clustering (categorical) or spatial
arrangement of a given set of concepts; (ii) the application of
mathematical procedures to proximity matrices (produced by either
individuals or a group), which were obtained either directly or indirectly from the subjects' responses, to produce these clusterings;
and (iii) lack of subject labels or explanations. Such probes thus
constitute high inference measures that need further interpretation by
the researcher. It is preferable to have low inference probes yielding knowledge structure representations which require lesser interpretation, such as ConSAT. Using this probe each student constructs
a cognitive map that shows the spatial arrangement of a given set of
concepts which includes the student's groupings and explanations,
thus avoiding or minimizing possible inference leaps. Sample cognitive maps are presented in the Appendix.

Initial findings indicate that the revised ConSAT interview has
satisfactory task test-retest reliability, and the classification
scheme for the bi-concept link has a high between-judges agreement
(95%) (Hoz et al., 1984). The reliability of the analysis scheme
developed for the biology domain was also assessed and a close
agreement was obtained for it (see next section). The ConSAT interview is administered individually, requiring about an hour to complete
the first time. Additional administrations once the interviewee is

acquainted with the task take about 30 minutes.

In the next section we describe the procedures by which knowledge structures are abstracted from cognitive maps, and illustrate them by analysing the disciplinary cognitive maps of one preservice biology student (participating in our larger study of teacher education). The concepts for the ConSAT were chosen by the methods course teacher who considered them central to both high school curriculum and the methods course. These concepts were given expert confirmations by several research biologists at the university. The students in this study were interviewed on two occasions and produced cognitive maps in both biology and pedagogy.

4. ABSTRACTING KNOWLEDGE STRUCTURES OF COGNITIVE MAPS

Concept maps are analysed at several levels which are illustrated below. The structural organization is characterized along several domain-specific dimensions that were identified by the discipline experts. Links between the concepts will be classified by a semantic scheme, developed from that of Dansereau et al., (1979), who devised it for the semantic classification of links in textual concept maps.

Cognitive maps are assessed on three dimensions pertaining to the elements of the map (concepts and groups), their composition, organization and relationships, as follows:

A. The *quality of concept groupings* is determined by the total number of groups, their nature and similarity to the experts' groupings, and the presence of focal concepts and kernel groups which are congruent with the expert's.

B. The *quality of links among concepts* is determined by their disciplinary characterization and relevance, and by their congruence with the experts' total set of links for these concepts.

C. The *semantic nature of links among concepts* is identified by a system developed for this purpose (Hoz et al., 1984).

We illustrate this scheme by applying it to the cognitive maps of one student on two occasions, 3 months apart. During this period he had completed the second two semesters of a biology methods course.

A. The quality of groupings in the cognitive map is determined by three dimensions: (1) the total number of groups, (2) the nature of groups and their similarity to the experts', and (3) the existence and nature of kernel groups.

(1) Regarding the existence and number of concept groups which are formed on a characteristic common to its component concepts, and labeled by this characteristic, in our example, on the first occasion the student formed three groups which he labeled, and three concepts remained ungrouped with no reasons given; on the second occasion he formed a large single group which he labeled.

(2) Three biology experts who served as consultants agreed on two "legitimate" partitions of the concept set, each having different structure and number of groups. *Partition A.* Group 1: hormone, enzyme, metabolism, photosynthesis, energy, diffusion, feedback. Group 2: biotope, evolution, classification. Group 3: cell, DNA. *Partition B.* Group 1: Cell, enzyme, metabolism, photosynthesis,

energy, DNA, diffusion. Group 2: biotope, evolution, classification. Group 3: hormone, feedback. These experts classified the students' cognitive maps according to their similarity to the experts' groupings on a three-level scale. Level 1: strong similarity, indicated by nearly complete group overlap and labels. Level 2: moderate similarity, indicated by some group overlap and labels. Level 3: weak similarity, indicated by a multi-group partition, with numerous small groups that do not overlap any of the experts' partitions.
(3) To identify focal concepts and kernel groups the three experts defined the "strength" of links between all pairs of concepts (with 13 concepts there are 78 pairwise links altogether). The strength of links between concepts was conceived as being directly proportional to the biological functionality of the two concepts. Link strength was measured on the following three-level scale, on which the between-expert agreement was 99%. Level 1: necessary links between concepts that are tightly connected and interact strongly. 25 of the 78 possible pairwise links are at this level. Level 2: possible links between concepts that are moderately connected and interact somewhat. 12 of the 78 possible pairwise links are at this level. Level 3: links between concepts for which a connection is biologically meaningless. 41 of the 78 possible pairwise links are at this level.

This classification of links were inscribed in a 13X13 array, termed the *experts' matrix*, on which the analysis of bi-concept links was based. It enabled the identification of errors or misconceptions about concepts and their links. The following features of knowledge structure were obtained using the experts' matrix:
1. The number and quality of links. A good map is characterized by a high percentage of first level links.
2. Focal concepts and kernel groups. We defined a focal concept as one which is characterized by a high percentage of both inter- and intra-group links of the highest strength level. We defined a kernel group as one in which all, or most intra-group links are of the highest strength level.

In our case, in each cognitive map (i) four concepts that were focal for the student were also focal for the experts, and (ii) two kernel groups were highly similar to the experts' kernel groups.

Using focal concepts and kernel groups enabled the identification of disciplinary misconceptions, by (i) detecting differences in focality between students and experts, and (ii) locating differences between strength levels for students and experts. In our case, "metabolism" and "diffusion" were miconceived: for the experts but not for the student they are focal concepts, and the link-strength of the concept "metabolism" is at the third level whereas it is at the first level for this student.

B. The quality of bi-concept links was assessed by the disciplinary characterization and relevance, measured on a three-level scale. Level 1: correct, precise and clear (9 points). Level 2: Correct but partial (7 points). Level 3: indirect and general, or imprecise and lacking in certain aspects (5 points). In our case, the median scores for the links in each map were 7 and 9 on the two occasions, indicating an improvement in the quality of biological relevance.

C. The experts' conception of the domain was obtained by using the experts' matrix to derive two indices, one external and one internal, to further assess the quality of cognitive maps. The external index is convergence with the experts' links, which is the percentage of links in a particular map which are at a given strength level out of the total number of experts' links at this level. The internal index is salience, i.e., the percentage of links of levels 1 and 2 out of the total number of links in the map. Its complement is the percentage of links of level 3 (i.e., misconceived links), which indicates overall misunderstanding of the relationships between concepts.

In our case, salience values were 61% and 81% on the two occasions respectively, with the respective misunderstanding values of 39% and 19%; and convergence values are 44% and 56% for level 1 links, and 42% and 25% for level 2 links. The changes in convergence and salience enable us to identify rather substantial improvements in the biological understanding of the student.

D. The semantic nature of the links between concepts was identified by the following system comprising 18 kinds of links: Part of, type/example of, leads to, analogy, characteristic, evidence, description, influence, precedence, relation, contingency, operation, aim, sameness, formation, neutral, nonexistent, and unclassifiable. (For more detailed description, see Hoz et al., 1984.)

In our case, the most frequent kinds were as follows: on the first occasion, 4 "part of" links and 4 "operation" links, and on the second occasion, 8 "operation" links and 4 "formation" links. This result reflects a better biological understanding of the relatedness among these concepts.

5. CONCLUSIONS

In this paper we have illustrated the use of concept mapping as a means of identifying and representing changes in the knowledge structures of student teachers. Here we have focused on the knowledge structures in the disciplinary domain, but the analysis schemes have potential for the other domains as well. In our larger study the students produced cognitive maps in pedagogy as well as biology, and in addition to the ConSAT the students took part in semi-structured clinical interviews designed to elicit their explanations regarding certain aspects of the training program and their impact on observed changes in the cognitive maps. We are currently developing classification schemes to analyse the clinical data to yield knowledge structure representations in every domain (along the lines of work by Leinhardt and Smith, 1984). We anticipate some difficulties in abstracting knowledge structures in certain areas (e.g., pedagogy) but the proposed methodology shows promise of further progress to be made in the understanding of teacher thinking.

Appendix. Cognitive maps of one student, on two occasions 3 months apart.

1. First cognitive map

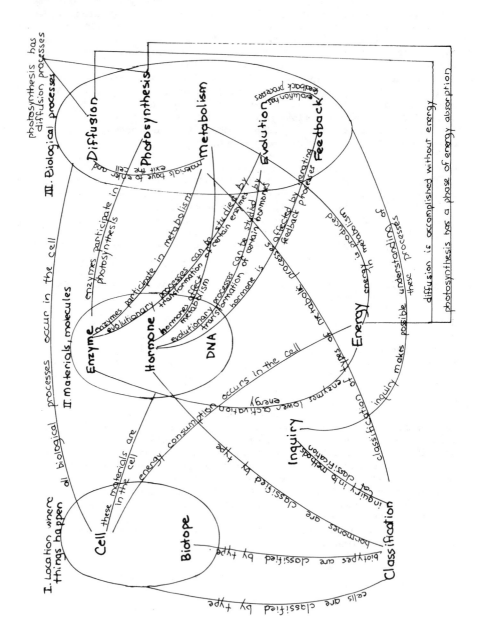

2. Second cognitive map

The map is characterized by the concepts being linked to each other from research processes to cellular processes.

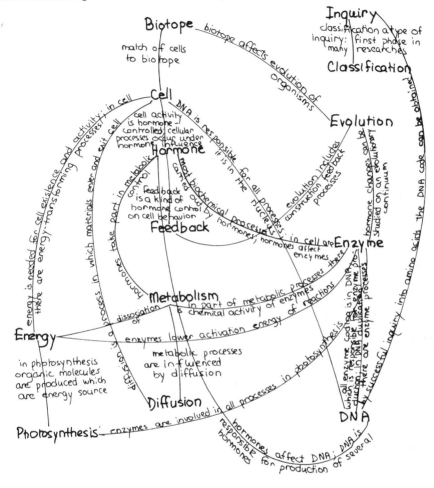

REFERENCES

Anderson, J.R. (1982). Acquisition of cognitive skill. *Psychological Review, 89,* 369-406.

Anderson, J.R. (1985). *Cognitive Psychology and its implications.* (2nd ed.) New York, Wiley.

Ausubel, D.P., Novak, J., and Hanesian, H. (1978). *Educational Psychology: A Cognitive View.* New York, Holt, Rinehart, & Winston.

Champagne, A.B., Klopfer, L.E. (1981). *Using the ConSAT: A Memo to teachers.* (Reports to educators R.T.E. 4). Pittsburgh, Learning Research and Development Center, University of Pittsburgh.

Champagne, A.B., Hoz, R., and Klopfer, L.E. (1984). *Construct valida-tion of the cognitive structure of physics concepts*. Pittsburgh, Learning Research and Development Center, University of Pittsburgh.

Chi, M.T.H., Glaser, R., and Rees, E. (1982). Expertise in problem solving. In: Sternberg, R. (Ed.) *Advances in the psychology of human intelligence*. Hillsdale, N.J., Lawrence Erlbaum Associates.

Clandinin, D.J. and Connelly, F.M. (1984) Personal practical knowl-edge: Image and narrative unity. In: Halkes, R. and Olson, J.K. (Eds.) *Teacher thinking: a new perspective on persisting problems in education*. Lisse: Swets and Zeitlinger.

Dansereau, D.F., McDonald, B.A., Collins, K.W., Garland, J., Helley, C.D., Diekhoff, G.M., and Evans, S.H. (1979). Evaluation of a learning strategy system. In: O'Neill, H.F. and Spielberger, G.D. (Eds.) *Cognitive and affective learning strategies*. New York, Academic Press.

Elbaz, F. (1983). *Teacher thinking: A study of practical knowledge*. London, Croom Helm and New York, Nichols.

Fuller, F.F. (1969). Concerns of teachers: A developments concep-tualization. *American Educational Research Journal, 6*, 201-220.

Hayes-Roth, B. and Hayes-Roth, F. (1978). *Cognitive processes in planning*. R-2366-ONR. A report prepared for the Office of Naval Research.

Hoz, R., Mahler, S., Yeheskel, N., Tomer, Y., and Elbaz, F. (1984). *Project for the Evaluation of Teacher Education*. PETE annual report 1984. Beer-Sheva, Ben-Gurion University of the Negev.

Katz, L.G. (1972). Developmental stages of preschool teachers. *Elementary School Journal, 73*, 50-54.

Leinhardt, G. and Smith, D. (1984). *Expertise in mathematics instruc-tion: Subject matter knowledge*. Paper presented at the annual meeting of AERA, New Orleans.

Lesgold, A.M. (1983). *Acquiring expertise*. Technical Report PD-5. Pittsburgh, University of Pittsburgh, Learning Research and Develop-ment Center.

McKloskey, M., Caramazza, A., and Green, B. (1980). Curvilinear motion in the absence of external forces: Naive beliefs about the motion of objects. *Science, 210*, 1139-1141.

Novak, J.D. (1980). *Handbook for the learning how to learn program*. Ithaka, Cornell University.

Novak, J.D. (1982). Psychological and Epistemological Alternatives, In: Modgil, S. and Modgil, C. (Eds.) *Jean Piaget: Consensus and controversy*. London, Holt, Rinehart and Winston, 331-349.

Preece, P.F.W. (1976). Mapping cognitive structure: A comparison of methods. *Journal of Educational Psychology, 68*, 1-8.

Preece, P.F.W. (1978). Exploration of semantic space: Review of research on the organization of scientific concepts in semantic memory. *Science Education, 62*, 547-562.

Schallert, D.L. (1982). The significance of knowledge: a synthesis of research related to schema theory. In: Otto, W. and White, S. (Eds.) *Reading expository material*. New York: Academic Press.

Schank, R., and Abèlson, R. (1977). *Scripts, plans, goals, and understanding*. Hillsdale, N.J., Lawrence Erlbaum Associates.

ROLE OVER PERSON: LEGITIMACY AND AUTHENTICITY IN TEACHING

Margret Buchmann[1]
Institute for Research on Teaching
Michigan State University

This chapter has been adapted from "Role Over Person" which originally appeared in *Teachers College Record,* Vol. 87, No. 4, Summer 1986. Reprinted by permission of Teachers College, Columbia University.

SUMMARY

This paper discusses competing norms for justifying teacher decisions, their effects on productivity and legitimacy in teaching, and the teaching profession as a moral and learning community. Drawing on philosophical analyses and studies of elementary and secondary schools, teacher preparation, staff development, and the adoption of innovations, it argues that personal orientations (centering on personal habits, interests, and opinions) remove teacher decisions from the realm of criteria for judging appropriateness. Personal reasons have explanatory value; they carry less weight when justifying professional action. Role orientation involves references to larger, organized contexts, including the disciplines of knowledge, group purposes, and societal issues.

1. CHOICE IN TEACHING

What teachers do is neither natural nor necessary but based on choice. Since choice may harden into custom or dissipate into whim, one asks for justification; it is a way of assuring that teaching will periodically pass muster. In justifying their actions, people give reasons. For teachers, personal reasons can be appropriate when explaining a given action to others, but they carry less weight in considering the wisdom of an action or decision. In other words, some contexts call for explanation and others for justification. When one wants to understand why someone did something, one wants to know what actually motivated him or her. But if one wants to know whether what was done was right, one wants to hear and assess justifications. Here it is important that the reasons be good reasons, and it becomes less important whether they were operating at the time.

The question, then, is what counts as good reasons in teaching. I argue that for many teacher actions, personal reasons are subordinate to external standards and that the scope of these actions is much broader than people often assume. Providing acceptable justifications requires the existence of a community to both set standards for adequacy and to determine a set of rules for guidance. The role obligations of teachers as members of such a community forge bonds which not only ensure compliance but generate effort and involvement.

Curriculum decisions may be at the top of the list of teacher actions for which one should expect adequate justifications, for, as Scheffler points out, it is not

> a matter of indifference or whim just what the educator chooses to teach. Some selections we judge better than others; some we deem positively intolerable. Nor are we content to discuss issues of selection as if they hinged on personal taste alone. We try to convince others; we present ordered arguments; we appeal to custom and principle; we point to relevant consequences and implicit commitments. In short, we consider decisions on educational content to be responsible or justifiable acts with public significance. (Scheffler, 1977, p. 497)

But decisions about the social organization of the class, how to deal with parents, and how to treat requests (or directives) from school administrators are also examples of teacher actions that are responsible acts of public significance. It is useful to recall the root meaning of responsibility; being a respondent has to do with one's answering for things and defending a position.

Personal reasons--centering on one's habits, interests, and opinions--are relevant for considering the wisdom of actions where the question is what the individual per se wants to accomplish, but not for professional situations where goals (and perhaps a range of means) are a given. People accepting a professional role are in the latter situation, and one must ask whether their particular actions and general dispositions are enacting and conforming to given standards and goals. Such people have no right to decide whether to act on their clients' behalf and in their interests: it is their obligation to teach school, put a leg in a cast, or appear in a court of law. This is why a professional's most significant choice is whether to take on the role (Fried, 1978).

What is close to people is always important to them; the personal will take care of itself. But professional aspirations, responsibility, and curricular subjects with their pedagogies must be learned. Tendencies in teacher preparation and staff development to stress individualism, self-realization, and the personal--even idiosyncratic-- element in teaching are therefore problematic. This would be true in any case. But such tendencies are extremely questionable in American education, where structural features (e.g., recruitment, induction, rewards) and the ethos of the profession already converge in conservatism, presentism, and individualism. The point is that attention to role is especially important for American teachers because it goes against many potent forces.

An understanding of teacher orientations (role versus personal) and their effects is particularly important now when there is a strong press to set policies that will improve schooling in the United States. It is well recognized that teachers have the final word on exactly what will be done in the classroom and what the actual curriculum will be (for a review, see Brophy, 1982). This implies that making good policy requires knowing how teachers are likely to act in answer to policy initiatives and why (Wise, 1979). It requires, furthermore, thinking about those competencies and dispositions that teachers should have as professionals (Kerr, 1983; Sykes, 1983).

2. TEACHING AS A ROLE

It is crucial to appreciate the fact that "teacher" is a role word. Roles embody some of our highest aspirations and provide social mechanisms for shaping action in their light. They are parts people play in society and do not describe individuals. Teacher obligations—those behaviors and dispositions that students and the public have a right to expect of teachers—actually have three important aspects that have no personal reference or connection. First, these obligations do not depend on any particular individuals (teachers or students). Second, they apply regardless of personal opinions, likes, or dislikes. Third, they relate to what is taught and learned. In schools, teachers are supposed to help students participate in "the community of subject matter" whose objective contents of thought and experience—systems, theories, ideas—are impersonal because they are distinct from the people who learn or discuss them. They are, to some extent, independent of time and place (Hawkins, 1974; Polanyi, 1962).

In an immediate sense, teachers have obligations toward their students; these obligations center on helping them learn worthwhile things in the social context of classrooms and schools. The view of students as learners underlies the distinctive obligations of teachers; and role orientation in teaching by definition means taking an interest in student learning. Thus, insofar as teachers are not social workers, career counselors, or simply adults who care for children, their work centers on the curriculum and presupposes knowledge of subject matter. This does not exclude their caring about children or being a person in their role.

Roles also indicate obligations toward more remote communitites; in teaching, these communities include the profession, the public, and the disciplines of knowledge. For instance, while it is important to communicate the fact that disciplinary knowledge is not absolute, teachers have to recognize and respect the constraints imposed by the structure of different disciplines on their decisions about how to teach, for:

> If a structure of teaching and learning is alien to the structure of what we propose to teach, the outcome will inevitably be a corruption of that content. (Schwab, 1978, p. 242)

Since teachers are supposed to look after the educational interests of children, they have to learn to live with the fact that they are not free to choose methods, content, or classroom organization for psychological, social, or personal reasons alone.

The teacher educator slogans of "finding the technique that works for you," "discovering your own beliefs," "no one right way to teach," and "being creative and unique" (see, e.g., Combs, 1967; Goodman,

1984) are seductive half-truths. They are seductive because anyone likes to be told that being oneself and doing one's own thing is all right, even laudable. Conduct sanctioned in this fashion--while consistent with professional discipline for those who already have the necessary dispositions and competencies--allows for both minimal effort and idiosyncrasy in other cases. These slogans are half-truths because--although identifying teachers' personal and commonsense beliefs is important--once identified, these beliefs must be appraised as bases and guides for professional conduct and, where necessary, changed.

Professional socialization marks a turning point in the perception of relevant others and of oneself, yet a reversal of prior conceptions is less clear cut and typical in teaching than in other professions (Lortie, 1975). Formal socializing mechanisms in teaching are few and short in duration, not very arduous, and have weak effects. The lengthy, personal experience of being in school as a student, however, provides a repertoire of behaviors, beliefs, and conceptions that teachers draw on. Where it is successful, genuine professional socialization trains attention on the specialized claims that others have on one. Thus the teaching role entails a specific and difficult shift of concern from self to others for which the "apprenticeship of observation" (Lortie, 1975) provides no training. Highet (1966) describes the nature of this shift:

> You must think, not what you know, but what they do not
> know; not what you find hard, but what they will find hard;
> then, after putting yourself inside their minds, obstinate
> or puzzled, groping or mistaken as they are, explain what
> they need to learn. (p. 280)

In general, a shift of concern from self to others comes more from acknowledging, "This is the kind of work I am doing," than from stating, "This is how I feel," or "This is how I do things." Subjective reasons refer to personal characteristics and preferences. They are permissive rather than stringent, variable rather than uniform. Appraisal requires distance, but detachment is difficult where things are simply seen as part of oneself. A danger is that personal beliefs and preferences are "no longer easily accessible to reflection, criticism, modification, or expulsion" (Schwab, 1976b, p. 37). This explains the air of finality that many subjective reasons have. Yet it is not that personal beliefs and preference must necessarily be misleading or selfish, but that--where such criteria rule--other and more legitimate concerns may become secondary (Lortie, 1975). This reverses the relation in which personal and professional reasons should stand in teaching.

Subjectivity and reasonableness

When people say, "This is the kind of person I am," they mean to close an issue and put an end to debate, whether the issues have been satisfactorily resolved or not. An emphasis on the self can block the flow of speculation, conversation, and reflection by which people shape habits of action and mind that affect others or the self; it

means cutting oneself and the collective off from some of the most
valuable human resources. Nor are teachers exceptions to the rule
that not everything people want is good. Imperviousness and finality--
of feeling, belief, or habit--interfere with learning and with getting
better at helping others learn.

Justification is always tied to reason and susceptibility to
reason; teaching is special in the sorts of reasons that are
acceptable. Professional decisions are tied to the public realm where
they are constrained by facts and norms, both forms of public
knowledge. Put differently, justification needs to reach beyond the
particulars of teachers' own actions and inclinations to consider
larger, organized contexts relevant to their work, such as the
disciplines of knowledge, laws, and societal issues (Thelen, 1973).
And teachers need not be creative to be reasonable. Rather, they must
be willing to act in accordance with rules, submit to impersonal
judgment, and be open to change for good reasons. To call an action
or person reasonable still is praise, for reasonable people are
neither inconsiderate nor rash, and their actions are unlikely to be
futile or foolish (Black, 1972).

Caprice and habit cut teaching off from thought, particularly
from its moral roots. In cause and origin, caprice is inherently
self-contained; it contrasts with cultiviation or improvement by
education, training, or attentive labor. Habit is the opposite of
impulse, and it confines in a different way. Yet caprice and habit
are alike in that they both allow for action without adequate reason,
removing teacher actions and decisions from the realm of criteria for
judging appropriateness. Part of reasonableness is the habit and
capacity of giving due weight to evidence and the arguments of others
who may offer new data or alternative explanations.

Workplace isolation and role orientation

Teaching is lonely work in the United States. Controls are weak and
standards low, rewards uncertainly related to achievement, and work
success uncertain, often elusive (Lortie, 1975). While an inner
transformation from person to teacher may be wanting, one can still
get a job teaching school. There is a sense of "easy come, easy go"
in teaching; such transiency does not support a sense of community.
Tenure and salary are based on years of service rather than competence
or commitment. An active interest in student learning does not come
with teaching experience, as some teacher development theories seem to
suggest (see, e.g., Fuller, 1969). To the contrary, teaching seems to
have a calcifying effect on teachers (McLaughlin & Marsh, 1978;
Waller, 1932/1961). The teaching career is flat, not providing
sufficient opportunities for changes in responsibilities and professional renewal. Together with the uncertainties of teaching, all
these things can affect even dedicated teachers. Thus Sizer (1984)
describes the feelings of Horace, a veteran teacher of 28 years:

> He is so familiar with the mistakes that ninth-graders make
> that he can sense them coming even before their utterance.
> Adverbs are always tougher to teach than adjectives. What
> frustrates him most are the partly correct answers; Horace

worries that if he signals that a reply is somewhat
accurate, all the students will think it is entirely
accurate. At the same time, if he takes some minutes to
sort out the truth from the falsity, the entire train of
thought will be lost. He can never pursue any one student's
errors to completion without losing all the others. (p. 13)

The organization of public schooling in America isolates teachers
from one another, and there is a lack of a common language and shared
experiences. Hence it is difficult to develop a role orientation that
one would be able and willing to use in the justification of teaching
decisions and actions. And what does the "inner self" do when left
unwatched and deprived of rules of conduct based on external standards
and role-specific sanctions? Anything that comes to mind? The degree
to which one's behavior can be observed and one's beliefs examined by
relevant others is crucial in role performance and professional
discipline. As Merton (1957) argues, "If all the facts of one's
conduct and beliefs were freely available to anyone, social structures
could not operate" (p. 115); however, insulation can lead people
astray, for "the teacher or physician who is largely insulated from
observability may fail to live up to the requirements of his status"
(p. 115). Where workplace structure insulates individuals, they are
also less likely to be subject to conflicting pressures--simply
because what they do is less well known.

With increasing size and a continuing accumulation of formal
policies, schools are becoming public-service bureaucracies. Teachers
adapt to conflicting policies and endemic uncertainties as best they
can. These adaptations can result in private, intensely held
redefinitions of the nature of teaching and of the clientele. In
resolving the tension between capabilities (often constrained by
workplace demands) and objectives, individuals may lower their goals
or withdraw from attempts at reaching them altogether. In responding
to a diverse clientele, they may reject the norm of universalism and
discount some groups as unteachable. Because such private, personal
conceptions can help individual professionals placed in difficult
situations, they tend to be held rigidly and are not open to
discussion. Also, though modifying one's conception of students is
private, the content of typical coping responses is likely to reflect
prevailing biases (Lipsky, 1980). There is thus a troubling relation
between the development and persistence of inappropriate coping
strategies in teaching--including racial, cultural, and sexual
stereotypes--and the relative likelihood of staying on the job.

Role orientation as a disposition can steady teachers in their
separate classrooms, helping them call to mind what their work is
about and who is to benefit from it. A disposition is a special kind
of orientation. While "to orient oneself" means to bring oneself into
defined relations to known facts or principles, a disposition is a
bent of mind that, once it is in place, comes naturally. Dispositions
are inclinations relating to the social and moral qualities of one's
actions; they are not just habits but intelligent capacities
(Scheffler, 1965). With role orientation as a disposition, no
extraordinary resolve is necessary to occasionally take a hard look at
what one does or believes in teaching. But instead of instilling role

orientation as a disposition, teacher educators often focus on the
personal concerns of novices and experienced teachers.

Personal concerns and teacher learning

In examining the process of learning to teach, teacher development,
and the adoption of innovations in schools, researchers and educators
have identified a shift from personal to "impact" concerns (how is my
action or innovation affecting my students?) as crucial. For example,
Hall and George (1978) found that among the teachers who do not use
innovations are those most concerned with the implications of change
for themselves personally, and Fuller (1969) identifies the emergence
of concern for student learning as a culminating point in teacher
development. Yet recently, Fuller's concept of personalized teacher
education has been questioned, even as an approach that may lead
teachers from self-oriented concerns to other-oriented concerns
(Feiman & Floden, 1980). The assumption that earlier concerns must be
resolved before later ones can emerge confuses readiness and motivation. Just because some concerns carry more personal and affective
charge, it does not follow that other concerns--less immediate, more
important--cannot be thought about. These criticisms also apply to
the work of Hall and his associates (e.g., Hall, Loucks, Rutherford &
Newlove, 1975; Hall & Loucks, 1978), who base the content of interventions in staff development on teachers' concerns. Actually, teacher
preparation and staff development that focus on personal concerns may
have the undesirable effect of communicating to teachers that their
own comfort is the most important goal of teacher education.
Zeichner and Teitelbaum (1982) draw attention to the political
attitudes that a personalized, concerns-based approach to teacher
preparation may promote.

> By advocating the postponement of complex educational
> questions to a point beyond preservice training and by
> focusing attention primarily on meeting the survival-
> oriented and technical concerns of student teachers, this
> approach (while it may make students more comfortable)
> serves to promote uncritical acceptance of existing
> distributions of power and resources. (p. 101)

One form of conservatism is to take the given and rest--an attitude
that bypasses an important source of learning and change, namely, to
take the given and *ask*. An emphasis on personal concerns is unlikely
to change the ethos of individualism, conservatism, and presentism in
teaching. There is, moreover, recent empirical evidence that both
elementary and secondary teachers base significant curricular
decisions on personal preferences. This empirical backing for my
claim that role orientation is not getting sufficient emphasis in
education is sketched below.

Teacher preferences and the curriculum

At the elementary level, Schmidt and Buchmann show that the allocation
of time to subjects in six elementary classrooms was associated with

teachers' personal beliefs and feelings concerning reading, language arts, mathematics, science, and social studies. Briefly, average daily time allocations went up and down in accordance with (1) teacher judgments on the degree of emphasis subjects should receive and, (2) indications (self-reports) of the extent to which teachers enjoyed teaching these curricular areas. When projected over the entire school year, differences in time allocations associated with teacher preferences amounted to significant differences in the curriculum, for example 45 hours more or less of mathematics instruction, 70 of social studies, and 100 of science.

Researchers also asked teachers to indicate how difficult they found teaching the five areas of the elementary school curriculum. Findings here were mixed and thought-provoking. For instance, in the area of reading, the six teachers studied did not seem to spend less time on reading just because they found it difficult to teach. But some such tendency could be observed in language arts, social studies, mathematics, and science. However, even here the results were less than clear. The mean differences between the teachers who found it difficult to teach social studies or mathematics and who found either subject easy to teach, for example, were small. It is possible that personal difficulties experienced in teaching a subject may to some extent be neutralized by external policies or a sense of what is an appropriate emphasis on a particular subject. Also, these unclear results may be due to the fact that "finding something difficult to teach" has two alternative senses, (1) the difficulty for children of the subject, and (2) the difficulty of the subject for the teacher.[2]

In a related exploratory interview study (Buchmann, 1983), 11 out of 20 elementary teachers showed some form of role orientation as they explained the ways they typically organized curricular subjects in their classrooms (integrated versus non-integrated). What united the responses of role-oriented teachers was the fact that they placed themselves within a larger picture in which colleagues, the curriculum, and accountability figured in some fashion. They looked outward rather than inward. This is not to say that they had no personal interests or preferences that influenced what they taught and how they taught it. But they felt bound by obligations; the personal element in their responses was framed by a sense of the collective.

Teachers demonstrating a personal orientation in their responses did not go beyond the context of their own activities. Most of them (six out of nine) explained their classroom practices by reference to themselves as persons. Their responses tended toward the proximate: affinity to self, immediate experience, the present characteristics of children. The "language of caprice" (Lortie, 1975, p. 212) pervaded several of their responses. In cases where they recognized that the needs of some children were unlikely to be met by their approach to teaching, these teachers would still explain what they thought and did by reference to personal inclination or habitual ways of working.

A three-year study of 14 fifth-grade classrooms examining curriculum and learning in science (Smith & Anderson, 1984), concluded that teachers' reliance on personal beliefs and teaching styles hindered student learning. For example, in using a text with an unusual and sophisticated teaching strategy, teachers did not pay attention to critical information provided in the teachers' guide,

62

depending on their previous ideas instead. In general, the researchers distinguished three approaches to teaching science that they identified by observing how teachers used textbooks and materials.

Activity-driven teachers focused on management and student interests rather than student learning; while following the teacher's guide rather closely, they omitted or curtailed class discussions meant to help students think about the science activities they were doing. Didactic teachers stayed even closer to the text that they regarded as a repository of the knowledge to be taught; their presentations, however, made little room for children's expression of their naive scientific conceptions, which therefore remained largely unchallenged. By contrast, discovery-oriented teachers avoided giving answers and encouraged students to develop their own ideas from the results of experiments; yet this distorted crucial intents of the text, which required direct instruction at certain points. While the texts were not perfect (failing, for instance, to spell out assumptions about teaching and learning science in the teacher's guide), the fact remains that these teachers relied on their personal approach to science teaching, with the result that the curriculum miscarried.

Cusick (1982) studied two large secondary schools, one predominately white and suburban, the other racially mixed and located in the central part of a smaller industrial region. Though there were exceptions, a self-oriented and laissez-faire approach to curriculum and student learning was typical in both schools. An American history class with a teacher who had served in World War II became a class on that European war; in a class on speech and forensics the teacher encouraged students (mostly black) to talk about the seamier side of their personal lives--with no one listening, or teaching about speaking. A premium was put on "getting along with kids," and this reward structure combined with isolation from colleagues, lack of scrutiny, and an open elective system turned these schools into places where teachers and students did what felt comfortable or what allowed them to get by. Though there was a pattern to these adaptations, they happened privately. These schools were not normative communities.

Cusick concludes that the secondary teachers he studied constructed "egocentric fields": They treated their job as an extension of self. The presumed needs of students accounted for most justifications of teaching practice ("This is the way to teach these kids"; "This is what they relate to"; or "I'm getting them ready for life"). However, curriculum and student needs were never discussed among teachers in these schools. This raises at least two important problems. First, though the freedom teachers enjoyed may bring high effort in some, other teachers can get by with doing little. Second, while able students with adult guidance may still learn worthwhile things under such conditions, others will pass through high school without learning much of anything.

3. IN TEACHING, SELF-REALIZATION IS MORAL

Autonomy and self-realization are indisputably personal goods. Schools, however, are for children, and children's autonomy and

self-realization depend in part on what they learn in schools. Thus
self-realization in teaching is not a good in itself, but only insofar
as pursuing self-realization leads to appropriate student learning.
The point is that in professional work reasons of personal preference
usually will not do; this applies to nursing, soldiering, and managing
a stock portfolio as well as to teaching. The idea of a surgeon keen
on self-realization at the operating table is macabre. A nurse who
brings up personality and preference in explaining why he changed
standard procedures in dealing with a seizure would not get very far.
There is no reason why such things should be more acceptable in
teaching. The fact that we may have come to accept them is certainly
no justification.

Everyone likes to be comfortable, free of pain and bother. But
the perspectives of psychology and profession are not the same.
Things charged with personal meaning may lead nowhere in teaching.
Even the integrity of self depends in part on suspending impulse.
Simply declaring "where one comes from" makes justified action a
matter of taste and preference, which expresses and reinforces a
massive moral confusion (MacIntyre, 1984; Shklar, 1984). In general,
conscience does not reduce to sincerity:

> While the "heart may have reasons of its own," when it
> simply chooses to assert these without critical inspection,
> then reason must condemn this as complacency. (Gouldner,
> 1968, p. 121)

A deeper analysis of self-realization shows plainly that the self
people aim to realize is "not this or that feeling, or any series of
particular feelings" (Bradley, 1876/1952, p. 160). Bradley maintains
that people realize themselves morally:

> So that not only what ought to be is in the world, but I am
> what I ought to be, and so find my contentment and
> satisfaction. (p. 213)

The self has a peculiar place in teaching as a form of moral action;
it is at once subdued and vital as a source of courage, spirit,
kindliness.

Profession requires community

What is characteristically moral presupposes community, both on
conceptual and pragmatic grounds. The concept of community is
logically prior to the concept of role. The very possibility of the
pursuit of an ideal form of life requires membership in a moral
community; it is extremely unlikely that minimal social conditions for
the pursuit of any ideal people are likely to entertain would in
practice be fulfilled except through membership in such communities
(Strawson, 1974; Schwab, 1976a; for an excellent review of empirical
literature relevant to this topic, see Purkey & Smith, 1983).
Membership in moral communities is realized in action, conversation,
and reflection. As a moral community, a profession

is composed of people who think they are professionals and who seek, through the practical inquiry of their lives, both alone and together, to clarify and *live up to* what they mean by being a professional. (Thelen, 1973, pp. 200-201; emphasis in original work)

The quality of aspiration--of aiming steadfastly for an ideal--is supported by the normative expectations of others. Individual and collective learning in the teaching profession depend, in particular, on norms of collegiality and experimentation. Norms of collegiality can reduce workplace isolation and help develop an orientation toward the teaching role. Norms of experimentation are based on a conviction that teaching can always be better than it is. If it is expected that teachers test their beliefs and practices, schools can be places where students *and* teachers learn.

Norms of collegiality and experimentation are moral demands with intellectual substance. They are not matters of individual preference but based, instead, on a shared understanding of the kinds of behaviors and dispositions that people have a right to expect of teachers (Little, 1981). These norms require detachment--a willingness to stand back from personal habits, interests, and opinions. What one does or believes in is not talked about as part of one's self but as something *other*--it becomes a potential exemplar of good (or not so good) ways of working, or of more or less justified beliefs. In teaching, what people do is neither private nor sacred but open to judgments of worth and relevance in the light of professional obligation.

Community provides not only constraints and guidance but succor. Collegiality, however, also depends on the degree to which another person is deserving and one's equal in deserts; it is not just loyalty and mutual help, but the enjoyment of competence in other people. Essential to collegiality in teaching is the degree to which its practitioners are good at talking with one another about their work and can be confident about their own ability, and that of others', as teachers and partners in the improvement of teaching. Without mental, social, and role competence, norms of collegiality and experimentation cannot take hold. There are some uncomfortable questions that need to be confronted here:

> What effect does the relative exclusion of ordinary teachers
> from the wider governance of education, their restricted
> access to educational theory and other kinds of school
> practice, and the consequent overwhelming centrality of
> classroom practicalities to teachers, have on the kinds of
> *contributions* they make to staff discussion? (Hargreaves,
> 1982, pp. 263-264; emphasis in the original)

Morality and authenticity in teaching

Of course, teachers are persons. But being one's self in teaching is not enough. Authenticity must be paired with legitimacy as opposed to impulse and inflexible habit, and with productivity or a reasoned sense of purpose and consequences (Thelen, 1973). Thelen places

authenticity in the context of action (authentic activities make
teachers feel alive and challenged) and gives legitimacy and
productivity the accent of thought:

> An activity is legitimated by reason, as distinguished from
> capricious-seeming teacher demand, acting out impulse, mere
> availability, or impenetrable habit. An activity may be
> legitimated by group purposes, disciplines of knowledge,
> career demands, test objectives, requirements, societal
> issues, laws, or by any other larger, organized context that
> enables the activity to go beyond its own particulars. . . .

> An activity is productive to the extent that it is effective
> for some purpose. . . . It is awareness of purpose that
> makes means-ends thinking possible, allows consciousness and
> self-direction, tests self-concepts against reality, and
> makes practice add up to capability. (p. 213)

Legitimacy and productivity are entwined, capturing social
expectations and aspirations central to teaching and to learning from
teaching. People's ordinary conception of morality describes this
interplay between ideals and the rule requirements of social
organizations (Strawson, 1974).

To the extent that roles have moral content, their impersonality
is not inhuman or uninspired. But rules, norms, and external
standards alone cannot account for moral action in teaching. First,
role orientation must be lodged concretely in someone's head and
heart. Where one's solid and full response to obligations is
withheld, the claims of others are not acknowledged livingly (James,
1969). As Dewey (1933/1971) stressed, thoughtful action does not only
depend on open-mindedness and responsibility, wholeheartedness is also
part of it. To the extent, then, that the content of role has been
absorbed into the self, role becomes a personal project--shaping the
inner self and the self as it appears to others. Thus moral
aspirations cannot be separated from the question of personal
identity, but conversely, responsibility for oneself, as a person,
does not mean that anything goes (Taylor, 1970).

Second, the moral quality of role relations between professionals
and clients draws on loyalty to concrete persons and analogues to
friendship in enacting role (Fried, 1978). The warmth and selectivity
of feeling implied by this contradicts the impersonality of role.
Loyalty as abstract duty is not the same as actually taking faithful
care of the particular people put into one's charge. All this is
complicated by the fact that, in teaching, professionals face groups
of young clients, not in school by choice. The role of the classroom
teacher, therefore,

> puts the major obligations for effective action on his
> shoulders; it is the teacher's responsibility to coordinate,
> stimulate, and shepherd the immature workers in his charge.
> . . . Task and expressive leadership in classrooms must
> emanate from the teacher, who, it is presumed, corrects for
> the capriciousness of students with the steadiness, resolve,

and sangfroid of one who governs. The austere virtues, moreover, must be complemented by warmer qualities like empathy and patience. It becomes clear, then, that the self of the teacher, his very personality, is deeply engaged in classroom work; the self must be used and disciplined as a tool necessary for achieving results and earning work gratifications. (Lortie, 1975, pp. 155-156; see also Waller, 1932/1961, pp. 385-386)

In sum, the moral nature of teaching--which also requires being genuinely oneself--does not remove the need for role orientation. Instead, a proper understanding of authenticity in teaching builds in the idea of external standards within which teachers make authentic choices. The need for authenticity hence supplies no argument against role orientation, but suggests that there are some teacher decisions that will be completely determined by role, some that are constrained by role but not determined, and some--not many--for which role does not and should not provide guidance.

FOOTNOTES

1) This chapter has been adapted from "Role Over Person: Morality and Authenticity in Teaching" which originally appeared in *Teachers College Record*, Vol. 87, No. 4, Summer 1986. Reprinted by permission of Teachers College, Columbia University. The author gratefully acknowledges Robert Floden and John Schwille who made valuable comments on various drafts of this paper. This work is sponsored by the Institute for Research on Teaching, College of Education, Michigan State University. The Institute for Research on Teaching is funded primarily by the Program for Teaching and Instruction of the National Institute of Education, United States Department of Education. The opinions expressed in this article do not necessarily reflect the position, policy, or endorsement of the National Institute of Education. (Contract No. 400-81-0014)

2) This idea was suggested to me by Joseph J. Schwab (personal communication, December, 1984).

BIBLIOGRAPHY

Black, M. (1972). Reasonableness. In R.F. Dearden, P.H. Hirst, & R.S. Peters (Eds.), *Education and the development of reason*. London: Routledge & Kegan Paul.

Bradley, F.H. (1952). *Ethical studies* (2nd. ed.). Oxford: Clarendon Press. (Original work published 1876)

Brophy, J.E. (1982). How teachers influence what is taught and learned in classrooms. *The Elementary School Journal, 83*(1), 1-14.

Buchmann, M. (1983). *Role over person: Justifying teacher action and decisions* (Research Series No. 135). East Lansing: Michigan State University, Institute for Research on Teaching.

Combs, A.W. (1967). *The professional education of teachers: A case study and a theoretical analysis*. Boston: Allyn & Bacon.

Cusick, P. (1982). *A study of networks among professional staffs in secondary schools* (Research Series No. 112). East Lansing: Michigan State University, Institute for Research on Teaching.

Dewey, J. (1971). *How we think: A restatement of the relation of reflective thinking to the education process.* Chicago, IL: Henry Regnery. (Original work published 1933)

Feiman, S., & Floden, R.E. (1980). A consumer's guide to teacher development. *The Journal of Staff Development, 1*(2), 126-147.

Fried, C. (1978). *Right and wrong.* Cambridge, MA: Harvard University Press.

Fuller, F. (1969). Concerns of teachers: A developmental conceptualization. *American Educational Research Journal, 6*(2), 207-226.

Goodman, J. (1984). Reflection and teacher education: A case study and a theoretical analysis. *Interchange, 15*(3), 9-26.

Gouldner, A.W. (1968). The sociologist as partisan: Sociology and the welfare state. *The American Sociologist, 3*(2), 103-116.

Hall, G.E., & George, A.A. (1978). *Stages of concern about the innovation: The concept, verification, and implications.* Austin: University of Texas, Research and Development Center for Teacher Education.

Hall, G.E., & Loucks, S.F. (1978). Teacher concerns as a basis for facilitating and personalizing staff development. *Teachers College Record, 80*(1), 36-53.

Hall, G.E., Loucks, S.F., Rutherford, W.L., & Newlove, B.W. (1975). Levels of use of the innovation: A framework for analyzing innovation adaoption. *The Journal of Teacher Education, 26*(1), 52-56.

Hawkins, D. (1974). I, thou, and it. In D. Hawkins (Ed.), *The informed vision: Essays on learning and human nature* (pp. 48-62). New York: Agathon Press.

Hargreaves, A. (1982). The rhetoric of school-centered innovation. *Journal of Curriculum Studies, 14*(3), 251-266.

Highet, G. (1966). *The art of teaching.* New York: Alfred A. Knopf.

James, W. (1969). The moral philosopher and the moral life. In J.K. Roth (Ed.), *The moral philosophy of William James.* New York: Thomas Y. Crowell.

Kerr, D.H. (1983). Teaching competence and teacher education in the United States. In L. Shulman & G. Sykes (Eds.), *Handbook on teaching and policy* (pp. 126-149). New York: Longman.

Little, J.W. (1981). *School success and staff development: The role of staff development in urban desegregated schools* (NIE No. 400-79-0049). Boulder: University of Colorado, Center for Action Research.

Lipsky, M. (1980). *Street level bureaucracy.* New York: Russell Sage.

Lortie, D. (1975). *School teacher.* Chicago, IL: University of Chicago Press.

MacIntyre, A. (1984). *After virtue.* Notre Dame, IN: University of Notre Dame Press.

McLaughlin, M.W., & Marsh, D.D. (1978). Staff development and social change. *Teachers College Record, 80*(1), 69-94.

68

Merton, R. (1957). The role-set: Problems in sociological theory. *British Journal of Sociology, 8*, 106-120.

Polanyi, M. (1962). *Personal knowledge*. Chicago, IL: University of Chicago Press.

Purkey, S.C., & Smith, M.S. (1983). Effective schools: A review. *The Elementary School Journal, 83*(4), 427-452.

Scheffler, I. (1965). *Conditions of knowledge*. Glenview, IL: Scott, Foresman.

Scheffler, I. (1977). Justifying curriculum decisions. In A.A. Bellack & H.M. Kliebard (Eds.), *Curriculum and Evaluation* (pp. 497-505). Berkeley, CA: McCutchan.

Schmidt, W.H., & Buchmann, M. (1983) Six teachers' beliefs and attitudes and their curricular time allocations. *The Elementary School Journal, 84*(2), 162-171.

Schwab, J.J. (1976a). Education and the state: Learning community. In *The great ideas today* (Annual yearbook of Encyclopedia Britannica, pp. 234-271). Chicago, IL: Encyclopedia Britannica.

Schwab, J.J. (1976b). Teaching and learning. *The Center Magazine, 9*(6), 36-45.

Schwab, J.J. (1978). Education and the structure of the disciplines. In I. Westbury & N.J. Wilkof (Eds.), *Science, curriculum and liberal education* (pp. 229-272). Chicago, IL: University of Chicago Press.

Shklar, J.N. (1984). *Ordinary vices*. Cambridge, MA: Belknap Press of Harvard University Press.

Sizer, T.R. (1984). *Horace's compromise: The dilemma of the American high school*. Boston, MA: Houghton Mifflin.

Smith, E.L., & Anderson, C.W. (1984). *The planning and teaching intermediate science study: Final report* (Research Series No. 147). East Lansing: Michigan State University, Institute for Research on Teaching.

Strawson, P.F. (1974). *Freedom and resentment: And other essays*. New York: Metheun.

Sykes, G. (1983). Public policy and the problem of teacher quality: The need for screens and magnets. In L. Shulman & G. Sykes (Eds.), *Handbook on teaching and policy* (pp. 97-125). New York: Longman.

Taylor, R. (1970). *Good and evil: A new direction*. London: Macmillan.

Thelen, H.A. (1973). Profession anyone? In D.J. McCarty (Ed.), *New perspectives on teacher education* (pp. 194-213). San Francisco, CA: Jossey-Bass.

Waller, W. (1961). *The sociology of teaching*. New York: Russell & Russell. (Original work published 1932)

Wise, A.E. (1979). *Legislated learning: The bureaucratization of the American classroom*. Berkeley: University of California Press.

Zeichner, K.M., & Teitelbaum, K. (1982). Personalized and inquiry-oriented teacher education: An analysis of two approaches to the development of curriculum for field-based experiences. *Journal of Education for Teaching, 8*(2), 95-117.

TEACHERS' STRATEGIES FOR UNDERSTANDING AND MANAGING CLASSROOM DILEMMAS

Magdalene Lampert
Institute for Research on Teaching
Michigan State University

SUMMARY

Many of the problems teachers face in classrooms are unsolvable because their solutions lead to contradictions in practice. This study examines several strategies available to teachers for coping with such dilemmas and analyzes common features of the thought and action involved in using these strategies. Case studies of teachers managing dilemmas are reported, both to describe the practical and intellectual tasks involved in this work, and as a framework for relating what teachers do about contradictions with their professional aims. These case studies illustrate strategies of negotiation, social reorganization, and structural reorganization. All of the strategies are exploratory and incremental; they reframe goals rather than accomplishing them.

DILEMMAS IN TEACHING

American social scientists have often characterized the work of the teaching profession as fraught with dilemmas, plagued by internal conflicts that are impossible to resolve, and hindered by essential contradictions among its aims (Waller, 1932; Bidwell, 1965; Dreeben, 1978; Jackson, 1978; Lortie, 1975). Ann and Harold Berlak (1981) have developed a taxonomy of these conflicts, relating them to the ambiguous role that schools play in social change. One way to think of what teachers do in the face of such conflicts is to assume that practitioners choose--between children and subject matter, between childhood needs and adult norms, between social equality and academic excellence. Much of what is written about teachers' work suggests that such choices are not only common but inevitable. The psychological theories which predominate in building models of teacher thinking also assume that teaching involves making dichotomous choices.[1] Yet choice between mutually exclusive alternatives may not be the only course of action a practitioner can take to cope with a pedagogical dilemma. And, furthermore, teachers may not perceive the same dichotomies in their work as those which trouble social scientists. As Richard Shavelson and Paula Stern (1981) observed in their review of the literature on teacher thinking, judgment, decision making, and behavior, descriptions of how teachers choose one practice over another based on the bilateral decision trees of cognitive information processing can only describe limited aspects of teacher thinking because "this formulation ignores multiple, potentially conflicting goals which teachers have to balance daily." (p. 471, footnote 2).

Conflicting Goals in the Classroom Context

We many think of the classroom as a workplace full of ideals to be realized. In the actuality of teacher's work, however, the practices intended to realized those ideals are often incompatible. In this sense, the classroom is a microcosm of the larger social world. In the words of William James, "The actually possible in this world is vastly narrower than all that is demanded; there is always a pinch between the ideal and the actual which can only be got through by leaving part of the ideal behind." (1891/1969, p. 183) The question is, which part? Which of the teachers goals can be sacrificed? Which is the higher good? Can rules be made a priori to help teachers decide what goals to sacrifice and what goals to satisfy? James concludes that such rules might be helpful but intuitions about the immediate situation will be more so: "For every real dilemma is in literal strictness a unique situation; and the exact combination of ideals realized and ideals disappointed which each decision creates is always a universe without precedent, and for which no adequate previous rules exist." (p. 187)

James' conclusion is congruent with the most recent analyses of what occurs during teachers' interactive decision making. Plans are brought to the teaching situation which relate teacher actions with desired outcomes. But these plans do not suffice to determine what a teacher will do or should do in the course of instruction (Leinhardt and Greeno, 1984). Because teachers work in a web of social relationships, and because the commitments of their students to the goals to be accomplished are both crucial and uncertain, they must weigh continuously changing evidence and make moment-by-moment choices about how to proceed, continuously creating what James called a "universe without precedent." Because teachers are personally present over time in classroom situations where conflicts arise, they have the capacity to alleviate conflicts using strategies that are unavailable to those intervening in practice from the outside (Lampert, 1985). The teacher herself becomes the instrument for managing contradicting ideals in education.

It is for these reasons that I have chosen to examine teachers' dilemma management strategies by looking closely at particular cases in which teachers face the incompatibility of their ideals as they recognize their consequences for conflicts in practice. The teacher, in each case, invents a set of strategies which enable her to avoid the contradictions among her goals while she practices in a way that maintains an ongoing productive relationship with students. The purpose of this study, then, is to conceptualize a particular aspect of teachers' work: What happens when teachers face a choice between equally desirable but conflicting practices?

By writing about teachers' strategies for managing contradictory
ideals, I do not seek to define a set of mechanical tools which can or
should be used by all teachers in all situations. Instead, my
intention is to explore the kinds of actions teachers might take when
they are confronted with contradictory aims. My purpose in presenting
case studies is to provide *examples* of what is possible rather than
models of "correct" teaching practice. Conflicts among professional
ideals and social norms are managed by persons in the context of their
idiosyncratic experiences (G.H. Mead, 1934). The case studies that
follow are examples of the idea that conflict can be managed, not
illustrations of the best or only way to manage it.

Conflict from the Teachers' Point of View: Methodological Issues

In order to study the many and potentially conflicting facets of
teachers' perspectives on their work as well as the actions teachers
take to manage dilemmas, it is necessary to both observe teachers'
actions and explore how they make sense of those actions in different
contexts over time. Conflicts in the way teachers view themselves and
their work will only emerge as they present themselvs in the stories
they tell about their work to different people and in different
settings (Hammersly, 1979). Such methods as journal keeping and
stimulated recall can only give a partial picture of the multi-faceted
self of the teacher as she does her work. In fact, when teachers are
asked to represent their thoughts, judgments, or decisions in any
form for review by researchers, distortions may be caused by the
assumed value of consistency and rationality (see Festinger, 1964;
Ericcson and Simon, 1980). In reconstructing an interactive decision
ex post facto, therefore, teachers might leave out conflicting aspects
of themselves which they could not accomodate in their actions, or
they might be reluctant to admit that the action they decided to take
was inconsistent with one of their goals or with a prior action
observed by the researcher.
        In order to address these methodological problems, I have used a
variety of strategies for collecting and analyzing my data. I
recorded discussions among a group of seven elementary school teachers
talking weekly over a two-year period with one another, as well as
with researchers, about the problems in their work. The tendency in
such a group for the teachers to respond to researchers' expectations
was restrained by the presence of several other practitioners. I also
observed the same seven teachers at work in their classrooms over a
three-year period, interviewing them individually and in small groups,
and read journals they kept over the course of the project. I
analyzed this data simultaneously with collecting it to discover
patterns and relationships within the teachers' perspectives on
particular classroom incidents. These were continuously tested
against later expressions of their points of view on the same
incidents. From this large set of data, I have drawn several case
studies of teachers' managing dilemmas in their classrooms.
        The data I collected from this group of teachers are
complemented by data from another souce less familiar to scholarly
research. I also work as a teacher and keep a journal of my
reflections on my practice. Autobiographical analysis has not been

used very widely as a technique for doing research on teaching, but it is particularly appropriate to the questions examined in this study. Being both a teacher and a researcher on teaching provides opportunities for scholarly deliberation which must meet two different sets of criteria for legitimate knowledge: those which obtain in the world of practice as well as those determined by academic research.[2]

The weekly discussions of teaching which I observed occurred in the context of an experimental teacher development project at Massachusetts Institute of Technology during 1978-1980.[3] The teachers who attended were volunteers who agreed to come together to examine their own assumptions about learning and teaching. They worked in large and small urban neighborhoods. They were all women, but they ranged considerably in age, years of experience, and educational background. Most of their classrooms were traditionally organized, but two of them taught in alternative "open" structures. My autobiographical data were collected while I taught fourth, fifth, and sixth grade mathematics in a private elementary school. The children I taught came primarily from middle and upper-middle class families living in the city and the suburbs. They ranged in academic competence from below average to very talented.

CASE STUDIES

1. *The Strategy of Social Reorganization*

In the school where I teach, students are grouped for mathematics instruction according to their ability. I had just begun teaching the "high ability" group what it means to multiply and divide fractions and they had seen several strategies for doing the complicated computations. I thought it would be useful to observe the children's facility with such computations, so one day I gave the class several problems to work on, and my assistant and I walked around the room watching them and answering their questions. Once they got settled down to their work, I decided to glance at their homework papers. The assignment revealed that although most of the class had a good sense of what fractions meant and how to compute with them, four children had some confusions. On closer inspection, I recognized that the errors of two students would be easy to clear up, but the other two were in need of considerable help.

My teaching goals led to a practical conflict at this point because of the particular character of the two students needing help. Noel and Terry, the boys who were confused about fractional computation, also have especially fragile egos. And both of them are likely to react destructively if their sense of themselves as competent students is threatened. One of my goals was to enable them to focus on their studies. The other boys in the class, in a manner typical of fifth graders, were always ready to pounce on Noel, who was the slowest problem solver in the group and particularly vulnerable to their scapegoating. Terry was among the brightest students in his class and math was his favorite subject. He had extremely high expectations of himself, and the other boys often looked to him for help. But he was a perfectionist; if he was "caught" by someone in even the slightest mistake, he became silent and unapproachable. So singling out Noel and Terry for help would also make them unteachable.

I devised a strategy of *social reorganization* to avoid the potential conflicts involved in the choice between singling out Noel and Terry for help or ignoring their difficulties in favor of classroom peace and emotional security. Instead of calling on only those students who had made errors on their homework for special attention at my desk, I changed my position to a less conspicuous corner of the room and called each member of the class there one at a time, in no particular order, for a discussion of the homework papers. As I took each paper in hand, I chose one element of the conceptual or procedural content on which to focus a question to the student who had produced it. By checking over everyone's homework individually, I would not call anyone's attention to the special help I needed to give to Noel and Terry but I also cut down the time that would be available to clear up their confusions. I had not planned to run this class this way, but it seemed to be an appropriate way to manage my dilemma.

The pedagogical thinking required in this case involved a redefinition of the problem to be solved rather than finding a solution to my original difficulties. What I chose to accomplish was neither the goal of Terry and Noel understanding fractions nor the goal of reducing their social and emotional vulnerability. Without drawing special attention to Noel's or Terry's difficulties, I conveyed the message to them that they were indeed confused, and prepared them for the fact that we would need to find a way to clear up their mistakes at some point. I was also able to collect more information about what they did and did not understand. Their position in the class group remained precarious, however, and I needed to continue to carefully monitor their interactions to avoid the eruption of major disorder in the classroom.

One way to characterize the thinking I needed to do in this situation is as "reframing" (Watzlawick, Weakland, and Risch, 1974). By removing myself from the conflict to choose between one goal or another when my goals would clearly lead to conflicts in practice, I was able to construct a strategy that would move me closer to my goals while not accomplishing them completely. The personal significance of this reframing of goals is that I did not need to give up either of my concerns. Choosing one accomplishment over the other would have required me to redefine myself in a way that would disregard goals that were important to my sense of professional identity. By changing the meaning of the situation to myself, I was able to put the choice between those goals aside and find a way to practice that was appropriate to the situation maintaining both my identity and my classroom equilibrium.

2. *The Strategy of Negotiation*

Suzanne is a fourth grade teacher. This case focuses on a teaching incident in which she had been working with one of the boys in her class, whom I will call Andre. She had been teaching her class some lessons about how to use prepositional phrases to elaborate on the action in a sentence. To assess their understanding, she wrote a simple sentence up on the blackboard ("The lady ran.") and asked her students to add to it using prepositional phrases. The class went to work, and Andre presented her with the following sentence: "The lady with the red hat ran to the parking lock to get her car." Suzanne reported that she was particularly pleased with this piece of work because Andre was usually quite reticent both in speaking and in writing. She said she expressed her satisfaction to the boy, but she also told him that he had one word "spelled wrong."

Because she usually had difficulty getting Andre to say or write anything, Suzanne perceived a contradiction in the work she needed to do here; she wanted to praise the boy for producing a long and complex sentence, but she also wanted to correct him for his misuse of the word "lock." She worried about how he might respond to a mixed message from his teacher about the quality of what he had produced. She was concerned about being in any way critical of his use of the English language because one of her goals was to encourage him to write and talk *more*, and yet she also had as a goal for him to learn to write and speak *correctly*. How could she teach in a way that would sidestep the seeming incompatibility of these goals? The two goals that Suzanne had for Andre, i.e., that he should spell words correctly and that he should feel comfortable taking risks with the processes of writing and speaking in the classroom, are not necessarily in conflict with one another. However, in this particular moment of teaching and learning they were perceived to be in conflict by this teacher. She saw her job at this point as trying to find a way to do two things that seemed to be in contradiction.

The first thing Suzanne tried was to ask the boy if he knew which of the words in his sentence was "spelled wrong." She was collecting information about what the boy knew rather than assuming she understood his abilities from what he had put down on paper. Instead of judging Andre directly, she asked him to judge his own work. If he recognized which word was spelled correctly, her conflict would go away. She would not need to say anything that might discourage him from trying again on the next assignment. Suzanne's strategy engaged her student as a partner in the correction of his own work. By doing this, she hoped to avoid the continuing conflict in her classroom identity between her role as judge and her role as supporter and deflect the possibility that the student sees her in only one way or the other. The way he sees her affects his response to her and thus determines the sort of learning that can occur in future interactions. Thus by using this strategy, she might succeed in preserving a productive relationship with Andre that would affect his future engagement in learning.

As a way to accomplish both encouragement and correction, however, Suzanne's strategy turned out to be a failure. Andre said he didn't know which word was spelled wrong. So she told him: "Lot. It's parking lot." But Andre did not agree; he responded, "No, it's lock." This exchange exacerbated Suzanne's conflict rather than alleviating it. She was back in the midst of the contradiction between her goals which she had faced initially. Should she insist on the correction and risk alienating Andre from the writing process? Or should she just leave him alone at this point in the hopes that she would not discourage him from writing more, even though he had used the word "lock" incorrectly? Again, there were good reasons for doing both; Suzanne needed a bargaining strategy that would provide an alternate to choosing between them.

Suzanne decided to be tentative. She did *not* say "*Lock* is wrong, and the correct word to use is *lot*." Instead she told Andre, "It was probably said, 'lot.'" By using the word "probably," Suzanne was again inviting Andre to make the correction himself rather than having it imposed by the teacher's authority. She did not bring out the full force of her authority to overwhelm whatever this student thought might be right. She also changed her opinion at this point about the nature of his error. She now was acting on the belief that he was pronouncing the word incorrectly rather than making a spelling mistake. With this change Suzanne was moving away from a subject in which her knowledge and authority were clear (Lock *is* spelled l-o-c-k.) into a hazier area where the determination of right and wrong is more dependent on social circumstances. Pronunciation is less determined by universal rules than spelling.

Andre did not respond to Suzanne's tentative suggestion however. He continued to hold firm to his position that "lock" was correct. But Suzanne still avoided a direct judgment of the mistake. Instead of telling the boy he was wrong and exacerbating her conflict with him, she used still another form of negotiation. She appealed to evidence from outside the situation, and continued to leave the judgment about which word was correct up to the student. She told the boy the meaning of the words "lot" and "lock" and asked him to choose which was the more appropriate word to follow "parking" in his sentence. Giving him this information could be seen as a further attempt to engage him in a partnership to correct his mistake. But Andre was not moved, and this time he mustered some evidence to support his argument that "lock" was correct. He said, "Well, over where I live it's parking *lock*, l-o-c-k, parking lock."

Andre was now drawing some boundaries which served to defend the original integrity of his written work. By qualifying his assertion with, "where I live" Andre inferred that "lot" might seem right *to her*, or perhaps "lot" was right *in school*, but he was not wrong to use the word "lock" because that's what was said in his neighborhood. (Perhaps he lived near a parking lot sign that said "Park and Lock.")

Andre and Suzanne did not need to decide what word was *absolutely* right or wrong, but what word was appropriate to a given setting. Their interaction had the character of a negotiation. Suzanne struck a bargain with Andre: "It's okay with me if you want to say 'parking lock' at home, but here in school, I expect you to say 'parking lot.'" She did not give him any reasons for her expectation. She did not say he should say it that way because she was the teacher or because that was the correct way to say it or even because that was how most people said it. She had respected his point of view, and now she was expecting him to respect hers. She left Andre feeling that he was right to say "parking lock" at home, but she also got him to write "parking lot" on his school assignment.

Suzanne recognized, in her conclusion of the story about her interaction with Andre, that the contradictions among her goals would remain even though she had managed them in this particular instance of instruction. She said:

> The boy accepted 'lot' and wrote it on his paper, yet I wonder
> if he really believed me, and if he will continue to say
> 'parking lock' at the place where he lives.
>
> There's a difference between *his* lanugage and how *I* expect kids
> to spell words. They've learned their spelling rules, but
> they're not spelling the same words as I am. He wasn't making
> a spelling error. It wasn't an error, it's part of his life.

Whether Andre learned that "lock" was wrong and "lot" was correct
remains an open question. But through this negotiation, Suzanne
maintained the possibility of keeping Andre interested in the writing
process because she did not directly criticize his work. The exchange
respected the boy's point of view throughout rather than being an
exercise of teacherly power.

This way of thinking about classroom problems suggests that a
certain inconsistency on the part of the teacher may be necessary to
get the job done. Suzanne was unyielding about the correct spelling
of "lock" and she persisted until her student got it down on his
paper. But at the same time, she also engaged him as a fellow human
being in the struggle involved in following such rules. She cajoled
him to go along with her and was sympathetic with his resistance.
Willard Waller (1932) recognized the centrality of expressing such
ambivalence in teachers' work:

> The teacher must alternate his roles because he is
> trying to do inconsistent things with students ...
> He is trying to maintain a definite dominance over young
> persons whose lives he presumes to regulate very completely.
> This requires of the teacher aggressiveness, unyieldingness,
> and determination. If persisted in, this attitude would
> exterminate in students all interest in subject matter and
> would crush out every faint inclination to participate in the
> public life of the classroom....Before this reaction has
> been carried through to completion, one says, 'But I am a
> human being and I try to be a good fellow.' (pp. 385-386)

If Suzanne had been absolutely authorative in her correction of
Andre, it would not be hard to imagine that she would have widened
rather than narrowed the gap between his acceptance and his belief,
exterminating, as Waller suggests, any further interest on this boy's
part in learning the rules of formal language.

3. *Structural Reorganization with Negotiation*

Vicki is a first and second grade teacher in an urban school. The
dilemma to be described here arose when she was teaching her students
to add three digit numbers. She had two instructional goals for these
lessons: one was to have the class learn how to record their answers
when the total in any column was more than 9 and the other was to have
them learn to judge the correctness of their own answers by checking
the additions with groups of base 10 blocks. The class had been
working successfully on adding numbers where no "regrouping" or

"carrying"was required, for example, the addition:

$$326$$
$$+143.$$

As long as there were no sums larger than nine they could treat each of the columns as a separate problem and it did not matter whether they began working in the hundreds column, the tens column or the units column.

They were using unit blocks (cubic centimeters), tens blocks (10 cubic centimeters attached together in a "rod"), and hundreds blocks (10 rods attached together to make a "flat" block 1 cm x 10 cm x 10 cm). The students would first represent each of the two numbers to be added as a pile of units, tens, and hundreds blocks, then push the two piles together, and finally count out the total of units, tens, and hundreds writing the total of each kind in the appropriate column on the paper.

When two of the boys finished all of their sums correctly, Vicki decided to give the problem of finding the sum of

$$309$$
$$+309.$$

She wrote the problem on a piece of paper between the two boys and went off to check the other students' work. The boys counted out two piles, each containing three hundreds blocks and nine unit blocks. They put the two piles of hundreds blocks together, and wrote a 6 under the two 3's and a zero under the two 0's so their paper now looked like this:

$$309$$
$$+309$$
$$\overline{60.}$$

Then they pushed the piles of unit blocks together and set to counting them. They came up with a total of 18. Under the two nines they wrote a 1, so the paper now looked like this:

$$309$$
$$+309$$
$$\overline{601.}$$

At this point, the teacher asked, "How did you get that answer?" One of the boys told her about the 18 unit blocks, and said there wasn't room to write 18 under the units column.

At this point, Vicki felt a conflict between her goals. She did not want to tell the boys the conventional solution to this problem of "not enough room." She wanted them to notice that the answer they had written down (601) was not the numeral that matched the total number of blocks (618), and she wanted them to figure out a way to make them match. Vicki believed that if she simply told them the conventional regrouping procedure they would easily forget it or misuse it. But she also worried that if she did not tell them how to "regroup" 18 into tens and units, they would continue to struggle and waste a lot of valuable classroom time.

Berlak and Berlak (1981) would call Vicki's difficulty the
"personal knowledge vs. public knowledge" dilemma: The public
knowledge that Vicki would have liked these boys to have is that the
18 units need to be regrouped as 1 ten and 8 units, and the total,
therefore, written as 618. Yet she also strongly believed that this
regrouping needed to make sense to the boys personally as a way of
solving their own problem with the blocks. She saw her conflict in
this way:

> Maybe I need to give them more direction than I do. Maybe it's
> not fair to make them struggle when I know how to help them. Yet
> at the same time, it can be so rewarding if they do figure out
> something for themselves. I know from past experience, if *they*
> figure it out they will always be able to use it and not forget it.

Vicki's mind was not made up. As she told me about the incident the
day it happened, she was arguing with herself about what to do.

The major strategy that Vicki constructed to manage her dilemma
was used in the math lesson the next day. She made several *structural
changes* in the way the lesson was presented. Instead of simply asking
the children to make informal "piles" of units, tens, and hundreds
blocks, she gave them charts:

hundreds	tens	units

and instructed them to place the blocks they were adding in the
appropriate boxes. She also told them: "Trade up whenever you have
more than 9 units or 9 tens, and make sure the blocks match the numbers
you write down on your papers *exactly*." By rearranging the workspace
and giving more precise directions for how to use the materials,
Vicki invented a tool for mediating between the public knowledge she
wanted to teach and the private knowledge the boys would derive from
solving their own problems with the blocks.

One of the boys who had been having problems the day before with
601 vs. 618 worked through two or three more sums, and Vicki noticed
him becoming quite frustrated with the mismatch between what he had on
paper and the blocks he counted on his chart. After watching him for
a few minutes, Vicki noticed that he did the appropriate trading with
his blocks, but had no way to record the trading on his paper; he did
not simply write the total number of blocks after trading and
counting. He treated the blocks and the paperwork as separate en-
deavors. On the paper, he always began with adding the hundreds
column first and made the same recording error he had made the day
before. One of his additions looked like this:

$$\begin{array}{r} 538 \\ +216 \\ \hline 741 \end{array}$$

while on the chart, he had 7 hundreds blocks, 5 tens blocks, and 4
unit blocks. He did not know why they did not come out the same.

Vicki did not judge his answer immediately. Instead she made a
few suggestions while he worked about how he might record what he was
doing with the blocks on paper. In both tone of voice and content
these were clearly not directives. She left it up to him whether to
use these suggestions in his work. The student continued to work and
the teacher watched. Once the boy noticed that his written sums were
beginning to match the total number of blocks, he loudly announced to
the other children at his table, "Hey, I just found a super-easy way
to do my math." He had learned what the teacher wanted him to learn
and yet he took credit for "finding" the way himself.

Vicki *restructured the learning space* so that she would not need
to confront her students with their errors directly. By creating a
way to use the math materials which in itself posed the problem of
their recording system, Vicki did not need to assert her authority as
the one who knows how to do math. She was able to teach and yet
foster independent discovery. In her interactions with this learner
Vicki used suggestion rather than direction. She did not tell her
student what to do, but she made a solution available for him to
choose which he could then feel some sense of owning. The management
of Vicki's dilemma depends on an interaction between the child's
concerns and her own. She assesses those concerns and responds to
them, not by constructing abstract resolutions of potential conflicts
and contradictions, but by constructing practical interactions like
those described above--balancing, mediating, trying one thing or
another and monitoring the child's response. The management of the
dilemma emerged for her in practice, whereas its resolution had been
elusive to her when she told me about her dilemma the day before.

COMMON FEATURES OF DILEMMA-MANAGING STRATEGIES AND THEIR IMPLICATIONS
FOR HOW WE THINK ABOUT TEACHER THINKING

These three cases illustrate three strategies teachers might use for
coping with the practical dilemmas that result from conflicts among
their aims: social reorganization, restructuring the materials of
instruction, and negotiating with students. There are no doubt many
other possible strategies to be considered, as there are many other
potential conflicts among teachers' aims. This list of strategies is
not meant to be a complete taxonomy with clear borders between
categories; rather it is meant to be a set of illustrations of an
aspect of teachers' work that merits further exploration.

What can we learn from these case studies about the practical
meaning of seemingly unresolvable conflicts to teachers? What do the
strategies analyzed here tell us about the work of teaching? The
instances of teaching practice described above have several common
features. These features suggest the sort of thinking that is
required to do the work of "dilemma-management" and they yield an
image of the teacher at work that has important implications for how
we go about improving practice.

In each case, the teacher accomplishes some instructional goal,
but it is different from the goals she had set out to accomplish at
the start of the interaction described. This *change in goals* is not

a whimiscal disregard, either for the plans established for a given lesson or for the importance and appropriateness of her original goals. Rather, practice in these cases involves an on-the-spot *reassessment of the means available to achieve desired ends*. When the cost of achieving those ends becomes too dear in any particular moment of the teacher's work, the problem to be solved needs to be redefined according to the means available for solution. In the case of teaching, the means available to the teacher include students; the knowledge and attitudes they bring to a lesson are among the resources a teacher calls upon to get her job done. But students' knowledge and attitudes are not only largely unknown quantities, they are also constantly changing as a result of forces over which the teacher has little control. So the teacher must take account not only of which problems should be solved in a particular teaching interaction but also of which problems can be solved given the information she gains along the way about the resources available to her. Although the teacher's initial goals in all these cases were attractive and desirable, they were not feasible. After looking at the homework papers and assessing the volatility of certain social relationships in my math class, I needed to define an instructional problem that could be solved using what I had to work with in the way of student attitudes and knowledge that day. Vicki similarly readjusted her goals in teaching addition to take account of the information she was gaining about a particular student's difficulties, and Suzanne continuously redefined the problem to be solved as she negotiated with her student about the correctness of the writing he had done. This sort of teaching enables learning in light of what the teaching itself reveals to be probably realizable.

The strategies that teachers used to *move* forward lead them *toward their goals in endless tiny increments*. They did not initiate large scale classroom reforms designed to finally accomplish their goals once and for all. Their moves toward recognized aims are small step by small step because taking larger steps in cases where goals are in conflict would have pushed them further away from other, equally desirable and appropriate aims. The actions taken in the instances of practice described above are not intended to achieve the somewhat Utopian ideals which inform teachers' thinking about what should be done; instead they are oriented toward coping with difficulties in a common sense manner, recognizing contradictions endemic to the work situation that will not be resolved. The point toward which they are moving constantly changes as they redefine where it is possible to go. Such mechanical devices as behavioral objectives give one the illusion of final accomplishment, often by equating quality with quantity, but in these three teaching situations, such objectives would only mask the underlying contradictions with which the teachers described must actively cope.

In addition to redefining problems and moving incrementally toward elusive and ever-changing goals, the teaching being done in these examples is *exploratory*. Actions are taken which have the capacity to produce new and useful information, both about what has been accomplished and about what can be accomplished next. The definition of what is possible and what is desirable emerges from the give and take of teaching students. Each of the teachers described had a different sense of what she could do and what she should do after doing something. Many of the choices they made about what to do had the purpose of postponing action or judgment until more information could be collected.

This relation between action and reflection in the context of teaching presents a view of teacher thinking that is broader than "decision making." The teacher is not only confronting choices about how to use means to arrive at desired ends, but continuously redefining what those ends can be. In this redefinition, the nature of teaching itself is being determined. This quality makes teachers' thinking "personal" in the sense that it was defined by George Herbert Mead: the demands of the context (social norms) and the teachers' actions together contribute to the possibility of what can be done.

If teachers are considered as persons in Mead's term rather than simply as role incumbants whose actions should be determined by the environment in which they work, they can be thought to manage the tensions in their work through their personal presence in situational acts of teaching. Seen in this way, teachers' thinking is not enhanced by the creation of logically correct solutions constructed outside of the situation in which a problem arises, nor is teaching practice improved solely by the invention of stable universal theories of professional decision making.

FOOTNOTES

1) See for a schematic description of these models: Clark, C. & Peterson, P. (1984).

2) See for a description of deliberation as a method of scholarly inquiry: Schwab (1983) and Shulman (1984).

3) See for a description of the project and my role in it: Lampert (1984).

BIBLIOGRAPHY

Berlak, A. and Berlak, H. (1981). *Dilemmas of schooling: Teaching and social change*. London, Methuen.
Bidwell, C.W. (1965). The school as a formal organization, in James G. March, Ed., *Handbook of Organizations*. Chicago, Rand McNally.
Braybrooke, D. and Linblom, C.E. (1963). *A strategy of decision*. New York, The Free Press.
Clark, C. and Peterson, P. (1984). *Teachers' thought processes*. (Occasional Paper No. 72). East Lansing, Institute for Research on Teaching, Michigan State University.
Dreeben, R. (1970). *The nature of teaching: Schools and the work of teachers*, Glenview, Scot-Foresman.
Ericcson, K.A. and Simon, H.A. (1980). Verbal reports as data. *Psychology Review, 87*, 215-251.
Festinger, L. (1964). *Conflict, decision, and dissonance*. Stanford, Stanford University Press.
Hammersly, M. (1979). Towards a model of teacher activity, in John Eggleston, Ed., *Teacher decision-making in the classroom*. London, Routledge and Kegan Paul.

Hofstaedter, D.R. and Dennett, D.C. (1982). *The mind's I: fantasies and reflections on self and soul*. New York, Bantam Books.

Jackson, P.W. (1968). *Life in classrooms*. New York, Holt, Rinehart, and Winston, Inc.

James, W. (1969). The Moral Philosopher and The Moral Life, in John K. Roth, Ed., *The moral philosophy of William James*. New York, Thomas Y. Crowell Company, Inc. (Originally published in *International Journal of Ethics*, April, 1891, Vol.1 pp. 330-354.)

Lampert, M. (1984). Teaching about thinking and thinking about teaching. *Journal of Curriculum Studies, 16*, (1).

Lampert, M. (1985). How do teachers manage to teach? *Harvard Educational Review, 55*, (2), 178-194.

Leinhardt, G. and Greeno, T. (1983). The cognitive skill of teaching. Paper presented at the Annual Meeting of the American Eduational Research Association, Montreal.

Lindblom, C.E. and Cohen, D.K. (1979). *Usable knowledge: social science and social problem solving*. New Haven, Yale University Press.

Lortie, D.C. (1975). *Schoolteacher: a sociological study*. Chicago, University of Chicago Press.

March, J.G. and Olson, J.P. (1979). *Ambiguity and choice in organizations*. Bergen, Universitetsforlaget.

Mead, G.H. (1934). *Mind, self, and society*, Ed., Charles W. Morris. Chicago, University of Chicago Press.

Schwab, J. (1983). The practical 4: omething for curriculum professors to do. *Curriculum Inquiry, 13*, 239-265.

Shavelson, R. and Stern, P. (1981). Research on teachers' pedagogical thoughts, judgments, decisions and behavior. *Review of Educational Research, 51*, 455-498.

Shulman, L. (1984). The practical and the eclectic: A deliberation on teaching and educational research. *Curriculum Inquiry, 14*, 183-200.

Waller, W. (1932). *The sociology of teaching*. New York, John Wiley and Sons.

Watzlawick, P., Weakland, J.H. and Fisch, R. (1974). *Change: Principles of problem formation and problem resolution*. New York, W.W. Norton and Co.

Wiezenbaum, J. (1976). *Computer power and human reason: From judgement to calculation*. San Francisco, W.H. Freeman and Co.

TEACHER BELIEFS
AND CLASSROOM BEHAVIORS:
SOME TEACHER RESPONSES TO
INCONSISTENCY

B. Robert Tabachnick and Kenneth M. Zeichner
University of Wisconsin-Madison
Department of Curriculum and Instruction
Madison, WI 53706

SUMMARY

This paper utilizes data from a study of two beginning teachers in
the United States and analyzes the strategies employed by the
teachers to reduce contradictions between their expressed beliefs
about teaching (in four specific areas) and their classroom
behavior. The individual and contextual factors related to the
choice of a particular strategy and to its eventual success or
failure are discussed. One of the teachers sought to change her
behavior to create a closer correspondence between belief and
action, while the other teacher changed her *beliefs* to justify
behaviors that were inconsistent with her expressed beliefs.

THE PROBLEM

This report of research examines consistency and contradiction in
teacher beliefs.
    This paper will draw upon the data from a two-year longitudinal
study of four beginning teachers in the United States (Tabachnick &
Zeichner, 1985; Zeichner & Tabachnick, 1985) and will analyze:
(1) patterns of relationship between teacher beliefs and classroom
behaviors; (2) strategies employed by teachers in an attempt to
bring about greater consistency between beliefs and behaviors;
(3) the individual and contextual factors that influenced the
relationships between teacher beliefs and classroom behaviors.
    In that two-year study, we aimed to explore the range of
diversity of individuals' responses to the student teaching semester
and, following that, to the first year of teaching. Our point of
emphasis was to discover what perspectives toward teaching were
developed by individual students during student teaching and how
these perspectives were influenced by the interplay of the
intentions and capabilities of individuals with the characteristics
of the institutions of which they became a part, first as student
teachers and later as teachers. The paper will be limited to an
analysis of the relationships between teacher beliefs and classroom
behaviors during the second phase of our study--the study of the

first year of teaching.

The construct of perspectives has its theoretical roots in the work of G. H. Mead and his concept of the "act" (Mead, 1983). *Teaching* perspectives were defined in our study as "a coordinated set of ideas and actions which a person uses in dealing with some problematic situation." This view of perspective is derived from Becker et al. (1961). According to this view, perspectives differ from attitudes since they include actions and not merely dispositions to act. Also, unlike values, perspectives are defined in relation to specific situations and do not necessarily represent general beliefs or teaching ideologies.

Teaching perspectives were defined in relation to four specific domains: *(1) knowledge and curriculum, (2) the teacher's role, (3) teacher-pupil relationships, and (4) student diversity.* Each of these four categories was further defined in terms of several specific *dilemmas* of teaching which had emerged in the analysis of our data from the study of student teaching (e.g., public knowledge vs. personal knowledge; knowledge as product vs. knowledge as process). Altogether 18 dilemmas of teaching were identified within the four categories of perspectives, and it was these dilemmas that gave direction to our data collection efforts during the second phase of our study.

A key assumption underlying the use of teaching perspectives as the organizing construct for our study is that teacher behavior and thought are inseparable and part of the same event. We assume that the meaning of teacher thinking cannot be understood in the absence of analyses of behavior engaged in by the actors to complete the ideas, to "express" them. Thinking and beliefs are, of course, not directly observable. We assume that classroom behavior expresses teacher beliefs in a way similar to the use of language to answer the question, "What are you thinking?" or "What were you thinking when you did that?" It may be that classroom behavior is a way of thinking about teaching analogous to the craftsperson or artist who "thinks with his (or her) hands." The interest here moves beyond a concern with either teacher thinking or teacher behavior alone to a concern for the ways in which teacher behaviors represent active expressions of thought and the ways in which teacher behaviors represent apparent contradictions of expressed beliefs. We are interested in knowing if teacher behavior and beliefs move toward some kind of internal consistency over time. What appear to be contradictions between behavior and belief are often revealed as more consistent, from the teacher's point of view, when behavior is thought about as a statement of belief.

We utilize the data from our earlier study to probe instances of contradiction and consistency between what teachers say they believed (e.g., about the role of teacher, knowledge and curriculum, etc.), their expressions of intent for particular classroom activities, and their beliefs as expressed in their classroom behavior. After identifying the strategies employed by the two teachers in an attempt to bring about greater consistency between belief and action, we discuss the various individual and contextual factors in each case that influenced the relationships between teacher beliefs and behaviors.

Much of the research that has been conducted to date on the
relationships between teacher beliefs and classroom behavior has
established that there are fairly close relationships between
teacher thought and behaviors (e.g., see Shavelson & Stern, 1981).
However, (1) most studies have relied almost exclusively on teacher
self-reports of their behaviors and not on analyses of observed
teaching; (2) few studies have explicated the processes by which
behaviors and/or beliefs are modified by teachers in an attempt to
move toward greater internal consistency. The paper addresses both
of these issues.

METHODOLOGY

The subjects for this study are two female first-year teachers who
were employed in different school districts in the United States
during the 1981-82 academic year. These individuals were selected
from a representative group of 13 individuals who had been studied
intensively during their student teaching experience at a large
midwestern university the previous spring (Tabachnick & Zeichner,
1985). Both of the teachers taught at the eighth-grade level.

Between August, 1981, and June, 1982, we spent three one-week
periods observing and interviewing each teacher. A specific
research plan was followed during each of the three weeks of data
collection. During four days of each week an observer constructed
narrative descriptions of events in each classroom using the four
categories of perspectives and related dilemmas as an orienting
framework. Each teacher was interviewed several times each day
regarding her plans for instruction (e.g., purposes and rationales
for particular activities) and her reactions to what had occurred.
One day each week, an observer constructed a narrative description
of classroom events with a particular focus on six pupils in each
classroom who had been selected to represent the range of student
diversity in each classroom.

In addition to the daily interviews with each teacher that
focused on particular events that had been observed, a minimum of
two in-depth interviews were conducted with each teacher during each
of the three data collection periods. These interviews sought to
explore teachers' views regarding their own professional development
in relation to the four orienting categories of perspectives and
also addressed additional dimensions of perspectives unique to each
teacher that had emerged during the year.

Additionally, we sought to investigate the influence of several
institutional elements of school life on the development of teacher
perspectives (e.g., school ethos and tradition, teacher culture,
administrative expectations about the teacher's role). During each
of the in-depth interviews we also asked the teachers about their
perceptions of the constraints and encouragements that existed in
their schools and about how they learned what was and was not
appropriate behavior for teachers in their schools. We also
interviewed each principal at least once and interviewed two other
teachers in each school concerning their views of the degree to
which each beginning teacher was free to employ independent judgment
in her work. Finally, we also collected many kinds of formal

documents in each school, such as curriculum guides and teacher handbooks.

Through the classroom observations and teacher and administrator interviews we sought to monitor the continuing development of teaching perspectives and to construct in-depth portraits of life in each of the classrooms. Tape recorded interviews and classroom observations were transcribed to facilitate a content analysis of the data. Several analyses of these data led to the construction of case studies that describe the development of each teacher and the individual and social influences on their development from the beginning of student teaching to the end of their first year of teaching. The paper will draw upon the induction year portions of these case studies to examine the relationships between teacher beliefs and classroom behaviors.

BETH: THINKING ABOUT TEACHING IN A CLOSELY CONTROLLED SCHOOL ENVIRONMENT

Beth was a student teacher in a middle-sized city (about 200,000) in a self-contained fifth-grade classroom, in an elementary school with grades kindergarten to fifth grade. In that community, this meant that her cooperating teacher was responsible for instruction in all subjects except art, music, and physical education. The prevailing style of teaching in her classroom was characterized by warm personal relationships, and some judicious sharing of curriculum decisions with pupils. Though most of the teaching was fairly routine (reading to answer questions about the text, drill in arithmetic), there was a genuine effort to encourage pupils' creative thinking and problem solving. Beth was encouraged to invent activities that would further these more diffuse goals as well as to further routine classroom learning activities with more precisely targeted goals. Students were from a mixed socioeconomic background, mostly middle class, but some from economically poorer homes. The principal supported an "active" curriculum which challenged and displayed the results of pupils' creative efforts. The teachers and principal believed that they had firm community and parent support for such an approach.

As a first-year teacher Beth taught eighth graders in a middle school enrolling pupils in grades six through eight. The school served a middle-class community suburb to a moderately large city. Very few homes could be characterized as near poverty level. The school's organization was quite different from Beth's school during her previous (student teaching) year. Groups of 75 to 100 children were taught all the subjects by teams of three or four teachers. Art, music, and physical education were taught by specialists, and other specialists were available for advice on teaching reading and language and for help in working with poorly achieving or psychologically disturbed children.

Beth and her two co-teachers together taught approximately 80 pupils. Their teaching was directed by lists of "Performances" in each subject. The curriculum was referred to by the teachers and the principal as Performance Based Education (PBE) with pupil achievement being judged on the basis of Criterion Referenced Tests

(CRT's). The lists of performances and the CRT's had been developed some years before by committees of teachers. Bureaucratic difficulty discouraged teachers from changing or adding topics. A CRT identified student inabilities, mainly in reading, language, and mathematics skills and in social studies and science information. Beth and her colleagues decided which of the teachers would be responsible for different groups of students in each subject, for the timing of instruction, and the scheduling of tests. Deviation from these time plans was discouraged. For example, taking longer to explore a topic or "going off on a tangent" (adding topics not specified in the PBE lists) might force one's colleagues to wait and waste time, since all pupils had to be tested at the same time. The school was built to an architecturally open plan so teachers could easily keep track of what was happening in other areas of the "pod." The principal frequently walked around the school and did not hesitate to discipline students or to point out to teachers deviations from established school procedures, either on the spot or in a later conference.

At the beginning of her first year as a regular teacher, Beth refers appreciatively to her student teaching when, from time to time, she decided on a topic to be taught, researched its content, and invented teaching strategies. Beth says she believes an "open and easy" approach to teaching is valuable because it stimulates pupils to think. In some interview statements she refers to the routine, or at least "follow-the-preset-pattern" nature of her teaching. In other statements she says she selects some of the topics for study, aims at stimulating pupils to "sit down and think about things," tries to think of ways to present the content that will capture the interest of pupils. However, she is observed to teach in a very controlled style. Her planning at the beginning of the year is almost entirely limited to deciding which textbook pages to use in working with groups of 10 to 25 pupils; which and how many math solutions to demonstrate, whether to repeat teaching on a topic or go on to the next item on the PBE list. (Beth is under considerable strain at first, finding her way into the system. This is noticed by the principal who tries to get her to relax, boosts her self-confidence).

One instance is recorded, in five consecutive days of observation, of the "open and easy" style of teaching; the most capable math group is encouraged to find alternative solutions to problems. The pupils respond eagerly and Beth smiles and says to the observer, "I love this!" But the bulk of her teaching behavior follows from (1) earlier decisions about how many questions to ask or problems to explain; (2) on-the-spot reactions to time remaining, to student actions (redirecting misbehavior, answering questions, correcting errors with on-the-spot explanations); and (3) the existence of available materials (booklets, film strips) with previously developed worksheets or test questions. Post-teaching behavior is mainly correcting tests and selecting the next day's questions, worksheets, drill practice.

At mid-year, five days of observation reveal no equivalent to the exciting math lesson. All the observed teaching is guided by getting through the PBE lists of objectives. Beth says the main influences on what happens in her classroom are:

> . . . the school curriculum in that they say what
> should be taught . . . us pod teachers in deciding who
> teaches what . . . and then me, myself as a teacher, as
> in how I'm going to teach it.

Selecting or identifying goals is *not* an important effort. She says
her goals:

> . . . [are] real sketchy . . . I really don't have any
> big ones set out . . . I'd like them to understand what
> I'm talking about, sure . . . and to retain some of the
> things that I've taught, definitely. But that would be
> it for goals.

Beth says she is satisfied with the amount of freedom she has
to control what happens in her class, "It sets out things you should
be doing, which is nice," she says, "because you know what's
expected." She comments that she can generally teach the kind of
curriculum that she thinks is important, "as long as it includes
what has been set out for me to teach."

At the same time, Beth says she thinks her talents are under-
utilized. She says,

> School isn't just the place for basic learning, you
> know; the teacher talks and you learn or absorb it.
> [It should be] more of an interesting kind of
> place . . . but it's just not coming through anymore.
> I guess I just don't take the time to sit down and
> think about it like I used to. Or I don't have the
> time to design some of the things that I designed that
> were really neat.

Asked about prep time, Beth says she has enough.

At the end of the school year, Beth's teaching is observed to
have changed little from the mid-year description, except that she
is more self-confident and practiced in implementing the PBE
curriculum. With the end-of-year tests to face, all of her
classroom behavior is focused on getting her pupils to perform well.
Observations describe days filled with assigning drill and practice,
giving information, and testing recall.

Beth's statements about her thinking during planning, during
teaching, following teaching, have changed in that they no longer
contain references to selecting topics, aiming to stimulate pupil
creative thinking and pupil reflection, as had appeared in earlier
statements of that type. She begins with the PBE lists of
objectives, uses materials for which there are information and
recall exercises (reading, social studies, science) or decides which
and how many math solutions to present, choosing items from the
textbook to illustrate. Decisions are often made on the spot
regarding what to say about a math problem or what questions to ask,
for example, about a story or a section of a science booklet.

Consideration for team decisions about time schedules are the strongest determinant for whether to extend or abbreviate teaching, give more time to slower learners or not.

What has also changed are Beth's statements about her perspectives toward teaching and about what she thinks she *should* be doing. Her earlier statements of belief placed high value on planning for active ("hands on") learning by pupils, with teacher research into content in order to invent activities that will challenge pupil thinking and stimulate pupil interest. Her statements of belief now indicate that she has learned that she can be successful as a teacher without doing much detailed planning and without the need to do much (or any) research on the topics she intends to teach. Presumably, she finds enough in the Teachers Guides and the pupil materials to support the explanations and presentations she gives.

Beth's thinking about teacher classroom behavior has also changed in that she no longer sees much value in open discussions and "hands on" pupil activities. She intends to move more quickly the following year, to spend less time explaining the work, leaving out discussions of topics which are not "on the test" and "covering more areas," especially areas that are tested.

HANNAH: THINKING ABOUT TEACHING IN A LOOSELY MANAGED SCHOOL

Hannah was a student teacher in a small village located near a middle-sized city (about 200,000) and worked as part of one of two fifth/sixth-grade teams in a grade 4-6 middle school enrolling about 500 children. There were four teaching teams in this school, each one of which was responsible for the instruction of approximately 120 children in all subject areas except art, music, and physical education. Hannah worked on a team with four certified teachers and had her own classes of around 30 pupils for each subject. During a typical week she taught almost all of the 120 pupils on her team, since the instructional program was totally departmentalized. The school community included few minorities and had a mix of parents ranging from a few who were very poor to some who were highly paid professionals. The majority of the parents were moderately well off financially.

Hannah was expected to follow very closely the highly structured curriculum of the school in all subject areas. She was provided with lists of specific objectives in each subject which she was expected to cover and with all of the materials and tests that she was expected to use. She was also expected to cover this curriculum within specified blocks of time and had very little choice about when subjects would be taught and for how long. Because of the open architectural design of the school where no walls separated the classrooms, all of Hannah's activities were totally visible to the other members of her team. She was told that very little noise and pupil movement would be tolerated so that the classes would not disturb one another. Hannah was generally provided by her colleagues with models of very formal and distant pupil-teacher relations.

Throughout the semester Hannah questioned the departmentalized

90

school structure, the rationalized curricular form, and the distant and formal relations between teachers and pupils which were a part of the taken-for-granted reality of her school and felt she was being asked to fit into a teacher role that she did not like. Despite isolated efforts, which continued throughout the semester, to implement what she felt was a more varied and lively curriculum and to relate to her pupils in a more personal way than was common in her school, Hannah for the most part outwardly complied with the accepted practices in her school and did not act in a manner consistent with her expressed beliefs. At the end of the semester, despite the lack of confirmation from her experience as a student teacher, Hannah was more convinced than ever ("having learned a lot of things of what not to do") that warm and close relations between pupils and teachers, getting kids excited about learning and feeling good about themselves as people (e.g., by integrating their personal knowledge into the curriculum) were the keys to good teaching.

Hannah's first year in a regular teaching position was spent as the only eighth-grade teacher in a nine-classroom K-8 public school enrolling about 190 pupils. The school was located in a rural farm community a few miles outside of a small city with a population of 9,000. Hannah taught all subjects except civics to her eighth-grade class and also taught science to the seventh-grade class. The parents of the children in her class were very diverse socioeconomically, ranging from those who were farm owners and professionals to those who were farm workers. All of the teachers lived in the immediate area with the exception of Hannah and one other teacher who commuted from a city 45 minutes away. Hannah was the youngest and the only first-year teacher in the school and the only one who had not completed a teacher education program at one of the relatively small state teacher's colleges which were now part of the state university system.

The culture, tradition, and organization of this school was quite different from the school in which Hannah completed her student teaching. On the one hand there was a very strong tradition of individualism in the school which sanctioned each teacher's right to do things in his or her own way, and there was very little cooperation or coordination among the staff. All of the classrooms with the exception of Hannah's and the seventh-grade class were totally self-contained, and each teacher was responsible for all of the instruction for a group of around 25 students. The principal of the school was also a full-time teacher and did not observe or confer with teachers except during weekly staff meetings.

Consistent with the individualistic tradition of the school, very few overt controls were exerted on teachers with respect to the planning and teaching of the curriculum. Teachers were given curriculum guides and textbooks for each subject area and were permitted to cover the content specified in the guides in whatever order, at whatever pace, and with whatever methods they thought were most appropriate. Teachers were also free to supplement the texts with any other materials and to go beyond what was listed in the curriculum guides as long as the curriculum was covered by the end of the year.

The only explicit controls which were placed on teachers'

handling of the curriculum were in the areas of grading and testing.
All of the teachers were expected to give each child 30 "marks" for
each subject during each of three report periods and to grade
pupils' work according to a standard grading scale. A great deal of
emphasis was also placed upon pupil performance on a national
standardized test given each spring.

Alongside the tradition of individualism in the school, there
was also a very strong and mostly unspoken agreement among all but
Hannah and one colleague in the seventh-grade class about the ways
in which teachers should relate to their pupils. This approach was
characterized by one teacher as "the old school method . . . you
can't have someone here who is too soft with the kids." Hannah
became aware of this consensus on teacher-pupil relations ("In this
school it's the teacher's role to be the disciplinarian.") through
observations of other teachers, through her pupils' comments, and
indirectly through the school "grapevine." Other teachers would
rarely confront Hannah directly with criticisms of her more informal
style of relating to pupils. On several occasions, however,
teachers complained to the principal, who in turn passed the word to
Hannah that she had violated the preferred formality between
teachers and pupils. All of the classrooms with the exception of
the seventh and eighth grades were very tightly controlled by teachers, and this strong, informal agreement among the staff initially
made Hannah feel isolated and alone.

> You begin to try new things; everything is not out of
> the textbooks or worksheet oriented. They look down on
> that. But they don't constrain you and say you can't
> do things. They would never say you can't do things.
> They'll do it in a roundabout way . . . when it comes
> back to you, you feel that everyone else is against
> you.

The community was characterized by Hannah and several other
teachers as extremely conservative, suspicious of new ideas, and as
holding expectations for teachers to maintain very tight controls
over pupils. Hannah initially felt more pressure from the parents
than from her colleagues to conform to the unspoken tradition
regarding the teacher's role and was initially reluctant to act on
her intuitions because she felt that she was perceived as an
outsider. From the beginning of the year, Hannah made many efforts
to win the trust and confidence of the parents and to learn more
about the ways and mores of the community.

At the beginning of the year, despite the lack of close
supervision and formal controls, Hannah relied heavily on the
textbooks in planning her curriculum; however, she also made efforts
from the very beginning to establish warm and close relationships
with her pupils in violation of the school's tradition. Hannah
continued to describe her basic orientation to teaching as
"humanistic" and emphasized the affective and interpersonal
dimensions of her work. She felt strongly that a positive
self-concept is the key to learning and wanted to find ways to make
school enjoyable for herself and her pupils. Hannah tried very hard

to present herself to her pupils as a "human being" by openly admitting her mistakes, her ignorance with regard to content, and by freely sharing aspects of her personal life with her pupils. She also made many efforts to understand the personal lives of each child in her class and to gain her pupils' trust and confidence.

Initially, Hannah's pupils were very suspicious of her efforts to break down the conventional barriers between teachers and students, and there was a lack of support from her colleagues. Hannah became confused and uncertain in the fall about the direction she should take, and established several classroom practices and rules which violated her own vision of "humanistic" teaching. Despite these isolated instances where Hannah flirted with more conventional methods of controlling her pupils, for the most part she exerted relatively little direct control over pupil behaviors, and the pupils gradually began to respond to her efforts.

Despite her efforts to establish warm and personal relations with her pupils which were gradually becoming more and more successful, Hannah was frustrated with her heavy reliance on textbooks and with her inability to establish a more varied and lively instructional program. While she was very sure of herself in dealing with children in interpersonal matters, she felt that she did not have a clear idea of how to implement her expressed preference for a more integrated curriculum which incorporated children's personal experiences, which gave pupils concrete experiences in relation to ideas, and which elicited their enthusiasm and excitement about solving problems in relation to the world around them. "I just feel like I'm spoon feeding them and opening their heads and pushing the knowledge in."

Knowing that her pupils had been taught "right out of the textbook" in the past and that they would probably be taught so in the future, and not confident that she was able to explain to others how particular methods were meeting specific academic goals, Hannah worried a lot about handicapping her students and about not giving them what they were "supposed to learn." By December, Hannah was so frustrated that she considered quitting teaching and accepting another job outside of education.

As the year progressed, Hannah became more and more satisfied with her classroom program, and her actions began more and more to reflect her expressed beliefs about teaching. She continued to rely mainly on the texts in planning her lessons, but she gradually made more and more independent decisions which resulted in a greater emphasis on providing concrete experiences for children and on incorporating their personal lives into the curriculum.

By April, Hannah felt confident enough to drop the basal readers and to have her pupils read novels and to let two pupils teach a unit on engines to the class that drew upon their experiences in repairing farm vehicles. Throughout the year Hannah continued to expose all of her pupils to the same curricular content and stayed fairly close to the texts in some subjects (e.g., math), but her work in language, reading, and science reflected more and more of the active pupil involvement and problematic approach to knowledge that she had hoped to create since the beginning of her student teaching. By the end of the year Hannah felt that she had come closer to her ideal where pupils are thinking critically and constantly and where they are always asking questions and trying to apply their in-class learnings to everyday life.

There were several reasons why Hannah was able to move from a point in December where she considered quitting, to a feeling of satisfied accomplishment at the end of the year. Among these were: (1) the support she received from her one teacher ally, the seventh-grade teacher; (2) her ability to mobilize parent support for her classroom program; (3) the pupils' traditions of mutual peer support and the warm acceptance of Hannah as a "teacher-friend"; and (4) her pupils' success on the national standardized test (scoring the highest of all of the eighth grades in the district). Because of this support from the pupils, parents, and the seventh-grade teacher, and because of Hannah's determination, her skills in dealing with people, and her sensitivity to the political dimensions of schooling, she was able to significantly redefine aspects of her school in relation to her own class and to modify her behavior to create more consistency between her beliefs and actions. Hannah maintained her beliefs regarding the importance of "humanistic" teaching throughout her student teaching and her first-year of teaching with little or no formal support from her schools and gradually, as her pupils and their parents began to respond positively to her approach, Hannah was able to find ways, by acting on her intuitions and through trial and error, of modifying her behavior to bring it into closer agreement with her beliefs about teaching.

CONCLUSION

Our conception of "perspectives toward teaching" is similar to what Clark and Peterson (1986) refer to as "teacher beliefs and implicit theories." There is some difference, since we treat classroom behavior as an expression of a teacher's beliefs or implicit theories about teaching and learning. The teachers we studied were also often able to articulate explicit theories of teaching; they often were aware of their beliefs and were ready to explain and justify them.

At the beginning of her first year as a teacher Beth made statements of belief about teaching that contradicted or were inconsistent with each other. Her teaching behavior was inconsistent with those statements of belief that referred to the need for active learning and creative problem solving. The teaching behavior was consistent with a belief in the value of a curriculum that encouraged pupils to learn prespecified information and skills. As the year passed, Beth's statements of belief contained fewer and fewer of the statements about the value of pupils' creative problem solving. Beth's beliefs changed until they were characterized by statements that affirmed and justified her teaching behavior; while her teaching behavior remains essentially the same throughout the year, it is more completely expressive of her statements of belief by the end of the school year.

Hannah also created closer agreement, as the year progressed, between her verbal and her behavioral "statements" of belief about teaching. She monitored her classroom behavior, modifying it to bring it into agreement with her beliefs about teaching. Her early lack of success led her to toy with the possibility of abandoning her beliefs (and abandoning teaching altogether), but by the end of the year she had reaffirmed her earlier commitments to an activity-oriented curriculum that encouraged pupil independence, initiative, and creative problem solving. At no time did her ideas or her behavior waver in revealing her belief that it was necessary to know children as people--and to be known by them as a person--in order to teach them successfully as pupils.

Both teachers reduced the inconsistencies in their statements of belief but used quite different strategies to do so. Partly, that was a result of their personal characteristics and history, their capabilities, their willingness to risk, their strength of commitment to a particular professional position. Hannah was both intuitively and consciously skilled in managing the political and social context of her classroom, her school, her school's community. She was also willing to make the effort. Beth avoided "political entanglements" and was content to affirm principles of action which she seemed to reject early in the year, but whose affirmation created solidarity between her and her co-teachers and the principal.

The schools offered very different opportunities to exercise professional judgment. Edwards' (1979) analysis of methods of control of a workplace are helpful in recognizing differences in the two schools. Hannah's teaching principal had little opportunity to control teaching behavior. In addition, efforts at control would have violated that school's informal cultural norms of independence (at least for adults). Beth's principal was able and willing to exercise control over what happened in the school. Bureaucratic control through the social arrangement of teaching teams was powerful in Beth's school but weak in Hannah's school, in which teachers could operate more independently behind their closed classroom doors. Control by technical elements--the physical structure of an open architectural plan that made it easy to monitor teacher behavior, the specificity of a PBE curriculum--was present for Beth but absent for Hannah. Indeed, under the conditions of strict control that characterized her student teaching school, Hannah suppressed the expression of her ideas as behavior, while reaffirming them verbally. Edwards' theory of control does not account for the presence of the informal school cultures in both schools which either encouraged conformity or else encouraged independent teacher action.

Teacher thinking as described in our study was not merely the result of an individual's personal history and psychological state. Though apparently highly context specific, thinking was not merely shaped by the sociopolitical conditions in the school. Rather, we discovered that in both cases the move to greater consistency between belief and behavior was the result of a negotiated and interactive process between individuals and organizational constraints and encouragements.

REFERENCES

Becker, H., Geer, B., Hughes, E., & Straus, A. (1961). *Boys in white*. Chicago, Illinois: University of Chicago Press.

Clark, C., & Peterson, P. (1986). Research on teacher thinking. In M. Wittrock (Ed.), *Handbook of research on teaching* (3rd ed). New York: Macmillan.

Edwards, R. (1979). *Contested terrain: The transformation of the workplace in the 20th century*. New York: Basic Books.

Mead, G. H. (1938). *The philosophy of the act*. Chicago: University of Chicago Press.

Shavelson, R. & Stern, P. (1981). Research on teachers' pedagogical thoughts, judgments, decisions, and behavior. *Review of Educational Research, 51*, 455-498.

Tabachnick, B. R., & Zeichner, K. M. (1985). *The teacher perspectives project: Final Report*. Madison: Wisconsin Center for Education Research.

Zeichner, K., & Tabachnick, B. R. (1985). The development of teacher perspectives: Social strategies and institutional control in the socialization of beginning teachers. *Journal of Education for Teaching, 11*, 1-25.

TEACHERS' INSTRUCTIONAL QUALITY AND THEIR EXPLANATION OF STUDENTS' UNDERSTANDING

Rainer Bromme
Universität Bielefeld
Institut für Didaktik
der Mathematik
Fed. Rep. of Germany*

Gudrun Dobslaw
Universität Bielefeld
Fakultät für Psychologie
und Sportwissenschaft
Fed. Rep. of Germany

ABSTRACT

"Instructional Quality" models stress the selection of tasks that are suitable for students. This study analyzes the cognitive tools that teachers use when they think about tasks and students. Mathematics teachers were asked how they explain the understanding of mathematical tasks to their students. The teachers´ replies reveal that task-related conceptions of the understanding process are present, as well as broader, task independent conceptions of understanding. There are also individual differences between teachers. In addition, the teachers were observed during lessons. Connections between the range of ideas of understanding, and the instructional quality of the teachers were examined. Teachers who were rated to be ´enthusiastic´ in their teaching tend to prefer task related or mixed explanations for their students´ understanding.

INTRODUCTION

It is of interest to explain understanding, since the teacher´s most important task is to promote this in her students. To achieve this, the teacher must realistically assess her students´s previous understanding. To be able to plan her lessons, and to make allowance for the difficulties some students might have, it is important that she be able to explain to herself the extent to which understanding has taken place.

We investigated explanations in order to learn something about the teacher´s professional knowledge. The investigation is based on viewing "teachers as experts" (Fogarty et al.,1983; Leinhardt 1983; Bromme 1986). Like other experts, e.g. doctors, chess-players or engineers, teachers use a network of professional concepts and concept relations. These concepts structure their conceptions of the

* The study was supported in part by the VW Foundation

tasks they have to cope with, and of the conditions they have to take into account in doing so, as well as the "image" or "model" they have of the situation in which their professional activity takes place (Schön 1983).

It is helpful to record professional knowledge while it is being used, that is in connection with concrete situations taken from the experts' field of experience. Then there will be less bias within verbal reports and the answers will be richer than if one tries to record a lexical or systematical representation of their knowledge. Asking for explanations for the understanding of mathematical tasks will create a situation for the teachers in which they may use their own knowledge about "understanding", and thus be able to explain it.

The professional knowledge with regard to pedagogical-psychological teaching problems, such as classroom-management, student aggression etc. has been extensively examined (e.g. Krause et al. in this volume). On the other hand, the teachers' concepts of more subject-specific issues i.e. problems linked to the subject matter taught, are less well understood (cf. Clark in this volume).

The models and findings in recent research on efficient teaching show that almost all teacher variables, which were found to be important for the students' learning, refer directly to dealing with the subject matter. They require at least subject-matter-relevant judgements from the teacher, such as allotting tasks according to the students' level of learning, evaluation as to which are unequivocal forms of presenting the subject matter etc. Judgements about the students, or his/her level of learning and his/her learning potential must be linked to the respective details of the task in order to be able to make a decision as to which action should be taken. This is only a hypothesis, taken from an analysis of the demands the teacher has to cope with. It must be investigated empirically whether this linking really takes place in teachers' minds.

Our question is whether evidence for such a linkage of subject matter components with observations and assumptions about the students' characteristics or students' behavior in the lesson, are to be found in the teachers' explanations, or whether these explanations refer to person characteristics and behavior not related to the subject matter.

The first type of explanatory concepts are called in the following, task-related concepts, because the subject matter in our study is represented as a mathematical task. All concepts about students' thinking, knowledge, behavior etc. directly dealing with the subject matter are called task-related concepts.

The second type of explanatory concepts are called task-independent. Examples are giftedness, general motivation, student's memory,

absenteeism, attention, support at home etc. Sometimes we will call
the second type of causes 'purely' psychological explanations. Obviously this is a quite narrow notion for 'psychological', but a
little exaggeration may help to clarify the distinction.

A similar differentiation is made in the empirical research into
conditions of students' learning at school. In this field, a divi-
sion is made between instruction independent predictors such as
intelligence, anxiety and sex, and more instruction dependent predictors such as instructional quality and previous marks, when trying to predict student performance. It has been revealed that the
causal effect on learning achievement of instruction independent
factors becomes increasingly weaker the longer the students are at
school, while the actual lesson quality, and the student's accumula-
ted knowledge become increasingly important for explaining and predicting school performance (Simons et al. 1975). For example,
Schwarzer (1979) showed that the students' subject-specific previous
experience formed the best single predictor of students' performance, when compared with intelligence and anxiety. Therefore the
question arises, whether the causal importance of such subject-related factors is also mirrored in the teacher's professional explanation.

A first study on students' understanding from a teachers' point of
view has shown that the subject content occupies a prominent space
in teachers' explanations of understanding (Bromme & Juhl 1984). The
objective of this study is to find out whether this result can be
generalized to other teachers and another type of school. Additionally we will investigate whether teachers differ in the extent to
which they include the subject matter in their explanations. Finally, we will inquire whether there are connections between the explanations and the quality of the teachers' classroom activity.

For this purpose, the quality of teaching is assessed according to
certain research variables into teacher effectiveness. As these
models stress the presentation of and the working with the subject
content, it will be of interest to see whether teachers who give
particularly "good" lessons with regard to these variables, will
also extensively refer to the subject content in their explanations.

Questions to be studied

1. Which concepts are named by mathematics teachers in order to
   explain their students' understanding of mathematical tasks?

2. Do teachers differ in their preferences for task related vs. task
   independent (pure psychological) concepts?

3. Is there a connection between the type of explanation and the
   quality of classroom activity in the teachers' subsequent teaching unit?

METHOD

Teachers´ explanations were obtained by using a table in which the teacher had to list a mathematical task that she had presented in her preceding teaching unit (cf. fig.1)

Fig.1

task
....

task understood	name name	reasons for understanding reasons for understanding
task not understood	name name	reasons for not-understanding reasons for not-understanding

For this task, each teacher had to select two students who had understood the task and two who had not. In the columns of the table, the teacher was asked to write down the causes of under-standing resp. not understanding this task. In constructing this table, we adopted a basic idea of Kelly´s (1955) repertory-grid test, that linking two given persons and/or facts requires the application of the subject´s existing system of concepts (Ben-Peretz 1984).

This method of attaining data does not impose predetermined items on the teacher, but permits us to obtain free answers. We considered this necessary as until now there are so few research results, that the presentation of items would be rather arbitrary (for this see also Huber and Mandl 1979). Using concrete mathematical tasks taken from the classroom assures that teachers will be able to base their answers on actual experience instead of "theorizing". Finally, the tables, by their standardized form offer the possibility of compara-tive and summarizing evaluation of the answers.

In each case, the teachers had to select the students from a list of 15 students chosen at random. Additionally, they had to note 4 tasks which had been actually worked on in the preceding teaching unit. Thus, we obtained eight explanations per teacher pertaining to understanding and pertaining to non-understanding. The teachers were permitted to give several reasons per student. The explanations were obtained immediately after the end of a teaching sequence - which had dealt with geometry for almost all of the teachers.

Lesson quality was then assessed by observers in the subsequent teaching series. Each teacher was observed in at least four lessons, her teaching being recorded in connection with another study. An observer who was familiar with the mathematical subject matter of this teaching series, and with the variables for the quality of teaching, assessed the teacher´s behavior according to six variables:

1. The teachers control of the course of the lesson

2. Clarity of organizational orders and subject matter instruction

3. Clarity when using blackboards and overhead projectors

4. "Warmth" of teaching style

5. The teachers' interest in the subject matter and emotional participation (enthusiasm)

6. Anticipatory approach towards disruptions and discipline problems
("withitness")

Active control was characterized by an active as opposed to a
reactive content-related and organizational lesson control.

Assessment of the clarity of teachers' remarks related both to
organizational and content-related instructions. This variable was
one of the five variables in the review by Rosenshine (1971) which
relate strongest to learning success.

In assessing the clarity of blackboard and overhead projector use,
behavior closely related to communicating subject matter was taken
into account.

The item "warmth" of teaching style concerned the extent to which
the teacher created a climate of understanding and personal acceptance in her lesson.

The variable of teachers' interest and emotional participation
described the degree to which the teacher was able to convey the impression that she personally found the subject interesting and the
course of the lesson exciting. This variable is also labelled
"enthusiasm".

The variable anticipation of disciplinary problems was introduced
to assess classroom management. This variable described whether the
teacher only intervened to deal with problems or events which had
already been developing for some time, or whether she acted at the
first signs of a disturbance ("withitness", as described by Kounin
(1979), cf. Rheinberg & Hoss 1979).

DATA COLLECTION AND SAMPLING

The study was carried out as part of a larger project on stocha-
stic education. 26 teachers participated in the overall study which
included pre-tests and post-tests and the recording of additional
data. The average professional experience of these teachers was
92 months.

For our purposes, the interest of these tests is merely that they
show, that our questions and our observation had no influence on

performance of the classes concerned in comparison to a control
group of ten other teachers who were not observed.

Thirteen teachers working with fifth and sixth year classes and
belonging to three different schools were included in the study of
teachers' explanations.*

DATA ANALYSIS

The free explanations were coded with a previously developed and
tested category system. They were subdivided into units of meaning
by one of the authors and subsequently processed by two trained
coders. The inter-coder reliability was 92 percent. Prior to further
analysis, agreement was reached on the remainder of codings after
discussion with the coders. The categories (see table 1) can be
assigned to two different fields according to our main questions:

- categories describing various stages of the process of solving
  mathematical tasks, or referring to subject-matter-related student
  behaviors or performance. These were named task-related categories.

- categories referring to pedagogical-psychological content such as
  student motivation, attention in the classroom, students' self-
  confidence etc. These were named task-independent categories
  ('purely' psychological categories).

There were also three remainder categories, the most frequent
being "mere description of the course of work".

The coding system was constructed after a survey both of the
literature on understanding as a cognitive process, and of studies
of teacher explanations which discuss personal, task, and teaching
variables (Bromme & Juhl 1984).

There is no unified model of conceptualization and explanation in
cognitive psychology for the process of understanding mathematical
tasks (cf. Greeno 1978; Resnick & Ford 1981; Michener 1978). Many
approaches, however, have been based on a problem solving model previously developed by Polya (1966) for working on mathematical problems.

Solving a task requires the following: previous knowledge, in
order to be able to understand the task; recognition of that which is
sought; knowledge concerning the proper solution algorithm and related problems. The particular importance of previous knowledge for

---

* Teachers' explanations were collected by G. Dobslaw (1983) and
  have been reanalysed for this paper.

understanding tasks is emphasized both by Ausubel and by the constructivist theory of memory.

The significance of the connection of the task with both other
tasks and the conceptual system of mathematics is due to the nature
of mathematical knowledge, as well as to the educational function
of tasks as special instances of concepts and rules which are to be
aquired.

Categories 6.1 to 6.7 are based on these elements of understanding. They refer to the process of understanding as a cognitive process and are used where task-related explanations appear. Explanations for the understanding of mathematical tasks can be given on
various dimensions and with different explanatory depth. This is why
causes like motivation, working behavior etc. were included twice –
both task-related and task-independent. Furthermore, we included explanations which are task-independent, such as influences external
to school or the students´ general speed of work. (The further evaluation steps are presented together with the results).

In the task-related categories, the teachers predominantly took
their previous knowledge into account. This can be seen in the frequency with which categories were named which involve the relationship to other tasks, and the work behavior when working on the task.
In the task-independent categories, the teachers´ predominantly
named style of thinking (e.g. "has a good imaginative ability"),
attention, concentration and general work behavior in the lesson
(e.g. "always cooperates well").

RESULTS

The first question: The procentual frequency distribution across
all categories (cf. Table 1) produces nearly the same number of
task-related and task-independent explanations (44% and 38%). Explanations of understanding and non-understanding were compiled for
the table.

In the task-related categories, the teachers predominantly took
their previous knowledge into account. This can be seen in the frequency with which categories were named which involve the relationship to other tasks, and the work behavior when working on the task.
In the task-independent categories, the teachers´ predominantly
named style of thinking (e.g. "has a good imaginative ability"),
attention, concentration and general work behavior in the lesson
(e.g. "always cooperates well").

Tab.1

Relative frequencies of the content analysis evaluation of
teacher explanations referring to understanding and
not-understanding of the mathematical task

Categories referring to tasks

2. Motivation ref. to task	3
6.1 Previous knowledge of the task related subject-matter	12
6.2 Recognizing the solution sought	1
6.3 Recalling or recognizing the idea of solution	4
6.4 Elaboration of an idea of solution by the student	1
6.5 Implementing the idea of solution	3
6.6 Recodgnizing the connection with other tasks	6
6.8 Other items of the process of problem-solving	2
8. Observable working behavior with regard to task	5
12. Giftedness ref. specifically to math. topics	1
13. Task characteristics	2
15. Characteristics of teaching whilst treating task	4
	---- ca.44%

Categories extending across tasks

1. General motivation	3
3. Attention	9
4. Self-Confidence	3
5. Memory	1
9. Speed	3
10. General styles of thinking	11
11. General giftedness	1
16. Homework	1
17. Gen. evaluation of achievement	4
18. Non-school influences	2
	---- ca.38%

Rest

6.7 Mere discription of the course of work	11
7. Observable working behavior in general	6
14. Gen. characteristics of teaching	1
19. Impossible to code	3

104

As far as the relative frequencies of the categories named can be used to draw a picture of the processes considered to be important for the students´ understanding, we get the following result:

Understanding mathematical tasks requires from the students both specialized previous knowledge (knowing the subject matter treated in previous lessons) and general, cognitive skills such as imagination, the ability to draw conclusions, reasoning etc. (which were summarized under category 10 as "style of thinking"). Likewise, students must be able to remember the special mathematical solution strategies necessary for a task, and must be able to apply them.

The second most frequent task-related category is that of recognizing the connection of the task with other tasks. Among the task-independent categories, the most frequent is that of styles of thinking, followed by attention, cooperation, and concentration.

The second question of the study was: Do certain teachers prefer task-related or pedagogical-psychological causes? The teachers were allowed to give several causes for each student, and did so. Combinations of causes were also given; the teacher stating, for instance, that the student did not pay attention and was therefore unable to retain a certain mathematical theorem and as a consequence could not understand the task. These combined causes can be purely task-related, purely task-independent or mixed, as in the example (attention and lack of mathematical knowledge). Decisions were reached by coding with the categories described above (see table 1).

When a combination of causes contained at least one category belonging to the task-independent and at least one from the task-related category, it was classed as a mixed combination of causes. Table 2 contains the frequencies of the preferred explanations under the headings "understood" and "not understood", broken down for each teacher.
The frequency with which different types of combination were used was significantly different, as shown by Friedman´s rank variance analyses (χ^2=147, p=.ooo understood, χ^2=258, p=.oo1 not understood). Mixed explanations were most frequently given, with purely subject-related explanations coming second. This holds for the explanation of both understood and not understood tasks.

No teachers provided exclusively task-related or exclusively task-independent explanations over all of their eight students. Rather, we found that they prefer either mixed and task-related, or mixed and pedagogical-psychological explanations or mixed explanations only.

This means that three groups can be clearly distinguished: Group A gives for the majority of its students task-specific, and for some

Tab.2:

teacher	task understood			task not-understood		
	task-rel. A	ped.-psy. B	mixed C	task-rel. A	ped.psy. B	mixed C
08	2	5	1	1	3	4
09	5	1	3	2	–	6
10	3	–	5	4	1	3
11	3	–	5	3	–	5
12	–	6	2	–	7	1
26	3	3	1	1	5	2
30	2	–	6	2	4	2
31	–	5	1	–	3	5
32	1	1	6	3	–	5
33	1	2	5	5	2	1
34	5	1	2	4	2	1
36	2	–	5	5	–	3
37	3	1	4	2	–	4

Sometimes a teacher has mentioned three students per table only.
Therefore the rows' frequencies do not sum up to 8.

students mixed explanations. Group B gives only mixed explanations for all students, and Group C consists of teachers who prefer task independent causes for the majority of their students, giving mixed explanations for the rest.

Hence, there are no teachers (one exception) giving, for some of their students, only task-related explanations, and only task-independent ones for others. It ensues that explanations are given according to individual emphasis, which is influenced, but not determined, by the facts (task/students) to be explained. The preferences for explanations for understanding and non-understanding differ only slightly. To illustrate the explanation preferences, we shall provide an example for each group of teachers; A, B and C.

In Group A (predominantly task-related explanations), the special previous knowledge with regard to the task concerned is frequently named in combination with recognition of the task's connection with other tasks.

In Group B (predominantly mixed explanations), teachers combine the deficits in previous knowledge with lack of attention and lack of self-confidence for most of their students who do not understand tasks. In the case of understanding, combining task-related categories with the students imagination and thinking styles is frequent.

In Group C (predominantly task-independent explanations), a teacher will name, for instance, general working behavior in the classroom, use of time, and influences external to school.

Consideration of the individual cases, however, does not only show that teachers place their emphasis differently, but it also additionally reveals that there are great differences in detail between the combinations of causes named by the teachers. The explanations thus do not adhere to a pattern which is stable across all behaviors to be explained and all teachers, but contain a variety of perceived combinations of causes.

<u>The third question under investigation:</u> As the quality of classroom activity is described in models of effective teaching, by variables which mainly concern the handling of the subject matter, we investigated the question as to whether a connection can be found between the teaching and the preferred explanation. In view of the small number (N=13) of teachers who were further interviewed regarding their explanations, such a connection can only be determined by considering the individual cases. The basis for this is a factor analysis which was performed for the entire sample with the observation variables listed above. The classroom observations were averaged across the four lessons and then submitted to factor analysis.

Using an obliquely rotated main component analysis with correlated factors, a factor structure was obtained that allowed clear interpretation. The assumption of a two factor structure was previously tested using an exploratory analysis without a preassigned number of factors.

This also produced two factors with eigenvalues greater than 1.0 (Kaiser criterion). For theoretical reasons, an independence of possible factors was not assumed. However, a low correlation was obtained between the two factors (r=.23).

The two factors explained 77% of the total variance, and also explained the six items concerning lesson quality to a satisfactory degree (communalities between .65 and .89). The contents of the two dimensions can be differentiated as follows: Factor 1 described aspects of subject-matter-related and student-related engagement, while Factor 2 concerns aspects of the organizational and content structuring of the course of the lesson.

In order to test whether it was acceptable to take an average across all lessons, we inspected factor solutions at specific timepoints. These produced the same factor structure with only slight variations.

The factor values for each observed teacher on each factor were known at the time of factor computation. We then tested the extend to which each individual teacher's values on both factors related to her career experience. No significant relationsships could be found.

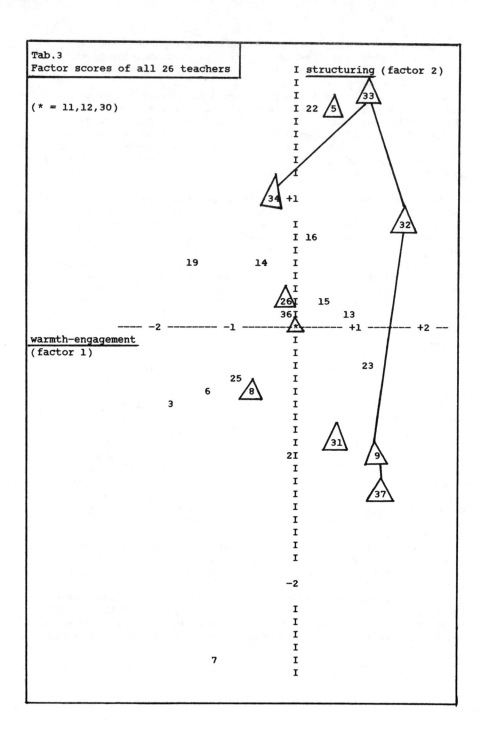

Tab.3
Factor scores of all 26 teachers

(* = 11,12,30)

structuring (factor 2)

warmth-engagement
(factor 1)

Table 3 shows the factor values of all 26 teachers participating in the study. The teachers whose explanations of understanding were collected, and are described in this paper, are marked by triangles. The letters serve to designate their preferences of explanation. To obtain these, the frequencies of understanding explanations were compiled from Table 2. Grouping as to A,B,C was performed according to the most frequent type of cause named.

A study of individual cases should focus on those teachers who have relatively extreme factor values compared to their colleagues. They are situated at "the margin" of the diagram and have been linked for purposes of illustration. It is evident that these "good" teachers belong either to A (predominantly task-related explanation) or to B (predominantly mixed explanations). The four teachers 33, 32, 9 and 37 are among the teachers in the overall sample who show the most "enthusiasm and warmth" (factor 1).

For the other dimension, no such connection can be determined. Here, teachers 33, 34 and 32 show rather high values, whereas 31, 9 and 37 show rather small ones.

This would seem to justify the cautious conclusion that the "enthusiastic" teachers prefer task-related and mixed explanations. The opposite conclusion, of course, does not hold; i.e. there are also teachers having these preferences of explanation who show only small or negative factor values on the dimensions of quality.

DISCUSSION

The teachers' explanations of causes make allowance for the cumulative character of learning in school. Mastery of the previous subject matter is considered to be a prerequisite for understanding a task. Tasks cannot be considered in isolation in the classroom. In order to understand them, it is necessary to recognize their relationships to other tasks and areas of the subject matter taught. This item is also frequently named by the teachers. The prerequisites of understanding, however, do not only lie within the student's knowledge and immediate cognitive processes. Understanding also requires activity and attention. Both the student's observable working behaviour and concentration are frequently named. The second most frequently named item is the style of thinking (for example: is able to think logically or spatially), which is a field-specific ability of the student that is relevant for the task in question.

This image of "understanding" from the teachers' point of view is quite consistent with basic assumptions of modern memory research and teaching/learning research, for instance in its emphasis on the importance of previous knowledge for learning, or in the frequent naming of task-related activities. The analogies to the importance of the "time on task" variable of empirical teaching research are obvious.

The frequency distributions of causes confirm the findings of Bromme & Juhl (1984) obtained from another sample taken from a different type of school (Gymnasium), but matched for age group and school subject. There is, however, a difference. While 69 percent of all items were task-related, field-specific explanations in the Gymnasium, there were only 44 percent in our present sample. In the case of the Gymnasium teachers, there were only 21 percent task-independent, general categories compared with 38 percent in the present study. It is possible that the difference can be explained by the fact that in the Gymnasium particular emphasis is traditionally placed on teaching subject-matter specific, curricular knowledge.

The relatively high proportion of task-related concepts of explanation, however, remains noteable, even if it is smaller than that in the Bromme & Juhl study (1984). The high proportion is possibly due to the method of obtaining data, as student and task were equally salient. This situation, however, is realistic, in that it conforms to teachers' everyday teaching experience.

The frequency distribution of the causes named does not yet clearly define the individual patterns of explanation. For the second question of the study, the explanation was thus evaluated for each teacher in order to see whether it was purely task-related, purely task-independent, or mixed. One half of the teachers used mixed explanations for most of the eight students they had to evaluate; the other teachers either preferred purely task-related or purely task-independent explanations. All teachers, however, gave mixed explanations, so that we have to assume teacher preferences rather than strong differences between teachers.

The variability of the individual patterns of explanation is remarkable. It indicates the presence of comprehensive and organized professional knowledge about "understanding" (cf. Rheinberg & Elke 1978). Among these explanations, the mixed ones best conform to that which is understood as an explanation according to what is called "understanding" within the philosophy of science, namely the linking of a specific observation to a more general assumption.

For the third question of the study concerning the connection between the explanations and the quality of teaching, we have behaviour observations from a teaching unit at our disposal, which was held after the explanations had been given. This enables us to obtain those connections between explanation preferences and quality of teaching which are very stable. In view of this difficulty, it is remarkable that the four teachers who show - compared to the overall sample - a relatively high amount of subject-specific interest and warmth (factor 1), prefer task-related or mixed explanations rather than task-independent ones.

This result can only be taken to be a first indication toward a possible connection of this kind. At least it is a hint that a connection between the quality of instruction and the teachers' explanatory concepts might actually exist.

REFERENCES

Ben-Peretz, M. (1984). Kelly's theory of personal constructs. A paradigm for investigating teacher thinking. In: Halkes, R. & Olson, J.K. (Eds.). *Teacher thinking: A new perspective on persisting problems in education.* Lisse: Swets & Zeitlinger.

Bromme, R. (1986). Der Lehrer als Experte - Skizze eines Forschungs-ansatzes. To be published in: Neber, H. (Ed.). *Angewandte Problem-lösepsychologie.* Münster: Aschendorff.

Bromme, R. & Juhl, K. (1984). *Students' understanding of tasks in the view of mathematics teachers* (Occasional Paper No. 58). Bielefeld: Institut für Didaktik der Mathematik. (ERIC Document Reproduction Service No. ED 254418). [German version published in: *Zeitschrift für Empirische Pädagogik und pädagogische Psychologie, 9,* 1-14.]

Dobslaw, G. (1983). *Zum Aufgabenverständnis von Schülern im Mathema-tikunterricht - eine Untersuchung zu Lehrererklärungen über den Verstehensprozeß von Schülern.* Unpublished master's thesis, Biele-feld University, Bielefeld.

Fogarty, J., Wang, M. & Creek, R. (1983). A descriptive study of ex-perienced and novice teachers' interactive instructional thoughts and actions. *Journal of Educational Research, 77,* 22-32.

Greeno, J.G. (1978). Understanding and procedural knowledge in mathe-matics instruction. *Educational Psychologist, 12,* 262-282.

Kelly, G.A. (1955). *The psychology of personal constructs* (2 vol.s). New York: Norton.

Kounin, J. (1970). *Discipline and group management in classrooms.* New York: Holt-Rinehart & Winston.

Leinhardt, G. (1983, April). *Overview of a program of research on teachers' and students' routines, thoughts, and execution of plans.* Paper presented at the meeting of the American Educational Research Association (AERA).

Michener, E.R. (1978). Understanding understanding mathematics. *Cognitive Science, 2,* 361-383.

Polya, G. (1966). *Vom Lösen mathematischer Aufgaben* (2 Bände). Basel: Birkhäuser.

Resnick, L.B. & Ford, W.W. (1981). *The psychology of mathematics for instruction.* Hillsdale, N.J.: Lawrence Erlbaum.

Rheinberg, F. & Elke, G. (1978). Wie naiv ist die 'naive' Psychologie von Lehrern? In: Eckensberger, L.H. (Ed.). *Bericht über den 31. Kongreß der Deutschen Gesellschaft für Psychologie* (pp. 45-48). Göttingen: Hogrefe.

Rheinberg, F. & Hoss, J. (1979). Störungen und Mitarbeit im Unterricht. Eine Erkundungsstudie zu Kounins Kategorisierung des Lehrerverhaltens. *Zeitschrift für Entwicklungspsychologie und Pädagogische Psychologie, 11,* 244-249.

Rosenshine, B. (1971). *Teaching behaviors and student achievement.* London: National Foundation for Educational Research.

Schön, D. (1983). *The reflective practitioner.* New York: Basic Books.

Schwarzer, R. (1979). Sequentielle Prädiktion des Schulerfolgs. *Zeitschrift für Entwicklungspsychologie und Pädagogische Psychologie, 11,* 170-180.

Simons, H., Weinert, F.E. & Ahrens, H.J. (1975). Untersuchungen zur differential-psychologischen Analyse von Rechenleistungen. *Zeitschrift für Entwicklungspsychologie und Pädagogische Psychologie, 7,* 153-169.

FORMING JUDGEMENTS IN THE CLASSROOM: HOW DO TEACHERS DEVELOP EXPECTATIONS OF THEIR PUPILS' PERFORMANCES?

H. Manfred Hofer
University of Mannheim
Department of Educational Psychology

SUMMARY

This experimental study investigates the question as to how teachers relate two different information factors about pupils and arrive at a prediction. Anderson and Butzin (1974) believe to have proved that it is by multiplication that adults integrate information about the motivation and the aptitude of a specific person to reach a judgement on his/her ability. Here it was assumed that there were major differences in the patterns by which individual teachers integrate information. An experiment was designed to allow a statistical evaluation for every teacher. The dependent variable was a prognosis of pupils' performances in the next examination of the teacher's subject. The findings of this study contradict the results mentioned above. Teachers arrive at their judgement by means of differentiated considerations, best explained by a two-staged process of information integration.

1. PROBLEM

How teachers process information to reach a prognosis on the future achievement of a pupil is the question under discussion. As a result of research, we already have sufficient knowledge of the variables which teachers use to reach a prognosis of the pupil: effort, aptitude and home environment. It is not known, however, in which way these variables are interrelated and how they are combined to arrive at a prognosis.

Expectancies of future pupil performance play an important role in guiding teacher behavior. In accordance with notions on the theory of action (Hofer 1986) these expectancies represent cognitions which are then compared with the teachers' aspiration level. The result of this comparison provides the starting-point for future activity.

This paper deals with the investigation of the rules teachers adopt when combining information about a given effort of individual students, in order to arrive at expectancies about their future achievement.

One possibility to elaborate such combinations is offered by the Information-Integration Theory by Anderson (1981). This theory was originally developed to represent judgements which can be measured in objective terms. Wilkening (1979), for example, presented test persons rectangles with various heights and widths and had them estimate the surface area. Children arrived at judgements by summing up the height and width of the individual stimuli. With adults, on the other hand, the judgement was reached by means of multiplying the information. Similar results were produced by the test persons who were given stimuli containing time span and speed of moving objects and who had to make judgements about the distance covered. This theory can also be used for psychological phenomena which are not measurable in objective terms (Anderson 1974).

The questions contained in this experiment have already been investigated in two other experiments, but not with teachers. Anderson and Butzin (1974) differenciated between four stages of motivation (low, moderate, moderately high, high) and intelligence (IQ = 100, 115, 125, 135). The tested persons were given descriptions of stimulus persons who were each characterized by a combination of these two variables. They were told that it was a applicant for admission to graduate school. On a twenty centimeter long graphic rating scale the test person was to indicate which performance this stimulus person would probably achieve. The statistical analysis showed an extremely significant interaction, 75% of the interaction showing a bilinear component. Kun and others (1974) were able to show that six year old children processed aptitude and effort information by addition to reach a prognosis on performance, while on the other hand eight and ten year olds, as well as adults, increasingly processed the information by multiplication.

In the present paper effort and aptitude were also used as indicators. The patterns according to which teachers combined these information factors were investigated statistically for each individual person (Rathje 1982).

2. METHOD

At first, a preliminary inquiry with seven teachers was instigated, in which the various aspects of the experimental structure was tested. Twenty-five teachers involved with all educational levels participated in the main inquiry. Forteen test persons were masculine and eleven feminine; the average length of teaching experience was 10.04 years. The teachers taught pupils from ages of 11 to 18 in the following subjects: Mathematics (11), English (6), German (6), Biology (1) and Sports (1). As a rule the teachers were contacted by a notice on the schools' bulletin board. The investigation was done in individual sessions. The design was a 3 by 4 variance-analytical design, with repeated measurements on both factors: Effort (very low, average, very high) and aptitude (well below average, slightly below average, slightly above average, well above average). The dependent variable was the expected achievement of the pupil in the next examination taken in the subject taught by the teacher.

The instructions said:

"With this experiment I would like to obtain information about the influence of certain traits of students on their future performance.

Let us presume you have just finished presenting a six week block in your subject, and to finish off the unit you would have your pupils take a written examination of average difficulty. A day before the exam you ask yourself how the pupils will perform."

For each student a card was prepared with his name and his distinctions (for example: Markus; ability: well above average, effort: willing to exert great effort).

"On the basis of your observation and experience, deriving principally from the completed block unit, you believe Markus (the given example) to have well above average ability and to be willing to put in great effort. Each time you have read a card please estimate the expected performance of the pupil in the projected examination by means of indicating on this scale by use of the pointer; on the scale there is a possibility of obtaining a maximum 15 points."

As a dependent variable a numerical scale was used. It was mounted on a wooden construction. The pointer was moveable and so constructed that the decision of the teachers could be read by the examiner on the reverse side. In each cell the test persons were confronted with three fictitious pupils, on whom they were asked to make judgements. A prior run through was regarded as practice and therefore not used in the evaluation. In addition the aptitude information was given four times without the effort information. Each test person had thus to give 64 single judgements. 64 registration cards were each labelled with a different masculine first name. The sequence of information within each stimulus was systematically varied in all the tests to eliminate a sequential effect. The complete processing time for the 64 stimuli was between 25 and 35 minutes. Together with the final interview the experiment took about an hour. Before beginning, the test persons were asked by the administrator to register spontaneously the impressions and thoughts that came to their minds while they were working on the cards.

3. RESULTS

3.1 First the opinions expressed by the teachers were evaluated and interpreted by the researcher.

a. Spontaneous comments:

More than half of the test persons reported that they had imagined their own pupils. Some teachers commented on particular students which they noticed particulary with remarks such as: "That will not do him any good either." (Combination of low aptitude - high effort). The comments show that the teachers translate the shallow information into personal experiences and realistic school situations.

b. Comments based on the stimulus material:

The test persons were most doubtful about the cases in which only the aptitude information was given. Well over half of the test persons had problems with the evaluation of the fictitious student and were unsure in their judgement or tried to evade the problem with the aid of assumed effort.

For some test persons there was not enough information given on the students so that they felt a judgement was very difficult based on these conditions; added information as to traits of character and home environment was desired.

c. Comments suggesting a prediction:

Aptitude and effort were regarded as the main factors for achievement. For various test persons, the aptitude of the student corresponded with an upper achievement limit; The attainment of the highest achievement is then dependent on the effort willing to be exerted by students.

The comments which were made about the combination of information are particulary interesting. In half of the cases, the presumption that one factor had greater importance turned out not to be valid. The prognosis about the compensating ability of the factors was proved predominantly correct. As a rule it was stated that the factors could compensate for each other.

More than half of the test persons stated that they based their valuation mainly on the aptitude information. Only two reported that the information on effort was more important to them. All that implies that a two-staged strategy has been used: Starting with the factor which is regarded as principal, the information of the second factor is added to reach a judgement.

Altogether qualitative results of this type show that:

- the persons tested could cope well with the instructions
- no definite judgement could be given on the basis of only one piece of information
- even with two factors of information the judgement was regarded as indefinite
- aptitude and effort were regarded as very important achievement factors
- the test persons are only partially conscious of their routine reasoning of combining information.

3.2 Statistical analysis

The evaluation of all the test persons simultaneously follows the randomized-block-factorial-design (Kirk 1969). Figure 1 shows the mean values. The effort factor is significant and constitutes 25% of the total variance. The aptitude factor even constitutes 68% of the totale variance. The proportion of significant interaction, on the other hand, is 2%. An analysis of the components of the interaction (following Anderson 1970) shows that the non-linear component alone is significant.

116

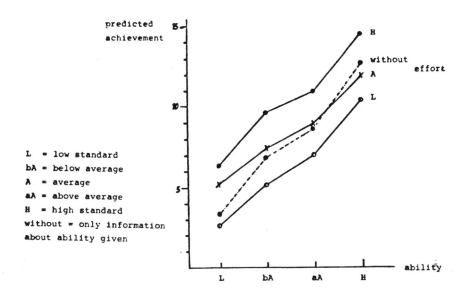

Fig. 1. Overall result of information integration

We are especially interested in the evaluation of each individual test person. The analysis followed a two-factor "Within-Subject Design" (Anderson 1976, p.685), in which each person was subject to all treatments. As an error term the average variance of the data within the cell of the design was used; the so-called "pooled error term". To test the multiplicative model, interaction variance was devided into a bilinear component and the residual variance. The calculation of the numerical values of the bilinear component followed Anderson (1970, p.157).

Table 1 shows the results for each person separately. In all cases both main effects were very significant. This was expected and indicates only that effort (A) and aptitude (B) were used by teachers as indicators for school achievement. Graphic illustrations reveal monotony: a higher degree of effort, or aptitude, on average leads to better prognosis. The relationship, however, is not linear; the stimuli were not observed as equally distant. The type of combination between both variables is shown in the form of interaction.

For seven teachers the interaction effect was not significant. The average model is confirmed in this case. These test persons assumed a stable influence of the factors: The effort has the same effect with low aptitude as it has with high aptitude.

The theory that judgement can be described by means of an additive model (Fishbein and Aijzen 1972) presumes that the first information results in a positive value, as does the following, and that each single piece of information contributes to the judgement in a quantitive way. If this were the case, then judgement based on only

	TEST PERS.	df=2 A		df=3 B		df=6 A×B		df=1 LIN×LIN		df=5 RES		TYPE
	1	77,80	**	95,07	**	2,73	*	3,71	ns	2,70	*	DIF
	2	78,25	**	491,11	**	5,36	**	5,36	*	5,35	**	DIF
	4	12,03	**	151,35	**	3,83	**	3,99	ns	3,80	*	DIF
	5	210,70	**	524,90	**	2,70	*	2,39	ns	2,76	*	DIF
	6	14,32	**	136,11	**	2,27	ns	0,17	ns	2,69	*	DIF
CS	7	1050,99	**	1326,55	**	27,88	**	12,16	**	31,03	**	DIF
	11	27,84	**	128,19	**	1,70	ns	1,55	ns	1,73	ns	ADD
	12	45,00	**	311,35	**	1,62	ns	2,79	ns	1,38	ns	ADD
	13	163,00	**	432,08	**	4,91	**	4,80	*	4,93	**	DIF
	14	95,13	**	49,43	**	4,00	**	6,75	*	3,44	*	DIF
SM	15	63,76	**	43,22	**	3,50	*	8,07	**	2,59	ns	MUL
	16	48,64	**	122,24	**	0,64	ns	0,25	ns	0,71	ns	ADD
	17	117,13	**	138,14	**	3,39	*	4,72	*	3,12	*	DIF
	8	38,86	**	128,07	**	0,41	ns	0,58	ns	0,37	ns	ADD
	9	342,16	**	468,61	**	7,27	**	0,071	ns	8,71	**	DIF
ST	10	384,12	**	269,12	**	9,62	**	33,35	**	4,87	*	DIF
	18	123,35	**	138,13	**	0,48	ns	0,005	ns	0,57	ns	ADD
	19	85,16	**	343,27	**	4,27	**	13,61	**	2,41	ns	MUL
	20	135,50	**	171,31	**	2,09	ns	1,42	ns	2,22	ns	ADD
	21	103,22	**	109,66	**	4,29	**	4,57	*	4,24	**	DIF
	22	228,00	**	542,66	**	4,38	**	16,05	**	2,04	ns	MUL
	23	79,40	**	1282,40	**	5,00	**	11,74	**	3,65	*	DIF
	24	187,35	**	121,21	**	4,78	**	18,23	**	2,09	ns	MUL
GS	3	162,92	**	293,80	**	11,59	**	2,89	ns	13,33	**	DIF
	25	16,91	**	19,06	**	3,28	*	16,73	**	0,59	ns	MUL

```
TYPE = Type of Information Integration      ** = p  < .01
DIF  = Differential Type                     * = p  < .05
ADD  = Additive Type                        ns = not significant
MUL  = Multiplicative Type
CS   = Comprehensive School            SM = Secondary Modern School
ST   = Secondary Technical School      GS = Grammar School
```

Table 1. Results of the variance analysis

one information factor (here: aptitude) would have to be lower in any case, than when two separate factors of information were given (aptitude and effort).

The figures show for all test persons that the judgement line, which was based only on information of aptitude, does not fall below the other lines. It intersects the other lines in such a manner that the following interpretation can be drawn: The test persons on the whole presumed with low aptitude a lower and with high aptitude a higher effort. (Except persons number 1, 10, 21, 23).

In a multiplicative model only the linear part of the interaction should be significant and the lines should spread out to the right like a fan: The higher the aptitude the stronger the effect of the effort on the prognosis. With five teachers (persons number 15, 19, 22, 24, 25) only the linear part of the interaction is significant. The lines do not run parallel. Only with four of them do the lines run close to the form of a fan. These teachers believe that with high ability a strong effort has greater effects on the achievement than with less able pupils.

There remains a large number of test persons with whom the non-linear part of the interaction is significant. Their judgements are to be described as differentially weighted models, since the weighting of the information combinations does not exclusively run in a linear fashion. There are six cases in which only the non-linear part of the interactive effect is significant, and eight cases in which both components reach the significance level. Various individual patterns occur. Five test persons considered the influence of effort as strongest with average aptitude. One teacher, on the contrary, regarded the influence of effort with average aptitude as less important in comparison to high or low aptitude.

In addition there is the extreme form of judgement from test person number six who saw at the two lowest levels of capability an average effort as more successful than a higher effort. This teacher seemed to believe that with lower aptitude an above average effort results in lower efficiency.

4. DISCUSSION

This paper has investigated by means of individual cases - but with the aid of quantitative and statistical methods - the thought processes of teachers integrating two kinds of information in making judgements of future pupil performance. It was shown that the way in which aptitude and effort information are combined in order to reach a judgement, varies substantially between different teachers. The relationship between predictors and criterium was monotone - with one exception. By no means did the integration follow the multiple regression model. Only in 24% of the cases did the judgements follow the average model. Here the contribution of the one variable to the criterium is independent from the distinction of the other. A compensation is possible. With 72% of the test persons the interaction effect between the indicator variables was significant. Within this group there were several different types. 16% of all persons judged (at least in tendency) in the manner of the multiplicative model in which the effect of the one variable increases with the presence of the other.

On the other hand, a further 20% considered the influence of effort to be strongest with average aptitude. One test person went even so far as to give a lower prognosis with lower aptitude and high effort than with low aptitude and average effort. Other judgement patterns were difficult to identify.

On the whole, the findings clearly run contrary to the results of the study of Kun and others (1974) and Anderson and Butzin (1974), which concluded from tests with adults that aptitude and effort information were used according to a multiplicative pattern.

From the verbal comments of the test persons, one can assume that the teachers did not process the information simultaneously but sequentially. First of all, the most important information is used, then the second information is taken into account. Aptitude is the most important information, because it contains a statement about a stable disposition. The information about effort then states in which way the persons can effectively control their dispositions. This two-staged process can be interpreted in two different ways:

a. The person processes the aptitude information and bases his/her final judgement upon the effort information.

b. A judgement is rendered on the basis of aptitude information and is corrected in respect of the differences offered by the second information.

One could possibly test this by means of presenting the persons with both factors of information in different sequences, asking them to give judgements after each one. The result, that the teachers' judgements are not, as a rule, based on the compensatory model of regression analysis, does not of course imply that their judgements are more valid than a statistical regression analysis.

REFERENCES

Anderson, N.H. (1970). Functional Measurement and Psychological Judgement. *Psychological Review, 77,* 53-170.

Anderson, N.H. (1974. Cognitive Algebra. In: Berkowitz, L. (Ed.). *Advances in Experimental Social Psychology, Vol.7,* Nw York: Academic Press.

Anderson, N.H. (1976). How Functional Measurement can Yield Validated Interval Scales of Mental Quantities.*Journal of Applied Psychology, 61,* 677-692.

Anderson, N.H. (1981). *Foundations of Information Integration Theory.* New York: Academic Press.

Anderson, N.H. & Butzin, C.A. (1974). Performance = Motivation x Ability: An Integration Theoretical Analysis. *Journal of Personality and Social Psychology, 30,* 598-604.

Fishbein, M. & Aijzen, I. (1972). Attitudes and Opinions. *Annual Review of Psychology, 23,* 487-544.

Hofer, M. (1986). *Sozialpsychologie erzieherischen Handelns.* Göttingen: Verlag für Psychologie Dr. C.J. Hogrefe.

Kirk, R. (1969). *Experimental Designs: Procedures for the Behavioral Sciences.* Belmont, Calif.: Brooks / Cole.

Kun, A. Parsons, J. & Ruble, D.N. (1974). Development of Integration Processes Using Ability- and Effort-Information to Predict Outcome. *Developmental Psychology, 10,* 721-732.

Rathje, H. (1982). *Untersuchungen zur Integration von schülerbezogenen Leistungsfaktoren im prognostischen Urteil von Lehrern.* Unveröffentlichte Diplomarbeit. Technische Universität Braunschweig.

Wilkening, F. (1979). Combining of Stimulus Dimensions in Childrens' and Adults' Judgements of Area: An Information Integration Analysis. *Developmental Psychology, 15,* 25-33.

RESEARCH ON ASSESSMENT PROCESS IN "NATURAL" CONDITIONS

Jean Paul Rapaille
Laboratoire de Pédagogie Expérimentale
Université de Liège
Belgium

ABSTRACT

Research on assessment process has been conducted so far in an indirect way, mainly by using experimental methods. The present research based on the "thinking aloud procedure" makes possible direct access to the thinking processes of teachers while correcting and assessing pupils' written work. The advantage of this method is also that it takes into account teachers' usual working conditions. These conditions are specified.

The theoretical framework of this research is the "model of assessment behavior" developed by Noizet and Caverni (1978).

Subjects are teachers in Belgian secondary schools, mainly in mother tongue. Teachers' comments were audio-taped. The data were submitted to five content analyses. Macro-analysis was used to clarify the general structure of the recording and the procedures used by teachers. Functional analysis was used to classify teachers' remarks into categories based upon the functions that the former play in the process of correction and assessement. Sequential analysis made it possible to identify patterns of behavior which occured repeatedly in a recording. Analysis of "verbiage" ("énonciation" in French) showed the effect that the requirement to think aloud had on the teachers' remarks and showed the teacher's attitude towards his pupils and his own statements. Finally, correlations between the results of previous analyses and the data collected from pupils' work were studied by micro-analysis. This latter analysis makes it possible to observe in detail the process of correction and assessment.

Provisional results are briefly presented.

Is it possible to study the process of correction and assessment of pupils' work without changing the usual conditions of teachers' work? This is the focus of our research (1).

1. THEORETICAL FRAMEWORK OF RESEARCH

The starting point of this question lies in a book published in 1978 by G. Noizet and J.P. Caverni entitled Psychology of scholastic assessment (Psychologie de l'évaluation scolaire). These authors present a model of "assessment behavior" which is explained and justified. This model has already been proposed at the International Congress of Educational Sciences, Paris, 1973 (Amigues et al., 1975). With this model the authors tried to integrate the numerous results of research conducted by a team of the University of Provence (France). They propose a general framework in which they discuss the assessment determinants, their interrelations and their place of impact. Their aim was to go beyond the simple recording of assessment defects in order to reach the determinants and processes of assessment behavior.

Their model will be briefly presented here. For more information and for further theoretical and experimental proofs, the reader may refer to the above-mentioned publication. The authors' terminology is preserved by the use of a literal translation.

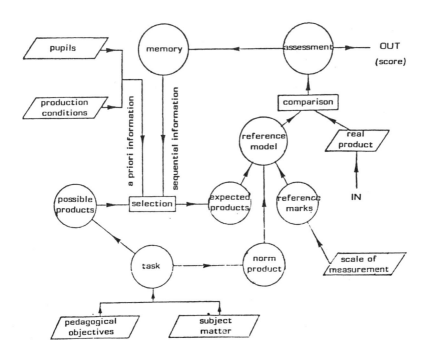

Figure 1 : Noizet and Caverni's model of assessment behaviour

Let us briefly comment figure 1: from the pedagogical objectives and the subject matter of the course (corps de connaissance), a task (tâche) is constructed: i.e. a question to be asked or an exercise to be given to the pupils. This task may be simple or complex. From this specific task, a norm product (produit-norme) and a set of possible products (produits possibles) are built up. The norm product is the most accurate answer. The set of possible products starts at the "no answer" level and ends at the "perfect answer" level. A selection among these possible products is made according to the information available about pupils (producteurs) and about production conditions (conditions de production). That clearly means that the teacher will not expect the same range of products from pupils of the first as of the sixth grade of secondary school, from pupils attending a "good" or a "weak" school, from gifted or less gifted pupils. Production conditions refer for instance to time limitation or to the availability of tools such as dictionary, grammar and so on. This information is called a priori information (informations a priori). The selection leads to a set of expected products (produits attendus).

At the same time, the teacher slects either an ordinal or an inter-val scale and determines reference marks: These are e.g. A B C D E or 10 9 8 7... out of ten (repères sur une échelle de mesure).

The reference model (modèle de référence) is then elaborated by pairing the reference marks and the expected products.

All the above-mentioned operations occur before correcting starts. But they generally happen in an implicit way.

Correcting and assessing procedures consist of comparing (compara-teur) a real product (produit réel) - i.e. the pupil's answer - with the reference model. The comparison leads to a score (évaluation).

The score however does not remain neutral as far as further evalua-tions are concerned. This score is kept in mind by the teacher (mémoire) and can influence his expectations, thus the reference model. Each "comparison" is susceptible to modify the model. Therefore, this information is called sequential information (informations séquen-tielles). This type of information explains both anchor effects and order effects.

This model is briefly the model proposed by the research team of the University of Provence.

First we would like to make a comment on this model. It does not take into account characteristics of the task. One of these characte-ristics seems however specially important as far as the proposed model is concerned: for some tasks, it is possible to define very precisely the norm product (e.g. dictation or calculation), for others, the norm product can only be specified in a more indefinite manner (e.g. essay). The discrimination between these two types of tasks (in fact, these are the extremes of a continuum) leads to the proposal of two models of assessment behavior, as has been shown in another paper (Rapaille, 1980).

All research conducted by the above-mentioned team follows the same procedure. As pointed ou by Noizet et Caverni (1978), the principle is very simple: it consists of choosing, for example, the same series of pupils' written work and having these corrected and assessed by several correctors under different conditions. The work can be real - i.e. written by pupils - or constructed by researchers. By description of appropriate statistics, significant differences are brought to light and explained by determinants or underlying processes.

This procedure has yielded very interesting results but one can raise some questions about their validity in relation to the usual conditions of teachers' work. Noizet and Caverni (1978) are aware of this fact when they raise the problem of the representativeness of experimental conditions as against the usual conditions where assessments occur.

Many questions can indeed be raised when one knows that for most of the research:

1. teachers receive no information about the pupils who wrote the answers (except this information is the variable under treatment);
2. scores have no influence upon pupils' results and upon the teaching process;
3. most of pupils' work comes from external examinations (e.g. baccalaurèat);
4. no information is given with regard to examination circumstances;
5. in a few cases, work is specifically constructed for the research.

Although the authors are aware of these limitations, they try to resolve these within the frame of the experimental procedure, i.e. comparing groups of teachers under fixed conditions (Noizet, Caverni, Fabre, 1977).

Beyond the criticisms of the experimental procedure, and even if it is conceivable that the experimentation constraints enjoin the acceptation of a few restrictions with respect to the usual conditions, it is important to wonder whether the study of the correction and assessment process can be satisfied by an indirect approach. As Rimoldi (1961) already pointed out in the early sixties when conducting research on problem-solving processes, "it is always possible to vary experimental conditions. stimulations, controls, and so on, in order to scrutinize answers, but this only leads to indirect information about the process... Analysis of the answers in not sufficient to establish the truth of inferences about the process. It is necessary to approach as close as possible the processes before stating hypotheses or postulating mediating variables in order to explain the answers".

More recently, the debate around the choice of models of analysis that has been raised in the study area of teacher thinking as well as in the study of judgment and choice processes, proceeds, in our opinion, from a similar desire to get a closer view of the processes (see e.g. Einborn et al, 1979; Yinger and Clark, 1982).

We tried therefore to set up a procedure which would help in studying the correction and assessment process with respect to teachers' usual conditions of work.

The usual conditions of work are first shown. They should conform to the following characteristics:

1. the teacher has constructed the tasks to be given to the pupils;
2. these tasks are carried out by the pupils in the usual class conditions;
3. the teacher has to correct pupils' work and to assess these in the usual way;
4. scores must have consequences for pupils and for the subsequent teaching processes and decisions.

Taking these characteristics into account, the most appropriate method proved to be the "thinking aloud procedure". Although data collected thus are considered less reliable by some authors (Nisbett and Wilson, 1977), Ericsson and Simon (1980) have analysed conditions and limitations of verbalization methods and have shown that such data are indeed reliable under certain circumstances. In the next section, the "thinking aloud procedure" as used by the present author, will be developed.

2. PROCEDURE AND METHODS OF ANALYSIS

Subjects participating in this research are teachers working in grades 7 to 9 at Belgian high schools. Most of them teach the mother tongue, but others teach maths or science. These teachers were asked to correct and assess the school work of their own pupils without changing anything in their usual way of doing this. They were asked to think aloud and to record themselves on a tape. These recordings and the pupils' work were collected. Recordings were entirely transcripted and pupils work was xeroxed. Each recording was then submitted to five content analyses which gave different and additional information.

2.1. Macro-analysis brings into light procedure followed by the teacher when correcting and assessing, and shows the general structure of the recording.

Regarding the procedure followed by the teacher, the researcher will wonder whether the teacher has corrected pupil by pupil or question by question; whether he has determined a norm product; whether he has established a reference model; and so on.

Regarding the general structure of the recording, the researcher will determine, beyond the distinction between pupils and questions, the times of reflection, the flashbacks to work corrected previously, provisional conclusions, etc. These specific incidents in the correcting process are often introduced by typical words (e.g. then, so,...) or idioms (e.g. it could be said,...) mostly idiosyncratic.

2.2. Functional analysis is used to classify teachers' remarks into categories based upon functions that these play in the correction and assessment process. Sixteen categories have been built. At the outset they refer to Noizet and Caverni's model. But some of them have been modified and some others have been added.

Here are examples of categories:
- referring to the objective;
- referring to the task, the question
- referring to external noise;
- referring to norm product;
- information "picking up";

- assessment;
- referring to sequential information;
- referring to a priori information;
- etc.

All these categories are divided into subcategories which specify the functions.

Silences are also categorized.

2.3. Sequential analysis is based upon functional analysis. It aims to discover patterns of behavior which occur repeatedly in the recording. Another approach considers the perturbations of a theoretical sequence that can be built if considering the assessment process as a rational one.

2.4. *The analysis of verbiage ("énonciation")* is proposed to answer questions such as: Is the teacher involved in his own remark? And how? "How are the verbalizations influenced by the communicative relation between reporter and reseacher?" (Huber and Mandl, 1984).(This question remains relevant for our research even if this relation is indirect: in this case, through recording.) How are pupils depicted? What attitudes are adopted by the teachers towards their own statements? Etc.

To find an answer, we turned to linguistics, particularly towards the theory of verbiage ("énonciation") proposed and developed by Emile Benveniste (1966). This theory is one of the foundations of what is now called pragmatics. Although it is not possible in the frame of this paper to enter into all the details concerning this rather complex theory, we can roughly describe it in the following way: verbiage ("énonciation") is the process by which the linguistic signs are actualized in particular circumstances of time and space and are assumed by the one who is speaking. The study of verbiage ("énonciation") can be applied to discover several linguistic cues within discourse, i.e. cues of the speaker, cues of the listener, cues of the relationship between these persons (e.g. speech acts), cues of the attitudes of the speaker towards his own statements, etc. In this paper, we used some elements of this theory for our analysis. But for better understanding, we used the traditional grammar terminology instead of the specific one.

When analysing the recordings, the following linguistic data were systematically picked up:

- personal pronouns;
- given names and surnames;
- familiar expressions;
- possessive pronouns;
- possessive adjectives;

- modal adverbs;
- modal expressions;
- adjectives used in a modal way;
- interjections.

Changes in tenses used are also noted.

To illustrate the method of analysis, we give an example of personal pronouns referring to the corrector (2).

Here are five sentences taken from the recording of a maths teacher. In some instances, we give two translations. The first one then is literal, the second one is more accurate.

a) "<u>Je</u> vais donner cinq points pour la définition en langage littèraire et cinq points pour la dèfinition en langage mathématique.
   "<u>I</u> am going to assign five marks for the definition in common language and five marks for the definition in mathematical language."

b) "<u>Je</u> vais quand même lui enlever un petit point parce qu'il faut quand même être précis dans la forme."
   "<u>I</u> am nevertheless going to take off a little mark because the formulation has nevertheless to be unambiguous."

c) "<u>Nous</u> ne tiendrons pas compte de sa deuxième présentation."
   "<u>We</u> will not take into account his second answer."

d) "Heureusement qu'<u>on</u> ne corrige pas l'orthographe."
   "Fortunately, <u>one</u> does not correct spelling."
   "Fortunately, <u>spelling</u> is not corrected."

e) "On sent tout de suite la différence, hein."
"One immediately feels the difference, doesn't one."
"The difference is obvious, isn't it."

The frequencies observed in the recording are as follows: three times "I", once "we", and five times "one". These frequencies are not very high although the work of twenty pupils have been corrected and although the recording lasted fifteen minutes. Therefore it is interesting to observe the circumstances in which these pronouns have been used. Hypotheses are also put forward to explain the use of the various pronouns.

The first sentence (a) occurs at the beginning of the recording just before starting the correction. The teacher specifies the weights of each question. It is a personal decision, and he therefore uses "I".

In the second sentence (b)... "I" also indicates that the teacher assumes a decision. But the circumstances of this use differ from in (a). In this case "I" used by the teacher when correcting the work of the ninth pupil. He has to assign a score, but he is wondering whether he should take into account a misspelling by the pupil. He has previously stated that such a mistake would not be taken into account (d). There is a discrepancy. Indeed, the use of "I" indicates that the corrector assumes the decision in spite of an inconsistency. However, it can also be considered as a cue to subjectivity within the decision-making (3).

It is also worth while to note that sentence (b) contains three modal words: twice "nevertheless", and "little". The latter is of particular interest because it shows off an attempt to minimize the penalization verbally.

The next sentence (c) contains "we". "We" usually refers to two or more persons including the one who is speaking. But, in this case of course, there is no one else present to whom the teacher could refer. "We" refers to the teacher, and only to him: it is the so called "royal we". The circumstances of the use are very illuminating. A pupil gave two answers to the same question. The first has been considered accurate by the teacher; the second is not as good as the first. The teacher decides not to consider the second answer. The use of a first person pronoun indicates that the teacher is assuming the decision. But, using the "royal we", he moreover shows that he is making a "royal gift" to the pupil.

In the fourth sentence (d), the pronoun "one" is used. As a subject, "one" is used more frequently in French than in English. It is considered as an indefinite pronoun" and it may stand for "I", "he/she", "they" or "we". By using this word, it may be that the teacher is referring to an habit or to a decision of the teachers' team. It has perhaps been decided by the latter not to take into account misspellings. The use of "one" instead of "I" can be interpreted as an attempt of the teacher to protect himself from blame from others in account of his behavior (and may be one of the "others" could be identified as the researcher who will listen to the recording).

In the last sentence (e), "one" seems once again to stand for "we". But with whom would the teacher "feel the difference"? It cannot be with other teachers as in the previous sentence because pupils' work is corrected by only one teacher. The only plausible hypothesis to explain the use of "one" is that the teacher tries to associate the one who will listen to the recording, the researcher. Just like the teacher, the reseacher will notice the difference between this answer and the previous one. The noticing of the difference cannot be contested: it is confirmed without any doubt by the modal "immediately". Our hypothesis is strengthened by the use of an end phrase. The teacher seeks to get approval from the person who will listen to him, through this. But what is the function of such usage? In my opinion, it is a way for the teacher to feel reassured about the accuracy of his own judgment.

This is only a short example of what can be obtained when analysing selected linguistic data. But it is sufficient to throw light on the influence - within certain limits of confidence - of the teacher-researcher relation upon verbalization.

2.5. Micro-analysis applies to pupils' answers. The first stage is the reconstruction of what is called by Noizet and Caverni the "norm product". It has te be done - when possible - with the help of the pupils' answers, their scores and the recording. The "norm product" is then split into different components. For example, here is a "norm product" in a mathematics test. The question was to define mathematically the cartesian product of two sets:
$$A \times B = \{(a,b) \mid a \in A, b \in B\}$$
This answer included fifteen components (following =).

The second stage deals with the pupils' answers. These answers may also be split into various components.

We compare, then, the components of each answer with the components of the norm product. Only those components which are different have been considered.

In the next stage, we relate the score of each answer to the components. We can therefore observe some differences in the way of considering certain inaccurate components. Even differences in taking into account a same component can be observed. For example, an inaccurate component leads to a penalization for one pupil, but not for another.

The last stage deals with the explanation of such differences in treatment. In order to give an answer, we move back once again to teacher's verbalizations. With the help of "functional" analysis and of the analysis of verbiage ("énonciation"), we try to determine what has caused the difference in the treatment of the components. For example, an inaccurate component is not taken into consideration because of a previous piece of information given by the teacher at the beginning of the correction of the present pupil's answer (halo effect) Or, an external component can lead to a penalization even though all components are correct (see sentence b).

The micor-analysis is the most interesting because it makes possible a very fine understanding of the correction and assessment process.

3. CONCLUSIONS

This research is still in progress. The results presented here are therefore provisional, - and thus are given briefly.
1. It is possible to study the correction and assessment process of pupils' work without changing the usual conditions of the teacher's work.

2. The "thinking aloud" method makes possible a direct approach to the study of the correction and assessment process.
3. Macro-analysis shows off different structures in the teachers' recordings. It has also been observed that no teacher defines a scoring table before starting the correction process and that most of them procede pupil by pupil even if several questions have been asked.
4. The "functional" analysis reveals a frequent use of specific categories. As expected, these are "picking up of information", "comparing" and "assessing". The frequencies of these categories differ however significantly according to the task and to the teacher. Moreover, idiosyncratic behavior can be observed when we refer to subcategories.
5. So far, sequential analysis has only been used for one recording. This analysis has pointed out two patterns of behavior which occured repeatedly.
6. The analysis of verbiage ("énonciation") brings to light changes in verbalization when "abnormal" phenomena occur during the correction and assessment of pupils' work. It also makes it possible to record allusions to the researcher in almost all the recordings. Consequently, it is possible to specify the influence of the research procedure upon verbalization. Teachers' attitudes towards their own statements have also been studied. Some of them are self-confident, others are more cautious. Most of the time, the pupils are alluded to in the third person.
7. The micro-analysis has confirmed most of the disturbance factors of assessment that have been shown by the experimental method. But, above all, it enables the researcher to scrutinize the process in detail and to observe how these disturbing factors act. New phenoma have also been discovered: e.g. the "intra-copy sequential effect" and the "pro-active sequential effect".
8. Finally, the results of previous analyses have led to the elaboration of a more sophisticated model of assessment behavior. Particularly, we are in a position to clarify what happens at the "comparison" level in Noizet and Caverni's model.

A better understanding of the correction and assessment process is essential - as G. De Landsheere wrote (1974) - "for an ethically more accurate and scientifically more rigorous scholastic evaluation". It is hoped that the present research will serve this aim, and that pre-and in - service teacher training would be able to make use of our results so that teachers may be aware of the process when it occurs during the correction and assessment of pupils' work and that this may eventually lead to a change in their marking routine.

REFERENCES

Amiges, R., Bonniol, J.J., Caverni, J.P., Fabre, J.M. & Noizet, G. (1975). Le comportement d'évaluation des productions scolaires: à la recherche d'un modèle explicatif. *Bulletin de Psychologie*, 28, 318, 793-799.
Benveniste, E. (1966). *Problèmes de linguistique générale*, I. Paris, Gallimard.

De Landsheere, G.(1974).*Evaluation continue et examens*. Précis de docimologie. Paris, Nathan & Liège, Labor.

Einborn, H.J., Kleinmuntz, D.N. & Kleinmuntz, B. (1979). Linear regression and process-training models of judgment. *Psychological Review*, 86, 5, 465-485.

Ericsson, K.A. & Simon, H.A. (1980). Verbal reports as data. *Psychological Review*, 87, 3, 215-251.

Huber, G.L. & Mandl, H. (1984). Access to teachers cognitions: problems of assessment and analysis. In: Halkes, R & Olson, J.K. (Eds) *Teacher thinking : a new perspective on persisting problems in Education*. Lisse, Swets & Zeitlinger.

Lampert, M. (1986). Teachers' strategies for understanding and managing classroom dilemmas. In: Ben-Peretz, M., Bromme, R. and Halkes, R. (eds.) *Advances of research on teacher thinking*,Lisse: Swets and Zeitlinger.

Nisbett, R.E. & Wilson, T.D. (1977) Telling more than we can: verbal reports on mental processes. *Psychological Review*, 84, 3, 231-259.

Noizet, G. & Caverni, J.P. (1978). *Psychologie de l'évaluation scolaire*, Paris, P.U.F.

Noizet, G., Caverni, J.P. & Fabre, J.M. (1977). Notes sur l'expérimentation hors du laboratoire en docimologie. *Psychologie française*, 22, 1-2, 55-60.

Rapaille, J.P. (1980). Le comportement d'évaluation : un ou deux modèles? *Bulletin de psychologie scolaire et d'orientation*, 4, 149-155.

Rimoldi, H.J. (1961). L'étude des processus psychologiques. *Le travail humain*, 24, 3-4, 225-234.

Wagner, A.C. (1984). Conflict in consciousness: Imperative cognitions can leed to knots in thinking. In: Halkes, R and Olson, J.K. (Eds.), *Teacher thinking a new perspective on persisting problems in education*, Lisse, Swets & Zeitlinger.

Yinger, R.J. & Clark, C.M. (1982). *Understanding teachers' judgments about instruction : the task, the method, and the meaning*. East Lansing, Institute for Research on Teaching, Research Series 121.

NOTES

1. Our research started out of the Teacher Thinking study field. It can however be related to this particular field in many ways: The main topic of the study focusses on the mental processes of the teachers. The thinking aloud procedures is one of the methods used in some teacher thinking studies. The correction and assessment task belongs to the post-interactives phase. And so on. Forthcoming papers will show the links between our research and the knowledge acquired in the teacher thinking study area.
2. We emphasized this analysis method at the request of the ISATT 1985 Conference Steering Comittee.
3. This discrepancy can be identified to what is called by M. Lampert (1986) a "dilemma", i.e., conflict occuring when teachers face a choice between equally desirable but conflicting practices, or to what A. Wagner (1984) defined as a "knot", i.e. a conflict in

consciousness arising from the perceived or anticipating violation of subjective imperatives, where subjective imperatives are cognitions which for the individual himself/herself have the character of a subjectively compulsory "MUST" or "MUST NOT". The discrepancy evoked in sentence (b) is in agreement with the type V knot of Wagner's taxonomy: a counterimperative knot, which occurs when an imperative collides with its own counterimperative.

INFORMATION TECHNOLOGY AND TEACHER ROUTINES: LEARNING FROM THE MICROCOMPUTER

J.K. Olson
Queen's University
Kingston, Ontario
Canada

1. INTRODUCTION: COMPUTERS AS A SUBJECT

We have undertaken case studies of forms of microcomputer in elementary and high schools using a variety of data collecting methods (interview, journal, stimulated recall, observation, repertory grid, and questionnaire).

The schools we studies were selected from a list of about 30 schools in a large suburban school board which were conducting action - research projects. We selected these schools in order to include different levels of schooling and different aspects of the curriculum. In each school we interviewed the principal teacher and one or more teachers involved in the action research. For each school we collected information about the history of computer use in the school and the background of the teachers. The information we collected was used to produce a policy oriented report to the Ontario Ministry of Education (Olson, J. and Eaton, S.,1986).

From the data we collected we constructed eight accounts of computer use which we have divided into two groups. The first group comprises four cases in which the computer is used as a way of teaching computers as a new subject in the elementary school curriculum. Within the subject domain we find activities like: programming, low resolution graphics and analysis of software. Our second group comprises four cases in which computers are being used as a teaching aid. Here we find drill and practice, tutorial, simulation and word processing activities carried on within the framework of existing subjects. The way the computer is used here is heavily influenced by existing plans for the scope and sequence of the subject and ways of teaching the subject; but there are interesting ways in which computer use affects these curriculum elements.

As we do not have space here to treat both of these areas, we will discuss how teachers use the computer as part of a new subject which they call computer "awareness" or computer "literacy" (see also Ragsdale, 1982; Amarel, 1984). Although some distinguish between these two terms, the common thread is that these teachers are experimenting with a new subject and with ways of teaching this subject within existing constraints of curriculum and resources. They have volunteered to do the additional work of teaching about computers and have been granted the use of at least one Apple 2e, one green screen and a disk drive; most of these teachers have printers and colour monitors, and some have peripherals like joy sticks and Koala pads.

There is no formal curriculum for the new subject, Teachers are making it up as they go along according to their own interests, and they express the uncertainties that come with such "unlicenced" practice. There are many questions that must be left aside here although they are discussed in the report of this research: Why these teachers? Why have they been allowed to experiment so freely? Why the computer promotion by their school aboard? Why choose the particular activities they have as definitive of computer awareness?

All four teachers we are considering adopted a similar strategy for using computers in the classroom which we call the "teach yourself" routine. We will outline the main features of this routine and describe the difficulties teachers had in maintaining it. We hope to show why teachers use the "teach yourself" routine and to see what their response to the difficulties of the strategy tells us about their approach to "newness" itself as an element in working life in the classroom.

2. THE TEACH YOURSELF ROUTINE

The routine has these composite features:
 a. The computer subject goes on all the time. Students go to the computer based on a rota; students are there while the teacher is teaching the rest of the class.
 b. Students engage in learning the subject mostly by programming the computer, but also through running assorted software.
 c. The teacher teaches the rest of the class and aims at minimal contact with the "class" working at the computer.
 d. To ensure minimal disruption and delay, the teacher may offer whole class instruction in key computer moves or refer students to manuals, and the teacher relies on computer "Whiz-kids" to help those who are "stuck" and to tutor their peers. The teacher also asks students to rely on the manual to help them "debug" their own problems.
 e. The teacher relies on certain students to preview software.
 f. The teacher chooses software and activities that require minimal teacher support. Thus Basic is favoured over Logo as a programming activity because they think there are more and more simpler steps in Basic.
 g. Access to the computer is part of the classroom reward structure.

These are the mean features of the strategy as teachers dexribed it,
Why such a strategy?

First we should say, and the teachers would say, that this
strategy is not new. It is an extension of self-directed seat work
that teachers are quite familiar with. There are many similarities
with sending children to the library to do library research using the
librarian as a support rather than "peer tutors",except that instead
of using software students use reference materials. These teachers
have taken a familiar strategy "off the shelf" and have used it to
support student self directed work on the computer.

Given that normally only one machine is available, it is not
surprising that teachers have chosen to "teach" the subject in
paralell with the teaching they have to do anyway, and given their
idea that doing the subject is doing programming, access to the
machine is critical. There are, of course, other ways of conceiving
of doing computers as a subject, but these teachers all chose doing
programming, or becoming familiar with types of software and
peripherals as their way of defining it.

We can think of reasons why it is not surprising that teachers
proceed this way. They find that some students are teaching
themselves anyway, and these few students stand out in the eyes of
these teachers. They are interested in computing and eager to explore
software. They seem to know how to "debug" it. Teachers see them as
members of the computer generation; it is a subject that is part of
their culture. Doing computers, one might say, a recess and lunch
time activity that now has a legitimate place in the classroom. The
new subject is one which has come from the student culture itself; so
these teachers seem to think. Some teachers feel they are on the
outside of it in some ways,and this feeling depends on whether or
not the teacher is a computer "buff" or expert, but even so the
sophisticated teachers realized that some of their students could do
things with the computer that they could not. It is thus not
surprising that teachers are prepared to let students teach
themselves computer skills.

Teachers are also short of time. How do you add another subject
and a non-licenced one at that on already heavy work? (see also
Shinegold, 1983). The teachers let the students work mostly on their
own thus freeing them to teach the rest of the class what had to be
taught. In any event teachers found themselves in the middle of two
lessons rather than teaching the main class, with the computer"class"
teaching itself. They were called upon to do two things at once;
much more so than they had hoped; and more so than normal when the
teach yourself method is used in other contexts, say in library work
or using work stations.

We thus became interested in why the teach yourself routine had
not worked as well as in other contexts. We found a number of
reasons.
1.   The programming required more support than teachers had imagined
     it would. Students could not handle messages like "syntax

error"; no teacher ever said "syntax error." Teachers give positive feedback which has a "warming" affect, but the machines gave negative feedback which could not be interpreted, and was read by students as unhelpful and cool.

2. Computer literate peers did not tutor. They would "debug" and move on, and the students they "helped" were not any the wiser about why they had run into problems.
3. Some students found that handbooks were difficult to use.
4. Some students had difficulty reading text on the screen.
5. Studens bacame bored with software they could not control, and some types of software were not that interesting as such. Logo was cited as a poor performer in the "teach yourself" strategy by teachers.
6. Students were posing management problems that could not be quickly dealt with like other seatwork situations.

Teachers were not able to do two things at once without flaw, and we saw examples of "slippage" that came about because the strategy did not work as planned. These incidents give a sense of wat "slippage" was like:

1. One student entered programming lines incorrectly, and was left for up to an hour before receiving corrective feedback by the teacher.
2. Another student entered a poem with a particular shape but did not know how to paragraph and ended up with a print-out quite unlike what she had hoped to get. What she saw on the screen was not what was printed because she lacked control of the word processing.
3. A student tried to produce a graphic without her coordinates which had been left at home; she guessed at the coordinates.

Teachers were aware of the "slippage". They could see it in the videotapes we showed them; yet they said they were satisfied with their efforts at running the "teach yourself" approach to computers as a new subject although they were frustrated that the strategy had not worked as well as they had hoped it would; that is that students would teach themselves. Because the students at the computer needed more support than anticipated teachers found themselves having to reconstrue the teach yourself routine. It became important to understand how the teachers construed the modified teach yourself routine. We shall call this modified approach the "two things at once" routine. It is, of course, common for teachers to do two things at once in the classroom, but we were interested in this special variant which involves the use of computers.

3. HOW TEACHERS CONSTRUED THE "TWO-THINGS-AT-ONCE" ROUTINE

We wanted to explore in greater depth how teachers construed their having to do two things at once and to do this we asked them to construe elements of computer use which involved episodes of delay and interruption and which required teachers to intervene in student activity. An example of an elements is: "One student does not want to work with another student at the computer." We asked them to sort these episodes (elements) into categories, and to subsequently construe all of the episodes using their own categories(Olson and Reid, 1982). We found the following constructs to be common:

1.   teacher-resolved vs. student-resolved episodes.
2.   student vs. technology problem episodes.
3.   quickly resolved vs. slowly resolved episodes.
4.   existing rules applied vs. new rules required.
5.   routine responses adequate vs. judgements called for.

From our analysis of the constructs we began to appreciate the problems teachers hoped to avoid in adopting the"teach yourself" routine in the first place, and the problems caused for them by its partial breakdown into their having to do two things at once. We could see that the "teach yourself" routine was intended to minimize interruptions from the computer "class", and that their views about software and machinery were based on their constructs of speedy resolution of classroom problems using existing routines. Indeed, for these teachers complex software was not the issue in the two things at once routine, complex student reaction to it was. These teachers did not want to have to invent new procedures for teaching; they hoped that the existing procedures would work. Ironically, the very way they defined doing computers as a subject ensured that their existing routines would not work well. The level of teacher support demanded by programming simply went well beyond what they were used to giving in other "teach yourself" situations, and although they thought that the peer tutoring would sustain the routine, peers did not tutor each other; computer literate student helped "debug" situations where they could, when they could, and the teacher had to be called in often as well.

We can see now how these teachers have "installed" the computer subject in their classrooms. The teacher reaction to newness might be put this way. The subject was taught using a well tried approach: the "teach yourself" strategy. The effect of the unforeseen elements of the new subject (for example, negative feedback of an imprecise kind) was that the well tried methods did not work well, and although the teachers professed satisfaction with them, we were not so sure they really were satisfied, nor sure whether they ought to be satisfied.

4.   EXPRESSIVE AND INSTRUMENTAL ELEMENTS OF TEACHING

Why did they express satisfaction? We have here an apparent paradox which we felt ought to be resolved. In spite of the fact that the teach yourself routine did not work as well as teachers hoped, they were prepared to continue with this conception and way of teaching the subject. They found that students enjoyed the new subject in spite of the difficulties of the "teach yourself" strategy. The teachers felt that the difficulties were worth the trouble because they enjoyed the children's pleasure at having a computer in their room. The teachers construed the using a computer as their way of being "modern", of expressing something about the kind of teacher they were. This purpose seemed to overrule the evidence that their chosen way of teaching about a new subject had not worked out that well. Their mild disquiet about the "slippage" was countered by the thought that their students had made significant gains in computer literacy. Evidence for these claims, however, seemed sparse, and negative evidence was ignored while claims about progress were made with little positive evidence available.

Why did the teachers act this way? Following the work of Harre (1979), we believe that teaching activities can be considered from two points of view: the expressive and the instrumental. Expressive teaching acts convey messages about how the teacher wishes to be seen by his/her students. As Harre suggests it is through the expressive dimension of our actions that we convey messages about the sort of person for which we wish to be taken. Instrumental teaching acts are those we commonly associate with the classroom--the "processes" of the "process-product" paradigm; acts which are directed as fostering learning; what we normally attend to in studying the influence of the teachers on the outcomes of classroom activity.

We argue that exclusive focus on instrumental acts of teaching is an insufficient basis from which to make sense of what happens in classrooms. One must understand both the expressive and instrumental dimensions of teaching activities. In our case we could not make sense of the paradox we had uncovered without appreciating the expressive dimension of teaching. We believe that the teachers value the computer as a symbol to be used expressively by them to enhance their standing in the eyes of the students, parents and principal. The minor difficulties in achieving computer literacy could be ignored for the time being since they were not as important as the expressive process. Let us consider how this is so.

These teachers spoke about the positive impact having a computer had on the class; how students were eager to use it; how much they enjoyed having it in the room. By having a computer in their room these teachers were able to say something about their interest in modern teaching methods and in the needs of their students, and about the relevance of their classroom to life outside it. The eight case studies reveal a common concern about the expressive dimension of using computers in the classroom. In the long run, of course, expressive and instrumental elements of teaching are linked, and as teachers work their way through the expressive dimensions of their task, it is likely that instrumental issues will receive more attention. How quickly the process occurs and how it might be facilitated are important further questions for research and policy (see Berg, 1983, O'Shea, 1984).

138

This study raises questions about how well existing routines can be modified to take advantage of new technologies; it also raises questions about what sustains these routines; what teachers have invested in them and how teachers can become more critical of the costs and benefits of the routines that they use.

5. ASSESSMENT OF ROUTINES AND PARADOXES OF TEACHING

Working with these teachers in the way we have involved them and us in a process of reflection-in-action (Schon, 1983). In confronting teachers with their practice we have asked them to consider the expressive and instrumental functions of their teaching; to bring to the foreground matters which often remain tacit. It has been said that action research is not an appropriate activity for teachers. Construed as "research" in the usual way, this claim is probably well founded. It is unrealistic to expect teachers to do research studies of the experimental or quasi-experimental type in their own class-rooms but it is essential that they subject their practice to critical, systematic reflection. We think this reflective process is in fact how action research ought to be construed--the careful consideration of specific elements of teaching, and that we ought to broaden how we construe research itself in education.

The systematic consideration of practice itself can yield the theories-in-action that are immanent in practice. As Schon (1983) has suggested tacit knowledge is not propositional knowledge, but is knowledge no less for that, and the recovery from practice of the theories implicit in the practice are what we take action research to be; thus verifying theory and practice in one process. In this study such collaborative action research has led to the identification and dissolution of a paradox. We think that apparently inconsistent or unusual practices might be usefully construed as paradoxical; that is "contrary to received opinion or expectation; sometimes with unfavourable connotation as being discordant with what is held to be established truth"(OED). Thus sometimes teachers appear to be doing things in ways contrary to orthodox opinion, and even their own espoused view.

Often teachers are viewed by outsiders as practising inconsistently when compared to certain ideologies. The teachers are said to be in the grip of a dilemma. In fact, what has happened is that the outsider often has perceived an apparent paradox and has failed to resolve it, or has not discovered the real paradoxes. It is not at all clear that teachers actually experience the dilemmas orthodoxy tends to make us think they experience.

Close attention to how teachers think about their practice is a way of surfacing and understanding paradoxes of practice. Some paradoxes are real; for example, the teacher may not be acting in accord with his/her own intentions. Other paradoxes may be only apparent; the teacher may be pursuing goals that are not those that are espoused, but valued nonetheless; at least by the teacher in relation to whom the practice is not paradoxical. Only orthodoxy renders the practice so. Thus the unusual practice seen in instrumental terms may appear paradoxical, but seen expressively is not paradoxical, at least not in relation to what the teacher is trying to do, and in relation to a holistic account of what teaching entails.

It is here, we believe, that the notion of expressive and instrumental dimensions of teaching is especially important. Teachers are conditioned by their education and by professional journals to pay attention to the instrumental dimensions of teaching as a way of assessing their practice; yet their practice cannot be other than paradoxical unless the expressive dimension is considered. As we saw in these cases, upon analysis of their practice, it became clear that expressive elements of their actions allowed us to account for the apparent paradox of persistence with ineffective teaching routines-- that is with the doing two things at once routine in spite of the difficulties that gave rise to. Such a routine left the teacher frustrated by interruption, yet in the absence of means to overcome these interruptions and wanting to continue to have students attend the computer "class" for expressive reasons, the teachers were prepared to continue with the routine. The paradox has disappeared.

Action research in the classroom enables teachers to explore paradoxes of practice and to learn from them more about what they value in practice and about the limits, and limitations of existing routines. In the cases we have been examining here the limits of the teach yourself routine can be clearly seen; such a routine does not effectively extend to teaching computers as a subject when construed as learning how to program. In discovering the limits of the routine, its limitations come to be known. As practice is recovered and analysed in this way there exists the possibility of a body of practical wisdom which could become the rational basis for practice istelf--a true educational theory based on practical wisdom derived from the interpretation of practice. This is the significance we attach to the research.

REFERENCES

Amarel, Marianne. (1983). "Classrooms and Computers as Instructional Settings." *Theory into Practice, 22*, 260-266.
Berg, Roger, (1983). "Resisting Change: What the Literature Says About Computers in the Social Studies Classroom." *Social Education*, 314-316.
Fraser, Rosemary et al. (Undated). "Learning Activities and Classroom Roles With and Without the Computer." ITMA Collaboration. University of Nottingham, Xerox.
Harre, R. (1979). *Social Being*. Oxford: University Press.
Olson, J. (in press). "Microcomputers and the Classroom Order." *New Education*. ERIC 245671.

Olson, J. and Eaton, S. (1986). *Case Studies of Microcomputers in the Classroom: Implications for Curriculum Design and Teacher Education.* Toronto: Ontario Ministry of Education.

Olson, J. & Reid, W. (1982). "Studying Innovations in Science Teaching: The Use of Repertory and Techniques in Developing a Research Strategy." *European Journal of Science Education, 4,* 193-201.

O'Shea, T. (1984). "The Open University Micros in Schools Project." CAL Research Group Technical Report No. 47.

Ragsdale, R. (1982). *Computers in the Schools: A Guide for Planning.* Toronto: OISE.

Schon, D. (1983). *The Reflective Practitioner.* New York: Basic Books.

Shenigold, K. (1981). *"Issues Related to the Implementation of Computer Technology in Schools: A Cross-Sectional Study."* Bank Street College of Education. Technical Report No.1.

PROFESSIONAL LITERACY, RESOURCEFULNESS AND WHAT MAKES TEACHING INTERESTING

Alan F. Brown
The Ontario Institute for Studies
in Education
The University of Toronto

SUMMARY

The purpose of this study was to understand what makes teaching interesting. To do this, we simply asked 22 teachers what they found satisfying, rewarding or stimulating and what was dull, bland or boring.
The analysis of their answers was done in two ways: (1) the substan-
tives of what they said and (2) the unique patterns of their thought
processes. The findings of the first analysis were familiar: Kids
are exciting and yard duty is tedious. The findings from the second
were surprising: Their self-estimates of quality of work life clearly
favoured those teachers whose ways of answering these questions showed
them to be (a) more resourceful in describing teaching and (b) more
articulate and aware of their own practical preferences, i.e., more
professionally literate. These findings are encouraging for persons
interested in teacher morale in that some previous studies carried out
for different purposes have demonstrated that series of workshops may
be deliberately designed to change those two variables.

INTRODUCTION

Quality of life, or when referenced to the workplace, quality of work
life (QWL), is of current interest particularly in management literature and research. Perhaps the interest arises out of the age old
evidence that it's cheaper to make a person feel good than to raise
pay. Whether or not either does affect output matters less in the
more professional levels of management and in the public service sec-
tor including teaching because in these tasks, quality of work life
itself becomes an output. If it's no place for you, you change it,
exit, or learn to put up with it one way or another. Thus quality of
work life as experienced by the teacher becomes as major a purpose of
the principal as did its earlier counterparts: dedication, organizational climate, commitment, morale, spirit, atmosphere, feeling tone,
vibes.
    Designing a program to improve the quality of work life--the main
purpose of good management (Stogdill 1965)--has engaged the attention
of consultant and researcher alike. In times of economic restraint,
university underfunding and the reticent marketplace, it seems that

any plan that looks promising is worth the attempt. Unfortunately this is usually not so. What may look promising appears so because its attention is directed more to conditions of the workplace than to the worker. The workplace is visible, is objective. The worker's intentions, wills, feelings are idiosyncratic, are subjective. Being less visible becomes seen as less accessible and thus researchers are less inclined to study it. Accordingly, the design of programs becomes based more upon the external manifestations of quality of work life than upon the cause itself. Inspired perhaps by Peters and Watermans' concept of excellence (1982), school systems may elect only those programs that are readily effected; changing how a person feels about work may mean changing how that person feels more than changing the workplace.

There have been several reports on how life at the school affects those who work there, e.g., Goodlad's *A place called school* (1983) and Batcher's *Emotion in the classroom* (1981). The study reported here examines not only what teachers find interesting and exciting or tedious and draining but why they may find it so.

A STRUCTURE FOR THOUGHTS BEHIND ACTIONS

Structured reflection is a term that has been used to describe some of our previous work trying to set out teacher's definitions of teacher effectiveness and teacher promotability (Brown 1984, Brown 1982, Rix 1982). In these studies it was discovered that it is not at all unusual for persons to have two quite different sets of definitions of the situation, the posted set and the operational set. The posted ones are those which we post as upon a billboard, to see and to be seen. The operational ones on the other hand are the ones which we actually are using, know it or not, as the tacit or implicit guides to our thoughts and actions.

There are three classes of posted constructions of reality, we have found so far. There are some posteds that are our ideals, some that are our thoughts-in-abstraction and some are outright lies, or perhaps at least our attempts at being diplomatic.

Taken in order, the ideals, or the first class of posted constructs, are the should-be's, or the ought-to-be's of Wagner (1984) so that it is not at all discouraging to find posted definitions differing from the operational, that is those definitions that are inferrable directly from our actions, or the "are's". When there is this discrepancy within our thinking it is perhaps a recognition that your reach must exceed your grasp (or what's a heaven for?). The chasm between the ideal and the real always seems to widen when you get grand visions of the possible but settle interimly at least on the mundane actual.

Posted definitions of a situation may also however be nothing more than our reflection-in-abstraction. Thus our second class of posted constructs are when we reflect first upon some abstract idea rather than upon an actual event; we have an arm-chair theory of reality in which we may actually claim to believe. This happens not so much because we are out of touch with reality as because we fail to attend to our own involvement within reality.

An example of the incongruity that may develop between a person's posted constructs which are reflection-in-abstraction and that same person's operational constructs--the ones actually in use at the time --is seen in the supervisor who stands and exhorts all teachers, every one of them in the very same way, to "individualize instruction." The possible contradiction between what is said and what is done is apparent only to the listener. This contradiction happens easily in administration so that one finds a superintendent waxing eloquently over a fascination with the intricately complex matrix of programs he/she has just drawn up for teachers' professional development, i.e., the growth of real live people. The necessary preoccupation with the processes for working with people comes to take precedence over the very people they were supposed to be about. The people get posted, the process prevails.

The third class of posted constructs in quite different. Whether it is called diplomacy, persuasion, salesmanship, hypocricy or just spinning lies, they all require you to know what you are up to and why. The teacher who claims to post that kids come first and then breaks a leg trying to beat them out of school at four o'clock (yes, one did but it was an icy Edmonton January) is an example. This is quite different from the second class of posted constructs; it is the difference between the smart hypocrite and the ignorant hypocrite: the former knows that he's lying, the latter does not and is therefore a dangerous phony.

It is now possible to suggest that all of us have different levels of what can be termed "professional literacy," that is our ability to articulate in some meaningful set of symbols, including language, the nature of our professional experience and what we do with it. This is the extended definition of the term and it is assisted by "From utterance to text" (Olson 1977) and *Literacy, language and learning* (Olson, Torrence and Hildyard 1985). We suggest that quality of work life is a matter of learning and that specific learning is aided by the concept of professional literacy and its development.

Whether or not teacher thinking and professional literacy are interdependent, as is implied here, remains a moot point. It is sometimes held, as did Cvitkovik (1986), that literacy and thought are quite independent. Thought, he argued, is not specifiable in terms of rules and representation while literacy is. Literacy is a special skill which may, nonetheless, provide some of the base on which this thought is carried out. Exploring that base is the central interest in the present study.

The notion of professional literacy deals mostly with the second class of posteds and their degree of correspondence to the operational sets. It is conveniently similar to what G. A. Kelly (1955, pp. 475-476) calls "level of cognitive awareness." At a low level of cognitive awareness, a person is dealing with elements that lie at the outer extremeties of the range of convenience of his available constructs, so that the opportunities for validation or invalidation of those constructs is minimized. Perhaps that's a good thing, not being able to see your own errors. But this person, says Kelly, "cannot be very keenly aware of what he is up to."

A high level of cognitive awareness could be thought of as the descriptor for persons whose constructs of what they are up to are indeed what it actually is that they are up to. Their thoughts and actions are integrated; they exhibit "integrity" in at least the conceptual sense. Similarly their priorities would correspond so that the constructs they *demonstrate* to be "of most importance" to the quality of their work life would, at perhaps some other time, be the same as the constructs they would upon reflection *claim* to be "of most importance." If you keep saying (even to yourself) that "working with people" is the most important thing that makes teaching interesting, then it should follow that "working with people" ought to be a construct that would differentiate strongly between those elements of your work you choose as interesting and those that are dull. You would then have a "high level of cognitive awareness" or perhaps get called "professionally literate" or even demonstrate integrity.

Thus the first question I wish to pose here is whether the level of one's cognitive awareness, or professional literacy, is a cognitive determinant of feelings of job satisfaction, itself related to sense of quality of work life. The question would seem to call for a linear relationship. The lower the level, the less chance there is for validation of your ruminations about work and thus the less likely you are to find the workplace satisfying. The higher the level, the more frequently you have been able to check back successfully and build new thoughts about the place. Thus you can come to feel better about it.

The next question uses the concept of cognitive complexity (Bieri 1955). According to this, the greater your cognitive complexity the more ably you cope with the tasks at hand. Many operational definitions of cognitive complexity now abound but the simplest estimate allowable would be your resourcefulness, or the number and variety of constructs you possess and are able to draw upon to confront a topic. In earlier studies on developing school principals' ability to make effective staff decisions (e.g., Brown, Rix, Cholvat 1983, for recommendations for promotion or selection) we found a wide range in their repertoire of operative criteria. Despite what they said or posted on the topic, some principals found their repertoires of operative criteria would be quickly exhausted when actually making selections among available candidates. They had to resort to repetitions or synonyms. On the other hand were the more discerning principals who could keep on finding unique characteristics in their candidates; they were thus able to make more sophisticated choices for more specific purposes. They had greater cognitive complexity.

The concept of cognitive complexity means being more resourceful, or having more strings for your bow when attacking a problem or reflecting on reality. Parry (1978) made the discovery that those principals who were regarded as more effective by their superintendents were those who used a significantly greater number of criteria than did the less effective; their superintendents had still more. Cognitive complexity also refers to construct interrelatedness but, because these two measures were once found to be highly correlated (Brown 1964), we will now use the simple number of different constructs used by a subject as a crude estimate of cognitive complexity. The question posed here is whether possession of this should turn out to bode well for the way you feel about your job, i.e., quality of work life. Again, a linear relationship will be looked for.

This study has three phases, one for each of the variables discussed above: (a) resourcefulness or estimate of cognitive complexity, (b) professional literacy estimated by level of cognitive awareness and (c) quality of work life. There were 22 experienced teachers and we met on several occasions in different groups in early 1985. I did not consider that demographic variables such as age, gender or ethnicity, or what I elsewhere call the organizational statics (Brown 1967) should have any effect in a study of organizational dynamics. Indeed they did not. Probably other variables such as level of education and length of experience would not have had any effect either but the subjects studied were relatively homogeneous on those variables. I knew these people well, had established rapport, and they responded with enthusiasm. This point I mention because of the crudity of some measures.

For resourcefulness or estimate of level of cognitive complexity, a variation of our Discriminant Perception Repertory Test (Brown 1964) was devised. This is distantly related to Kelly's Role Construct Repertory Test (Kelly 1955) but has no roles or poles. Several measures of the reliability and validity of our test have been carried out (for summary report see Brown 1982, pp. 17-18) when used for organizational decisions but none when used for job satisfaction. Because the format is quite similar and because our subjects were familiar with its personnel decision use, we infer its use to be sufficiently reliable and valid for the present. The instructions given to my teachers this time were:

> Think of three elements of your work or workplace in which you are very interested, find stimulating or exciting, derive satisfaction or reward from, or make you want to stay with it or are otherwise a positive element in what you do and why you do it.
>
> These elements should now be identified below as Element A, Element B, Element C. Note that these elements may be any tasks, persons, challenges, groups, committees, staffs, work routines, events, duties, responsibilities, opportunities, good times, bad times with adults or children or both or neither so long as--to you at least--they are thought of as part of your work or somehow associated with it.
>
> Think of three elements of your work that are bland, dull, boring, tedious, irritative, annoying, uninteresting, a nuisance to bear, make you want to avoid it, cause bother or are otherwise a negative element in what you do and why you do it.
>
> Now enter these as Elements X, Y and Z below noting the same range of conditions as above.

The purpose of these instructions was to elicit a representative sample of the respondent's positive and negative elements about job satisfaction. Following these instructions was a series of forced comparisons among these elements. There were 18 such comparisons, which exhausts the combinations of six elements taken three at a time, excluding the two homogeneous sets. The intent of this instruction was to exhaust their repertoires of constructs attributable to these elements. Because my teachers were already familiar with this format, I allowed them to process their own protocols thus avoiding any problems of scorer verification.

Their 18 constructs, understood at least to them, now became a simple 18-item Likert scale against which in turn each of the six elements was rated. Processing the protocol meant subtracting, for each construct, the summed weights of its X, Y, Z elements from its A, B, C elements, to arrive at an estimate of the power of that construct upon the critical decision made earlier: what makes teaching exciting and dull? This may be termed the decision power of each construct, showing its strength or weakness as a criterion for job satisfaction, at least for that idiosyncratic respondent. The respondent's complete set of criteria may now be compared to each other to show a scale of the priorities of their constructs, ranked according to the strength or weakness of each construct to discriminate between positive and negative environs at work.

The second phase of the study was approximately three weeks later, with no intermittent reference. The purpose was to obtain an estimate of what can be termed professional literacy which is similar to Kelly's level of cognitive awareness. The estimate is arrived at by making a simple comparison of a person's posted and operational criteria. It is done this way: from the foregoing first phase, each teacher was able to develop a scale of priorities among their operational criteria. They did this by rank-ordering their own criteria according to the decision power of each criterion. To arrive at a comparable scale of posted criteria requires a person to contemplate concepts-in-abstraction.

Contemplating concepts in abstraction is what we do all the time, whether reading journal articles or the daily newspaper. Making preferences among these concepts we also do regularly. That is particularly so of teachers, school administrators or others in helping professions. The larger problematic of this phase occurs when our concepts in abstraction come out-of-synch with our concepts in use; that happens when the abstractions become disconnected from that from which they were to have been abstracted: the real events, actual people, specific acts. Or perhaps some never were connected: like the *pater noster*, we acquired it in the abstract and kept it there.

It involves an inferential leap of perilous dimension to thrust the value-laden term "character" onto the innocent test-taker whose posted and operational definitions of reality happen to coincide. But then, for the son of a Presbyterian minister, Kelly was admirably agile in keeping morals out of cognitive theory. Guilt, for example, is only that response to the discovery that what you did does not congrue with your set of personal constructs. So in this paper there is the assumption that the congruence of one's priorities in the abstract with their priorities as shown in actual behavior is an indication that they are integrated. Lack of cognitive integrity, or low level of cognitive awareness, simply means you "better smarten up."

The procedure for this second phase was to give the teachers back their own lists of 18 statements. As a point of procedure, the actual processing of the first phase, described above, was not completed until <u>after</u> the second phase so as not to contaminate the task. They were simply asked to:

Read all your 18 statements and decide which
of your criteria are most important to you and your
work. Try to decide the relative importance to you
of the effect on the quality of life at work of each
of these 18 and rank-order them from 1st to 18th or
from 1st to however many different criteria you have,
not counting synonyms, antonyms.

This was not a memory-check. With the elements having been re-
moved, they were studying attributive statements in the abstract, not
identified directly with a concrete referent such as their six elements. The likelihood that these rankings of posted attributions
would correspond to their earlier operationally-derived rankings of
element-referenced attributions is the likelihood that the terms they
talk about lie within their broad range of convenience, or are the
operational ideas that they are easily able to articulate meaningfully.
The likelihood they would not correspond is greater when the teacher
has a lower level of cognitive awareness, has less connection between
ideas forced out of experience and terms taken off the shelf. That
is, he is "less keenly aware of what he is up to." The correspondence
between the two sets of rankings is the second variable.

For the third variable, quality of work life, the crude global
estimate was used. This was sought on a different occasion. No claim
can be made for its reliability although at that moment for that person it was probably a valid answer to the question of "where, on a
scale of 1 to 10, would you place your own quality of work life?" I
would like to have attempted this, which is the dependent variable
here, in a more definitive fashion but was convinced none exists.

THE FINDINGS

The main directions of this study were confirmed: the bigger your
resourcefulness or level of cognitive complexity, possibly the higher
too is your correspondence between what you do and what you talk about
(among school administrators: goal-directed behaviour), and the
better the both of these, the more likely you will be to find yourself
sitting on a comfy cloud when it comes to estimating your quality of
work life. That is indeed an overgeneralization but at least there
is enough to encourage a more penetrating study of the inner dynamics
that help to turn chaos into challenge or to make a nightmare just a
nuisance. The encouragement seems to come from the cognitive nature
of the determinants. The encouragement lies not in the idiosyncratic
nature of these determinants; it is encouraging because we are much
more likely to be successful in changing cognitions than in working
directly on people's wills and feelings.

Why this possibility is thought to be more likely is because of
the reasonably temporary nature of results of inspirational professional activity days on the one hand and the successes we have had
with professional development projects resulting in an increase in
the number of personal constructs (Brown 1982), change in the
structure of professional criteria which changes held for a period of
eighteen months (Rix 1981). An interesting example of personal change
through cognitive structuring is in Rix (in press), "Understanding the
disoriented senior as a personal scientist: the case of Dr. Rager,"

where three months of intensive personal attention brought back an older man's constructs, poetry and will.

Table One sets out the cognitive structure findings and seems to say "the more strings to your bow the more fun is the hunt" but less clear is the relation with level of cognitive awareness. This ambiguity cleared during interviews with those showing anomalous results. Some seemed to say, "we're quite happy with how we think we see things so don't confuse us with reality."

In the last column of Table One, Anomalies, attention is drawn to those teachers whose results are "anomalous" to the general trend posited earlier. The As are anomalous in that they showed a high degree of cognitive awareness but a medium, low or very low estimate of quality of life. Their comments were the classic ones found in studies of worker satisfaction implying or stating "of course we know the way it is and even if it's not that bad it could be very much better." The thinking of the "A" teachers is that of the hard-headed idealist who, without any cognitive disjunction, lives with realistic visions of improvement. What would a staff be without the divine discontent?

The Bs comments however were to the contrary and equally believable. These teachers all displayed, if not quite the classic "bovine contentment," at least an equanimity with reality and a willingness to accept cognitive disjunctions as part of the taken-for-granteds of life in complex organizations especially schools with its comings and goings of unpredictable people.

The Cs remind us against temptations to go running gleefully into predicting personal behaviour: individual personal problems and challenges set them askew.

Looking at the substantive content of teacher thinking provided no surprises. The what and the why of interest in the workplace are familiar to educators: children are challenging and paper work is boring. One of them, Don (3), has high cognitive awareness, high cognitive complexity and high quality of work life. He especially finds rewarding the personal relationships developed through coaching a sports team and is frustrated by school board trustees because he has no control over them (note, as compared with his team members).

Several negative attributions of teaching—yard duty, futile trustees—were seen as not enriching or even related to the essence of being a teacher while others—grading, report cards—were seen as detractors from joy but were nevertheless something that just has to be done.

By defining their attributions to the task of being a teacher, our 22 participants re-emphasized the finding (Blackshaw 1982) that personal constructs underly satisfaction.

The purpose of this paper was not to identify or propose some new way of making teaching more exciting. Teachers do that themselves. Indeed from what we see, those highly resourceful and professionally literate teachers will derive a rewarding satisfaction from it and, what is more significant, if they do not they will know why not.

REFERENCES

Batcher, E. (1981). *Emotion in the classroom*. New York: Praeger.
Bieri, J. (1955), Cognitive complexity-simplicity and predictive behavior. *J. abnormal and social psychology*, 51: 2, 263-268.

Table One: 22 Teachers Grouped by Self-Estimates of Quality of Work Life (QWL), Measures of Cognitive Complexity (CCX) and Level of Cognitive Awareness (LCA).

		QWL		CCX*		LCA**		Anomalies
1.	Nel	10	v. high	12	high	11	high	
2.	Bob	9	v. high	13	v. high	8	med.	B
3.	Don	8	high	14	v. high	11	high	
4.	Pete	8	high	12	high	10	med.	
5.	John	8	high	11	h. med.	10	med.	
6.	Len	8	high	10	h. med.	13	high	
7.	Jim	8	high	7	low	4	low	B
8.	Mal	8	high	6	v. low	10	med.	C
9.	Jayne	7	med.	12	high	10	med.	
10.	Lois	7	med.	12	high	10	med.	
11.	Geri	7	med.	8	l. med.	12	high	A
12.	Candy	7	med.	9	med.	9	med.	
13.	Jan	7	med.	8	l. med.	5	low	
14.	Donna	6	med.	8	l. med.	10	med.	
15.	Guy	5	low	8	l. med.	12	high	A
16.	Gaye	5	low	10	h. med.	9	med.	C
17.	Fred	5	low	7	low	13	high	A
18.	Alf	4	low	8	l. med.	6	low	
19.	Vern	4	low	7	low	12	high	
20.	Lorri	3	low	8	l. med.	6	low	
21.	Dona	3	low	6	v. low	5	low	
22.	Thom	2	v. low	10	h. med.	10	med.	A

Possible range	1-10	1-18	1-14

*Number of different constructs used when comparing work situations.
**Congruence of priorities within sets of posted-operative constructs.

Anomalies:

A's know very well what they are up to and claim that as a result their QWL could take improvement.

B's are quite happy thank you with the way they see things now and show little desire to delve deeper.

C's are a mix of personal hopes, problems, opportunities and temporary inconveniences.

Blackshaw, D. (1982). Personal constructs underlying satisfaction. Unpublished Ph.D. thesis, University of Oregon.

Brown, A. F. (1984), How to change what teachers think about teachers: affirmative action in promotion decisions. In R. Halkes and J. K. Olson, eds. *Teacher thinking: a new perspective on persisting problems in education*. Lisse, Holland: Swets & Zeitlinger, 197-209.

Brown, A. F. (1982), Interpersonal administration: overcoming the Pygmalion effect. *Interchange* 13/4, 15-26.

Brown, A. F. (1967), Reactions to leadership. *Educational Administration Quarterly*, 3: 1, 62-73.

Brown, A. F. (1964), Exploring personnel judgments with discriminant perception analysis. *Proceedings of 3rd Canadian conference on educational research*. Ottawa: CCRE, 229-238.

Brown, A. F., Rix, E. A. and Cholvat, J. (1983), Changing promotion criteria: cognitive effects on administrators' decisions. *J. experimental education*, 52: 1, 4-10.

Cvitkovik, M. (1986), Literacy: the problems in literacy seminar. McLuhan Program in Culture and Technology *Newsletter*, 7, March 1, 3.

Goodlad, J. I. (1983), *A place called school*. New York: McGraw-Hill.

Kelly, G. A. (1955). *The psychology of personal constructs*. New York: Norton, vol. 1.

Olson, D. (1977), From utterance to text: the bias of language in speech and writing, *Harvard Educ. Review*, 47, 257-281.

Olson, D., Torrence, N. and Hildyard, A., eds. (1985). *Literacy, language and learning: the nature and consequences of reading and writing*. Cambridge U. K.: Cambridge University Press.

Parry, R. (1978). Elementary school principal effectiveness: perceptions of principals and superintendents. Unpublished Ed.D. thesis, University of Toronto.

Peters, T. J. and Waterman, R. H. (1982). *In search of excellence*. New York: Harper & Rowe.

Rix (Hill), E. A. (in press), Understanding the disoriented senior as a personal scientist: the case of Dr. Rager. In F. Fransella and L. Thomas, eds. *Personal constructs*. London: Rutledge & Kegan Paul.

Rix, E. A. (1982), Sift and shift effect: a cognitive process in understanding the psychological dynamics of administrators' personnel decisions. *Interchange*, 13/4, 27-30.

Rix, E. A. (1981), Dynamics of promotion decisions. *Comment on education*, 12: 1, 4-12.

Stogdill, R. M. (1965). *Managers, employees, organizations: a study of 27 organizations*. Columbus: Ohio State University.

Wagner, A. C. (1984), Conflicts in consciousness: imperative cognitives can lead to knots in thinking, in R. Halkes and J. K. Olson, eds., *Teacher thinking: a new perspective on persisting problems in education*. Lisse, Holland: Swets & Zeitlinger, 163- 175.

SELF-EVALUATION A CRITICAL COMPONENT IN THE DEVELOPING TEACHING PROFESSION

Miriam Ben-Peretz and Lya Kremer-Hayon
University of Haifa
Israel

SUMMARY

The study relates to several questions concerning teacher thinking in the process of self-evaluation. Teachers' goals and criteria for self-evaluation, their perceptions of the evaluation process, their main concerns and personal styles of thinking about this issue are investigated. Findings are based on questionnaires responded to by two groups of ninety teachers and in-depth interviews with nine teachers. Teachers' goals of self-evaluation cover a wide range of topics including students' needs and teachers' needs--professional and personal. A progressive view of education was found to underlie these needs. All traditional means of self-evaluation were perceived to be used much more than desired, probably because they are relatively more observable and operational. As far as the style of self-evaluation is concerned, several categories emerged: Professionalism; cognitive/affective orientation; structure; externality/internality; criticism; self vs. other emphasis;negative/ positive image; difficulties. Findings may serve as a basis for reconsidering teacher education and staff development toward a higher degree of professionalism.

PERSPECTIVE

Teachers' self-evaluation is one aspect of the overall process of teachers' thinking. Studies of teachers' thinking represent an attempt at revealing covert, tacit processes conceived of as affecting teaching acts. Research findings indicate that teachers' thinking in the process of planning instruction plays an important role in bringing about student cognitive and affective achievements (Marx, 1978; Clark et al.,1978). While a good deal of work has been done on teachers' planning, there have been very few investigations of teachers' self-evaluation. The investigation of teachers' planning must, however, be followed by studies on self-evaluation as a form of feedback, which is considered a necessary condition for the enhancement of learning and change. Psychologists may differ on the principles of learning they suggest, but there is agreement on the importance of feedback. Since the professional development of teachers is a process of constant learning on the part of the teacher, feedback becomes an indisputable need (Moustakas, 1972).

There are several sources from which teachers may derive feedback; supervisors, colleagues, principals, students and parents. Supervision of instruction has been extensively studied as a tool for providing feedback. Within this context, various strategies of supervision have been developed and put to use, such as clinical supervision (Cogan, 1973), conferencing techniques (Hunter, 1980) and interaction analysis (Blumberg, 1980).

Teachers themselves as a possible "self-feedback system" is a relatively neglected topic. Techniques and strategies for teacher - evaluation that have been developed, investigated and proved to be effective in improving instruction, are based on criteria, that are derived from educationists' and supervisors' views. All these factors are located outside teachers. A few examples will suffice to illustrate the point: rating forms (Ryans, 1960), micro-teaching (Allen,1966; Fuller, 1973), interaction analysis (Flanders 1970). The anthology of instruments "Mirrors for Behaviour" (Simon & Boyer, 1967) suggests a variety of such instruments. The fact that self-evaluation based upon teachers' own criteria has not been thoroughly studies, is surprising in view of the extensive demands for professional growth and for teachers' autonomy in planning and in processes of instructional decision making. Fostering teacher self-evaluation is perceived as deriving from the need for constant feedback, from trends toward professionalization and the development of an autonomous teacher.

The present study attempts to answer questions related to teacher thinking in the process of self-evaluation.

Specifically, the objectives of the study were:
- to determine teachers' goals in the process of self-evaluation;
- to identify specific topics of concern of teachers in the context of self-evaluation;
- to identify main criteria used by teachers for self-evaluation purposes;
- to disclose sources of evaluation teachers use in order to evaluate their professional work;
- to disclose the extent to which teachers' self-reported evaluative activities are congruent with their stated preferences;
- to explore whether teachers perceive their training as contributing to the process of self-evaluation;
- to detect personal styles of teachers in the manner in which teachers discuss the process of self-evaluation.

METHOD

Two investigative procedures were used in the study - a questionnaire and interviews.

A questionnaire "Teacher Self-Evaluation" (TSE) was developed on the basis of answers given by teachers in an open-ended interview regarding goals, criteria and sources of self-evaluation. Analysis

of answers yielded a long list of items. After the removal of
duplications the remaining items went through a process of item
analysis. The questionnaire in its final version consisted of 21
items cast into a 5 point interval scale ranging from 1 (low) to 5
(high). Respondents ware asked to relate to each item three items
as follows: (a) to what extent do they actually act as stated in the
items? (b) to what extent would they prefer to act accordingly?
(c) to what extent were they trained to act as specified in the
items? Background data were included in the questionnaire and
analyzed with regard to the questions raised and was processed by
the aid of SPSS programs, yielding frequency distributions, means,
standard deviations and t-tests.

A group of 90 teachers, randomly selected from the northern
district of Israel from various school levels, with differing
seniority and training background served as subjects for questionnaire
administration. (Partial findings were reported elsewhere, Kremer and
Ben-Peretz, 1984). A series of in-depth interviews were carried out
with nine elementary school teachers, ranging from 10-12 years
of seniority.

The interviewers were a group of graduate students in education,
who had been especially trained for this purpose. Following the
literature on interviewing, the interview focussed on one open-ended
question, stated as follows:"What can you tell about yourself as an
evaluator of your own teaching?" Interviewers were instructed not
to interrupt the flow of talk unless they were sure that the
participants concluded their responses. In this case, probing
questions could be raised and some elaboration could be asked for, if
needed.

Protocols of the interviews were analyzed by the investigators
using the process of analysis described by Miles and Huberman(1984).

FINDINGS AND DISCUSSION

Analysis of teachers' goals of self-evaluation points to a wide
variety of interests, starting with perceived students' needs and
followed by varying professional and personal needs. In descending
order, teachers indicated their goals of self-evaluation as follows:
"Improving students' achievement" ($\bar{x}$= 3.75, sd= .72), "improving
the teaching profession" ($\bar{x}$ = 3.08, sd = 1.07), "satisfaction of
personal needs" ($\bar{x}$ = 2.83, sd = 1.03), "career promotion"
($\bar{x}$ = 2.20, sd = 1.09),

With regard to various criteria suggested for diagnosing
developmental stages of teachers' concerns, the listed goals of
teachers' self-evaluation may be classified relatively high (Fuller,
1969). Thus, teacher educators may derive some satisfaction from the
fact that 'improving student achievement' achieved the highest score
and that the next three listed goals pertain to professional
development, because these interests may serve as a sound basis for
improvement. Since the highest rated goal of self-evaluation focusses
on students, a progressive orientation may be implied. This
implication is supported by additional findings regarding differences
between actual and preferred criteria of self-evaluation;

for instance: traditional-oriented criteria perceived by teachers to be used more than is desirable, whereas progressive-oriented criteria are used less than is perceived to be desirable. This direction of discrepancies may be related to the nature of the traditional characteristics of teaching which are observable and relatively operational as compared with progressive teaching characteristics (Hofman and Kremer, 1980), and hence more easily evaluated. However, the possibility of social desirability of progressive orientations should also be kept in mind.

Except for 'tests', the traditional means of evaluating students' achievements, all sources of self-evaluation are considered to be used less than desired.

The general declared lack of training for self-evaluation is not surprising in view of this relatively neglected topic in teacher education programs. However, some additional interpretations of this phenomenon may be suggested. Even if attempts at training for self-evaluation are included in the processes of pre- and in-service education, teachers may not be sensitive to their implications for the daily practice of teaching. These findings indicate the need for developing programs which integrate and foster self-evaluation in the process of teacher education.

In-depth interviews with teachers provided more specific insights into their main concerns.

Eight out of nine teachers interviewed in the study mentioned pupil achievement as their main concern of evaluation. A clear tendency to classify the achievements into information, intellectual skills and values was observed. These were related to by way of a hierarchy. Increase in information was perceived to be the easiest to assess and evaluate and value education was perceived as the most difficult area of evaluation. Teachers expressed their frustration, because of the high importance they attached to value education on the one hand, and lack of professional knowledge to evaluate their works in this area. Another topic of concern was teaching methods. The eight teachers who mentioned this topic related it to pupil achievement, wondering if they chose their teaching methods wisely and whether they performed well. Discipline was an additional topic of concern mentioned, however only by four teachers. Interestingly, no connection was found between seniority and discipline concerns.

While topics of concern pertain mainly to the content of self-evaluation, personal styles pertain to the form and manner in which these concerns were expressed by teachers.

The following categories for defining styles of self-evaluation emerged from our analysis;

1) Professional approach, namely, the use of professional educational terms in discussing the process of self-evaluation. Such terms as, for instance, "taxonomy of objectives", "affective domain", "learning for mastery", are used by teachers with different frequencies ranging from 12% - 56% of statements. These varying frequencies, as well as the nature of the terms used, form part of the personal style of teachers commenting on self-evaluation processes.

2) Cognitive and/or affective approach to self-evaluation.
   Examples of statements reflecting a cognitive approach are:
   "How does a teacher use the educational potential of a given
   content... what does he do to ensure its being learned...how
   does he transmit its cognitive messages."
   Examples reflecting an affective approach are:
   "Self-evaluation is accompanied by negative side effects...
   One has to remember that the professional status of teachers is
   low in comparison with other free professions."
3) Structure is another characteristic of teachers'personal style in
   thinking about self-evaluation. Some teachers exhibit a quite
   rigid structure which is reflected in the fixed sequence of their
   description of self-evaluative attempts. Examples of this style
   relate to the necessity of defining objectives which will serve as
   guidelines for assessing one's teaching efforts.
4) Reliance on external sources
   A surprisingly high percentage of statements, ranging in frequency
   from 3% - 39%, reflected an expressed need for external sources as
   aids in teachers' self-evaluation. Thus we find teachers who say:
   "I need the feedback of colleagues in order to assess my teaching",
   or: "when one sees how complicated the issues are, it is best to
   turn to external experts."
5) Emphasis on difficulties
   Several teachers who participated in this study emphasized the
   difficulties associated with self-evaluation. The percentage of
   such statements ranges from 3% - 20%. Among the difficulties
   mentioned were the following examples: "It is not so simple to
   evaluate oneself, the classroom climate may suffer as a result",
   or: "there is the danger of not being able to accept criticism."
-- The last three categories deal with teachers'perception of self
   in the process of evaluating their work.
6) Self-criticism
   Relatively few statements expressed teachers' readiness to view
   their professional activities critically. The frequence of such
   attempts ranged from 3% - 16%. Statements in this category were,
   for example:" If you believe that things are not going well, you
   have to examine yourself and not blame the students" or "I am
   able to judge what I am doing, I strive to be satisfied with my
   professional activities."
7) Emphasis on self
   This is the style of teachers who put themselves in the center
   of the stage and tend to emphasize their own personal satisfaction
   in the process of self-evaluation. The percentage of such
   statements ranges from 3% - 25%. Statements reflecting this
   style are:" I am reinforced when I perceive how hard I work",
   or: "The question is what do you expect of yourself..."
8) Negative image
   Sometimes the personal style of teachers discussing self-
   evaluation reflects a negative image of themselves. The following
   statements exemplify this style:"I was stunned, I understood
   that something is wrong with me." The percentage of such
   statements ranged from 1% - 14%.

156

CONCLUSIONS

It is interesting to note that much of teachers' concern in evaluation focussed on their pupils' achievements. This finding may be interpreted as reflecting a high developmental level in their profession (Fuller, 1969).

It seems clear that teachers exhibit different personal styles of relating to self-evaluation. Some are highly cognitive in their approach while others are predominantly affective. Some rely heavily on external support for self-evaluation while others seem to be oblivious to such possible assistance. The use made of professional terms varies greatly. Most interesting, some teachers are burdened with the difficulties of self-evaluation, while others neglect this aspect completely.

Can we detect any regularities in the personal profiles of teachers as they relate to self-evaluation?

Several tendencies emerge.

There seems to be a consistent positive relationship between a structured approach reflected by teachers and their use of professional terms. A possible interpretation is that awareness of professional terms allows for a more structured, systematic way of handling self-evaluation.

In almost all cases reliance on external sources is linked to a low level of self-criticism. This seems logical, if one relies on others to assess one's professional activities there is no need to be too self-critical. Some relationships are inconsistent. Thus, the perception of difficulties is sometimes related to a great emphasis on self, while in other cases the opposite phenomenon emerges - the more awareness of difficulties the less emphasis on oneself.

This study is an explanatory attempt to reveal some of the personal styles of thinking about self-evaluation. It is contended that the categories for defining personal styles of teacher thinking about self-evaluation can be used in further research.

Many questions call for further investigations:
- Are teachers' personal styles in self-evaluation reflected in other evaluative contexts as well. For instance, if teachers reveal an affective approach to their own evaluation, do they use the same approach toward peers or students? If they tend to focus on negative views about their teaching, do they do the same when evaluating their students or peers?
- What is the nature of relationship between personal styles in self-evaluation and personal background or situational variables? Is there any connection between self-assessment style and professional achievement?

Insights into ways in which teachers think about evaluating their own work may provide important knowledge about professional modes of teaching.

The more we learn about teachers' self-evaluation the closer we may come to the enhancement of professionalization of teaching.

REFERENCES

Blumberg, A. (1980). *Supervisors and teachers: A cold war*, Berkeley, Calif. McCutcheon Publ.

Clark, C.M. , Wildfong, S. & Yinger, R.Y. (1978).*"Identification of salient features of language and activities"*, Mimeographed, East Lansing, Michigan State University.

Cogan, M.L (1973). *Clinical Supervision*, Boston, Mass.

Flanders, N. (1979). *Analyzing Teaching Behaviour*, Mass. : Addison-Wesley.

Fuller, F.F. & Manning, B.A. (1973). "Self-Confrontation Reviewed", *Review of Educational Research*, 43:469-528.

Fuller, F.F. (1969). "Concerns of teachers - a developmental conceptualization", *American Educational Research Journal* 6, 2:207-226.

Hofman, J. & Kremer, L. (1980). "Attitudes towards higher education and course evaluation", *Journal of Educational Psychology* 72, 5:610-617.

Hunter, M. (1980). "Six types of supervisory conferences", *Educational Leadership* 5:408-413.

Kremer, L. & Ben-Peretz, M. (1984). "Teachers' self-evaluation - concerns and practices", *Journal of Education for Teaching*, 10, 1, pp. 53-60.

Marx, R.W. (1978). *"Teacher Judgments of Students' Cognitive and Affective Outcomes"*, Doct. Dissert. Stanford University.

Miles, M.B. & Huberman, A.M. (1984). *Qualitative Data Analysis*, Beverly Hills, Sage Publications.

Moustakas, C. (1972). *Teaching as learning*, New York, Ballantine Books.

Ryans, D.C. (1960). *Characteristics of Teachers, their Description, Comparison and Appraisal*, Washington, D.C. American Council on Education.

Simon, A. & Boyer, G. (1968). *Mirrors for Behavior - An Anthology of Classroom Behavior*, Philadelphia, Research for Better Schools.

SUBJECTIVE THEORIES OF TEACHERS: RECONSTRUCTION THROUGH STIMULATED RECALL, INTERVIEW AND GRAPHIC REPRESENTATION OF TEACHER THINKING

Frank Krause
Universität Konstanz
Sozialwissenschaftliche Fakultät
Fed. Rep. of Germany

SUMMARY

A specific method for analyzing subjective theories of teachers is presented. Specific features of it derive from the author's focus on action-theory and from an interest in aggression-relevant inter-actions in the classroom.[1] The method includes stimulated recall, interview, and graphic representation of the data so obtained which are submitted to a 'communicative validation' (Groeben, 1981). Analysis of data from 23 teachers depicts how these teachers describe their actions in response to aggressively behaving students and the inferences they make in respect to their own actions. Although methodological and empirical aspects are emphasized, theoretical assumptions are included as well as considerations regarding the utility of the method for teacher training purposes.

1. INTENTIONS AND AIMS

It is not our intention to measure subjective theories of teachers per se. Guided by personal interests, prior experience, and theoretical assumptions we aim at a very specific kind of subjective theory:

Important considerations for our methodology derive from our interest in <u>conflicting and (potentially) aggressive episodes</u> during classroom interactions.

Another reference point is our interest in <u>teacher training</u> (Tennstädt, Rimele & Krause, 1984). We think that to be effective, any interaction-oriented teacher training should start where the individual trainee stands at that moment in reference to the aspect in question. This implies reconstruction of his thoughts and feelings as undistorted and accurate as possible and, preferably, in his own (logical and verbal) terms.

Two goals derive from the desire to contribute kwowledge not only to practical problems but also to basic psychological research:
- To arrive at general, <u>intersubjectively comparable descriptions of subjective theories</u>, their qualities and their structure, and
- to help answer the questions, <u>if and under what circumstances these theories are linked to overt actions</u>, or even guide them.

2. THEORETICAL ASSUMPTIONS

It is obvious that theoretical assumptions about the structural and functional qualities of subjective theories may have strong implications for the development of an appropriate method and, later on, for the interpretation of the data. Therefore, our central presuppositions are made explicit here:

(a) Subjective theories are <u>accessible to the actor's conscience</u>, at least under some specific conditions (compare Morris, 1981; Wegner & Vallacher, 1981 with Nisbett & Wilson's (1977) very sceptical position on this subject).

(b) We conceptualize subjective theories as relatively <u>stable cognitive representations</u> that, at least as to their central aspects, may only be altered through long-term processes.

(c) We conceive of subjective theories as having <u>similar structural qualities as scientific theories</u>; that is, they can be adequately represented as having an argumentative structure (see Kelly's notion of the everyday man as a scientist and Groeben & Scheele, 1982, but also Bromme's (1984) critical comments on this point.).

(d) Subjective theories, besides other factors, <u>influence the actual behavior of their owners</u>, again, at least under some specific conditions (e.g., 'normal' levels of cognitive and emotional activation and of situational demands; see Tomaszewski's (1978) action-theory framework [2]).

3. THE METHOD

Main features

Unlike our approaches of measuring subjective theories by using psychometric scales (see Dann et al., 1982), the method presented here relies mainly on an interview technique. It is based on work of several authors (Wagner et al., 1981; Wahl et al., 1983; Feldmann, 1979; Scheele & Groeben, 1984). Its main features are:

(a) The instrument is based on <u>real-life episodes</u> during class hours. Thus, episodes from everyday teaching practice are used as reference for reconstruction.

(b) The reconstruction focusses on concrete, <u>observable behavior</u> of teachers and students, and the corresponding thoughts and feelings that preced or accompany teacher's actions.

(c) It is <u>aggression-</u> or at least <u>conflict-oriented</u>.

(d) It is <u>teacher -centered</u>: Every information is seen and reported exclusively through the eyes of the teacher. Students' actions, thoughts, and feelings are represented only insofar as the teacher observes or implies them.

Basically, the reconstruction is realized in three steps. In the first step, the relevant data are collected during an interview. In the second step these data are arranged by the researcher into a graphic draft. Finally, the draft is corrected and supplemented through an intensive dialogue between researcher ant teacher.

More specifically, the interviews are repeated over three to five days for each teacher. Each interview takes place immediately after the class being observed by the interviewer and an independent obser-ver. To minimize memory-related disortions and gaps, tape recordings are made during class hours.

Before each interview, both interviewer and interviewee agree on a specific episode out of the preceding classroom hour which, in the teacher's opinion, contains aggressive or at least potentially aggressive student behavior. To insure a clear identification of the episode in question and to stimulate the reactualization of what 'really' went on in the teacher's mind during the original event, the tape recordings are playedback before each interview.

The interview procedure is directed by an interview-guide: In the first section, the guide thematizes the overt behaviors and the re-spective cognitions and feelings that were experienced during the critical episode. General questions are formulated aimed at leaving the teacher a maximum of freedom as to the content and structure of his answer, e.g.: "Could you please describe the whole episode in your own words?"; "What was going on inside yourself at that very mo-ment?".

The second part of the interview could be labeled as the 'focussing phase'. The questions raised gradually become more and more specific, e.g.: "What did you think then?"; "Did you pursue a specific aim at that moment?" and so on. In addition, a specific set of potential 'preconditions' or 'determinants' of actions is ad-dressed systematically in order to supplement the already sponta-neously mentioned list of factors which, in the teacher's mind, guided his decisions, e.g., the behavior of other students, his own emotional status, etc.

During the final phase of the interview the specific episode which had been the constant anchor of reference until then is left behind. The teacher is instructed to reflect on other situations which are similar in respect to the initial (aggression-relevant) behavior of some student, but different in respect to the relevant 'determinants' of behavior inside or outside the acting teacher. This leads to a certain generalization of the reported cognitions originally directed to a very specific and unique event.

An important feature must be added that characterizes the inter-view throughout: Once the teacher has described the events in his own words he is asked to 'translate' specific elements of his report (mainly his and the students' behavior) with the aid of a set of pre-defined terms. These terms (cf. part 4) are explicitly described to the teacher in advance. They originate from our manual for syste-matic observation of teachers' and students' behavior (Humpert & Dann, 1984).

After the interview, the interviewer tries to convert the inter-view data into a graph which represents the assumed argumentative structure and the complexity of the teacher's ideas as a whole. This proposal is then revised through an intensive dialogue - Groeben (1981) and Lechler (1982) refer to this procedure as 'communicative validation' - with the teacher who is encouraged to alter and sup-plement the draft until he can fully agree with its content. The interviewer's part during this dialogue is intentionally restricted to aspects of the formal correctness of the graphic design by follow-ing clearly defined rules.

Figure 1 illustrates the general design of the graphs: the formal structure, the elements and their relationship between them. Figure 2 shows and original graph of how a single teacher describes his (real and hypothetical) interactions with a specific type of student behavior ('verbal aggression'), specifying his inferences about what makes him react the way he does. (As a special case it contains first-order actions and first-order determinants only). For further details see Krause & Dann (1986).

The sample

After several pretests and improvements of our method, reconstructions of aggression-relevant subjective theories were carried out with 23 mostly experienced teachers - their average seniority being 9.8 years - from rural and urban areas of Southern West-Germany. The sample consisted of 8 females and 15 males with an average age of 35.7 years.

The German 'Hauptschule' (student age 11 to 15 years) was chosen for the study because this type of school is known to have a high incidence of disciplinary problems involving aggressive behavior.

Participation was voluntary. It was offered to a number of teachers that as we knew had problems in dealing with aggressive and/or undisciplined students. A willingness to invest considerable amounts of time for this problem and a readiness to reveal glimpses into one's professional life were further selective factors for the composition of our sample.

4. RESULTS

The original reconstructions can (and should) be analyzed in different ways, depending on the purpose pursued. In a teacher training context for instance, the unique features of each graph and its content are essential for diagnosis and evaluation and should therefor be conserved in their original, highly differentiated, idiosyncratic status. Here, however, we aim at giving a first insight into the data of all 23 teachers, pointing out common features and tendencies in the way these teachers reconstruct their behavior cognitively. Two topics will be focused upon:

(1) The main categories through which the teachers describe and explain their own actions, and

(2) The predominant inferences they make when choosing a specific action.

Teachers' categories of description and explanation

To describe the teachers' view of their interactions we shall first direct our attention to the central components they refer to: their (self-reported) actions, their (self-reported) goals, and the (perceived) determinants of their actions.

(a) Teachers' actions: The numerous action categories originally chosen by the teachers may be condensed to three overall types of actions:

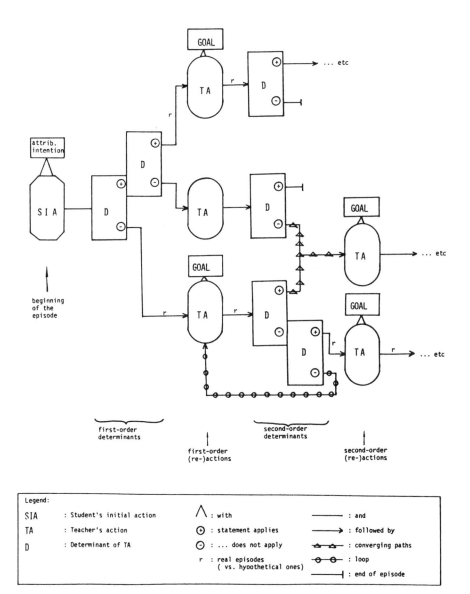

Legend:

SIA	: Student's initial action	$\bigwedge$: with		——————	: and
TA	: Teacher's action	$\oplus$: statement applies		————→	: followed by
D	: Determinant of TA	$\ominus$: ... does not apply		▵—▵	: converging paths
		r : real episodes (vs. hypothetical ones)		⊖—⊖	: loop
				——⊣	: end of episode

Fig. 1. Formal structure of the graphic representation
of the teacher's action-oriented thinking

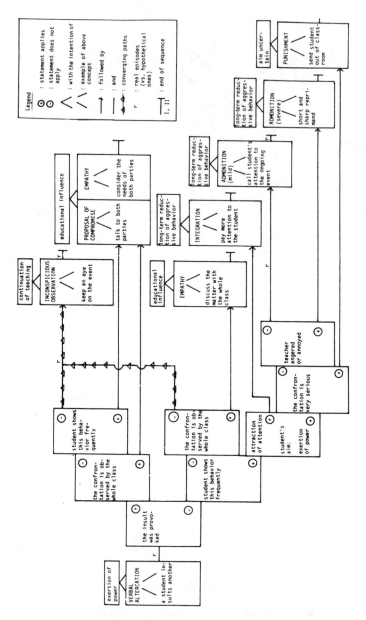

Fig. 2. Example of the action-oriented thinking of an individual teacher in response to aggresively behaving students

- Neutral actions, comprising the categories of 'unconspicious observation, 'interruption', and 'admonition'
- Punitive actions, comprising 'threat', 'punishment', and
'disparagement'
- socially integrative actions, comprising 'proposal of compromise',
'integration', 'encouragement', and 'empathy'.

According to this classification, most actions taken by the
teachers accross al first-, second-, ...to sixth-order actions
(see Figure 1) were neutral (57%), followed by punitive actions
(33%), and only 10% of socially-integrative actions. In the course of
their interactions, however, (that means comparing consecutively the
actions of first to sixth order), the teachers tend to reduce the
proportion of neutral actions substituting them accordingly by
punitive measures. Socially integrative actions, meanwhile, remain
quite constant at their initial low level (see Figure 3).

(b) Teachers' goals: From several pretest interviews with
teachers, three kinds of goals emerged as relevant in connection with
aggressive-undisciplined student behavior: short-range goals (mainly
'continuation of teaching'), long-range goals of reduction of
aggressive and undisciplined behavior and, finally, goals which
combine short- and longe-range perspectives simultaneously (mainly
refered to by the teachers as 'educational influence'). When these

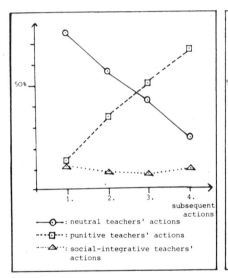

—O—: neutral teachers' actions

---□---: punitive teachers' actions

····△····: social-integrative teachers'
actions

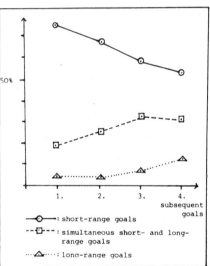

—O—: short-range goals

--□---: simultaneous short- and long-
range goals

····△····: long-range goals

Fig. 3. Subsequent actions of
teachers towards aggres-
sive or undisciplined
students as perceived by
the teachers themselves
(relative frequencies;
n=1666 actions)

Fig. 4. Subsequent goals of
teachers in interaction
with aggressive or undis-
ciplined students as per-
ceived by the teachers
themselves (relative fre-
quencies; n=1625 goals)

165

three types of goals were offered in the reconstruction work, short-range goals were by far (69%) the most frequent ones chosen, followed by goals of simultaneous short and long range (25%). Goals of long-range reduction of aggressive and undisciplined behavior were chosen only 6% of the time.

Again, a shift can be observed in the course of the episodes: from their first to the following actions teachers' readiness to act with short-range intentions (to continue teaching) decreases constantly and is supplemented accordingly by an increasing proportion of educational and long-range modificatory goals (see Figure 4).

(c) Determinants of teachers' actions: Seen through the teachers' eyes and in their actor-specific perception of the flow of events, each of the critical episodes starts with a student behavior labeled by them as aggressive or at least undisciplined and further specifications of the situation which, in their view, determine together the choice of their first reaction.

As for the initial student behavior, our teachers, in their recon-structions discriminated between several classes:
- physical altercation, e.g., hitting, scratching, pulling chair away, etc.
- verbal altercation, e.g., insulting, discriminating others verbally, etc.
- refusal, verbally or factually refusing to follow teachers' instructions or to cooperate with co-students,
- disruptive non-participation in classwork, e.g., talking aloud with co-student, throwing paper airplanes, etc.
- other aggressive or undisciplined behavior, e.g., taking possession of objects of others or damaging objects purposefully, threatening, blackmailing or rejecting co-students, etc.

The distribution of these initial student behaviors shows that refusal and disruptive non-participation are the most frequent student behaviors which the teachers choose to reconstruct (making up 26% and 25% of all initial student behaviors, see Table 1).

As for further attributes relevant for the teachers' first appraisal, four major categories derive from their graphs:
- characteristics of target-students' personalities, e.g., 'easy/difficult to handle', 'ringleader/follower', etc.
- characteristics of target-students' behaviors, e.g., 'intensity of the offence is high/low', 'first/repeated alteraction', 'other students watching/not watching', etc.
- Self-related cognitions and emotions, e.g., 'afraid of loosing face', 'feeling angry/relaxed', etc.
- External circumstances not directly related to the episode but, nevertheless, relevant for the teacher's reaction, e.g., 'first/last hour', 'gym-lessons/mathematics', etc.

Since most determinants by far - absolutely and in terms of their variability - are mentioned before the episode's first action we restrict the following data to first-order determinants (cp. Figure 1).

Our data indicate that the (attributed) characteristics of the target-students' personalities (making up 24% of all first-order determinants) and their actual and past behaviors (39%) are judged by

the teachers as being the most relevant complex for their first
reaction to aggressive and undisciplined behavior (together 63%).
Self-related cognitions and emotions (21%) and external circumstances
(16%), instead, are seen as less influencial.

Teachers' inferences

How do the cognitive inferences look in more detail? Again we limit
this question to data "predicting" first-order teachers' actions
only.

(a) Students' actions and contingent teachers' actions: As we have
seen already (cp. Figure 3), three out of four first reactions of
teachers are "neutral" ones, while the punitive and social-integrative
actions occur significant less frequently, 13 and 12% of all first
reactions respectively.

Keeping these proportions in mind, Table 1 indicates that chances
for neutral actions to occur are especially high following
'disruptive non-participation in classwork' as well as following
'refusal'. Chances for neutral actions are especially low, however,
following 'other aggressive or undisciplined behavior'. Punitive
reactions are most likely to occur with students showing 'other
aggressive/undisciplined behavior' and 'refusal' and least probable
in response to 'disruptive non-participation in classwork'. Social
integrative measures, finally, are especially linked to 'verbal
altercations' and 'refusal', and most seldomly chosen after
'physical altercations'.

Students' actions	General categories of teachers' actions				
	neutral	punitive	social-integrative	Total %	(abs.)
physical altercation	16.9	22.5	9.0	16.7	(112)
verbal altercation	17.0	12.4	34.6	18.5	(124)
refusal	26.4	25.8	26.9	26.4	(177)
disruptive non-participation	29.8	10.1	15.4	25.4	(171)
other aggressive or undisciplined behavior	9.9	29.2	14.1	13.0	(87)
Sum % (abs.)	100.0 (504)	100.0 (89)	100.0 (78)	100.0 (671)	

Tab. 1. Students'actions and contingent teachers'
actions as perceived by the teachers themselves
(first-order actions only; relative frequencies)

(b) Further determinants and contingent teachers' actions: The
values of Table 2 indicate that all kinds of teachers' actions
– neutral, punitive or social-integrative ones – are most
frequently preceded by determinants of the type 'characteristics of
the target-students' behavior': 39% – 37% – and 39% respectively. In

the second place, neutral and social-integrative actions are
contingent on 'characteristics of students' personalities' (25% -
25%), while punitive reactions are especially linked to 'self-
related cognitions and emotions' of the teacher (26%). For neutral
and punitive reactions the weakest interrelations, in contrast, can
be observed with 'external circumstances' (16% - 15%), meanwhile
social-integrative teacher actions are least often (16%) preceded by
'self-related cognitions and emotions'.

Determinants of teacher-actions	General categories of teachers' actions				
	neutral	punitive	social-integrative	Total %	(abs.)
characteristics of target-students' personality	24.5	21.0	25.2	24.0	(389)
characteristics of target-students' behavior	39.3	37.3	38.7	38.9	(630)
self-related cognitions and emotions	20.4	26.6	15.5	21.0	(339)
external circumstances	15.8	15.1	20.6	16.1	(261)
Sum % (abs.)	100.0 (1212)	100.0 (252)	100.0 (155)	100.0 (1619)	

Tab. 2. Additional preceding determinants and contingent
teachers' actions as perceived by the teachers
themselves (first-order determinants and
actions only; relative frequencies)

General categories of goals	General categories of teachers' actions				
	neutral	punitive	social-integrative	Total %	(abs.)
short-range goals	82.7	59.1	56.0	76.6	(497)
short- and long-range goals	14.9	30.1	34.7	19.1	(124)
long-range goals	2.4	10.8	9.3	4.3	(28)
Sum % (abs.)	100.0 (491)	100.0 (83)	100.0 (75)	100.0 (649)	

Tab. 3. Teachers' goals and their related actions
as perceived by the teachers themselves
(First-order goals and actions only;
relative frequencies)

(c) Teachers' goals and the actions linked to them: Data from
Table 3 indicate that short-range goals are predominant for every
kind of teacher reactions with neutral actions being almost exclusively (83%) linked to these goals. Punitive and social-integrative
actions, however are additionally matched to a considerable extent

(30% and 35% of their frequencies) with combined short- and long-range
goals and also, to some extent, with long-range goals (11% and 9%
respectively).

5. CONCLUSION AND SOME PERSPECTIVES

The method described here reconstructs thoughts and feelings of
teachers involved in concrete aggression- or discipline-relevant
interactions with students in the classroom. Its basic features are
an action oriented interview, a transposition of the interview data
into a holistic graph, and its 'communicative-validation' in a
dialogue between the interviewed teacher and the researcher (or
another teacher). The method may be applied for basic-research
purposes as well as for in-service training. Therefore it must meet
two potentially conflicting expectations: First, it should provide
for 'naturalistic' reconstruction of how each teacher thinks, feels
and acts in his own - strictly speaking - unique terms. Second, it
should yield generalized descriptions of teachers' thinking, feeling,
and acting in inter-individual terms. In order to bridge that gap
multiple codings of the data on different levels of abstraction are
carried out: original verbal quotations of individual teachers,
categories of actions and goals set by the teachers themselves, and
general categories of these events established by us in the course
of data aggregation.

The empirical data presented can only give a first impression of
teachers' action-oriented cognitions. According to these data, the
23 teachers of our sample interacting with aggressively behaving or
undisciplined students (think/say they) cleary prefer 'neutral'
reactions, mostly pursue short-range goals and consider primarily
characteristics of the students' behavior and personality in their
decision to react.

This strong overall tendency determines to a considerable degree
teachers' inferences as to what specific reaction is contingent upon
specific goals or preceding determinants of the situation.

In the course of episodes with several subsequent teachers' (and
students') actions, however, this overall tendency is modified:
punitive teacher-actions and long-range goals are chosen more
frequently the longer the episodes last. These results seem remarkable to us, since through other independent efforts (see Dann &
Humpert, 1986) there is evidence that teachers themselves are quite
aware of the ineffectiveness of punitive actions as a means of
reducing aggressive or undisciplined student reactions in the long
run. For further empirical data in the domain of teacher cognitions
and teacher behavior see Hofer's, 1986, compilation of pertinent
research.

In further analyses we shall try to determine if and under which
circumstances subjective theories of teachers (co-)determine their
actions. This will be done mainly through comparison of the above
data with independent observation of teachers' and students' behavior.
This 'falsificatory validation' (Groeben, 1981) could yield some
insights into the 'classical' theme of 'cognition and action'.
Moreover, it could contribute knowledge to practical attemps to
modify teacher behavior through cognitively oriented training programs.

FOOTNOTES

1) The author is a member of the project "Aggression at School" at
   Konstanz University, Federal Republic of Germany. The project is
   sponsored by the Deutsche Forschungsgemeinschaft. Co-members are
   at present: Hanns-Dietrich Dann (chairman), Winfried Humpert, and
   Kurt-Christian Tennstädt.
2) TOMASZEWSKI's (1978) action-theoretical framework does not refer
   to subjective theories explicitely. It offers, however, attractive
   perspectives for integrating 'routines' into purposeful 'theory-
   guided' behavior.
3) To compute the frequencies of all elements emerging in the graphs
   every thinkable (real or hypothetic) path from the initial student
   behavior to the end of each different episode is run through,
   counting every element (initial student behavior, determinants of
   actions and teachers' actions) as often as they are met on these
   pathways. Through this procedure identical elements may be counted
   repeatedly depending on the position they hold in the graph (cp.
   Figure 1). From the 23 teachers, 41 graphs were obtained containing
   a total of 671 pathways.
4) and 5) The differences between the frequencies of actions and
   those of goals result from the fact that some teachers, for certain
   actions, explicitely denied to pursue any goals.

REFERENCES

Bromme, R. (1984). On the limitations of the theory metaphor for the
    study of teacher's expert knowledge. In: Halkes, R. & Olson, J.K.
    (eds.). *Teacher thinking: a new perspective on persisting problems
    in education*. Lisse: Swets & Zeitlinger.
Dann, H.-D. & Humpert, W. (1986). *Eine empirische Analyse der Hand-
    lungswirksamkeit subjektiver Theorien von Lehrern in aggressions-
    haltigen Unterrichtssituationen* (in prep.)
Dann, H.-D., Humpert, W., Krause, F., v. Kügelgen, T., Rimele, W. &
    Tennstädt, K.-CH. (1982). Arbeits- und Ergebnisbericht des Pro-
    jekts "Aggression in der Schule". In: Zentrum I Bildungsforschung/
    Sonderforschungsbereich 23 (Ed.) *Wissenschaftlicher Arbeits- und
    Ergebnisbericht 1979-1982*. Konstanz.
Feldmann, K. (1979). MEAP - Eine Methode zur Erfassung der Alltags-
    theorien von Professionellen. In: Schön, B. & Hurrelmann, K. (Eds.)
    *Schulalltag und Empirie. Neuere Ansätze in der schulischen und
    beruflichen Sozialisationsforschung*. Weinheim: Beltz.
Groeben, N. (1981). Die Handlungsperspektive als Theorierahmen für
    Forschung im pädagogischen Feld. In: Hofer, M. (Ed.). *Informations-
    verarbeitung und Entscheidungsverhalten von Lehrern. Beiträge zu
    einer Handlungstheorie des Unterrichtens*. München: Urban &
    Schwarzenberg.
Groeben, N. & Scheele, B. (1982). Einige Sprachregelungsvorschläge
    für Erforschung subjektiver Theorien. In: Dann, H.-D. et al.
    (Eds.) *Analyse und Modifikation subjektiver Theorien von Lehrern*.
    Zentrum I Bildungsforschung/Sonderforschungsbereich 23, Forschungs-
    bericht 43. Konstanz.

Hofer, M. (1986). *Sozialpsychologie erzieherischen Handelns. Wie das Denken und Handeln von Lehrern organisiert ist.* Göttingen, Hogrefe.

Humpert, W. & Dann, H.-D. (with contributions from T. v. Kügelgen and W. Rimele) (1984). *Das Beobachtungssystem BAVIS. Ein handlungstheoretisch orientiertes Beobachtungsverfahren zur Analyse von aggressionsbezogenen Interaktionen im Schulunterricht. Entwicklung - Beschreibung - Anwendung.* Projekt "Aggression in der Schule", Arbeitsbericht 8. Konstanz.

Krause, F. & Dann, H.-D. (1986). *Die Interview- und Legetechnik zur Rekonstruktion Kognitiver Handlungsstrukturen ILKHA.* Projekt "Aggression in der Schule", Arbeitsbericht 9. Konstanz.

Lechler, P. (1982). Kommunikative --Validierung. In: Huber, G.L. & Mandl, H. (Eds.). *Verbale Daten. Eine Einführung in die Grundlagen und Methoden der Erhebung und Auswertung.* Weinheim: Beltz.

Morris, P. (1981). The cognitive psychology of selfreports. In: Antaki, Ch. (Ed.). *The psychology of ordinary explanations of social behavior.* London: Academic Press.

Nisbett, R.E. & Wilson, T.D. (1977). Telling more than we can know. Verbal reports on mental processes. *Psychological Review 84,* 231-259.

Scheele, B. & Groeben, N. (1984). *Die Heidelberger Struktur-Lege-Technik (SLT). Eine Dialog-Konsens-Methode zur Erhebung Subjektiver Theorien mittlerer Reichweite.* Weinheim: Beltz.

Tennstädt, K.-CH., Rimele, W. & Krause, F. (1984). *Das Konstanzer Trainingsmodell (KTM). Entwurf eines integrativen Lehrertrainingsprogramms zur Bewältigung von Aggression und Störung im Unterricht auf der Basis subjektiver Theorien.* Projekt "Aggression in der Schule", Arbeitsbericht 7. Konstanz.

Tomaszewski, T. (1978). *Tätigkeit und Bewußtsein. Beiträge zur Einführung in die Polnische Tätigkeitspsychologie.* Weinheim: Beltz.

Wahl, D., Schlee, J., Krauth, J. & Murek, J. (1983). *Naive verhaltenstheorie von Lehrern. Abschlußbericht eines Forschungsvorhabens zur Rekonstruktion und Validierung subjektiver psychologischer Theorien.* Zentrum für pädagogische Berufspraxis, Oldenburg.

Wagner, A., Maier, S., Uttendorfer-Marek, J. & Waidle, R.H. (1981). *Unterrichtspsychogramme. Was in den Köpfen von Lehrern und Schülern vor sich geht.* Reinbek: Rowohlt.

Wegner, D.M. & Vallacher, R.R. (1981). Common-sense psychology. In: Arnhold, W. (Ed.). *Social cognition. Perspectives on everyday understanding.* London: Academic Press.

POST- INTERACTIVE REFLECTIONS OF TEACHERS: A CRITICAL APPRAISAL

Joost Lowyck
Department of Educational Sciences
Leuven University
B-3000 Leuven (Belgium)

SUMMARY

Many researchers in the field of teacher thinking restrict their work to one specific phase of teaching : the pre-interactive, interactive or post-interactive one. Most attention has been paid to the planning phase, less to the interactive thought processes and very few to post-interactive thinking.
This research has been set up as a contribution to a better understanding of the post-interactive reflection of teachers. Both the methodological refinement and the content of after-lesson thoughts are emphasized. The results reveal the problem of reducing the study of teacher thinking to the isolated phases as chronological dissections of the teaching activity. From the teachers'standpoint, planning, interaction and post-interactive reflection are strongly connected, because they think rather in terms of a meaningful content than in chronological terms. The study of the interrelations between the phases needs more attention, to contribute to a more integrative concept of teaching.

INTRODUCTION

In most of the publications on teacher thinking the distinction between the three phases of teaching has been taken for granted. It seems to be a workable scheme for several reviews of research (Clark & Peterson, 1985; Shavelson & Stern, 1981).

Whereas process-product studies focused almost exclusively at interactive classroom behaviors (Dunkin & Biddle, 1974), research on teaching mainly stressed the planning phase (Bromme, 1980; Jackson, 1964; Morine, 1973; Stolurow, 1965; Yinger, 1977; Zahorik, 1970). However, some outcomes of these studies reveal problems, due to the isolation of the planning phase from the interactive one (Lowyck, 1980).

Besides the question of the compatibility between the pre-interactive and interactive phase of teaching, there is few insight in what happens after the lesson is over, and how possible reflections during the post-interactive phase influence both future planning and teaching.

In order to gain insight into the relationship between the different phases of teaching, a descriptive-empirical study has been set up (Fets, 1984; Lowyck, 1985).

POST-INTERACTIVE REFLECTION : CONCEPTUALIZATION

It always seems difficult to agree upon definitions, mainly because of the lack of both conceptualization and empirical research. What teachers do after their lessons often has been qualified as "evaluation" (Shavelson & Stern, 1981). This concept "refers to the phase of teaching where teachers assess their plans and accomplishments and so revise them for the future" (Shavelson & Stern, 1981, p. 471).
These authors attribute the lack of studies in the domain of post-interactive reflection to some psychological evidence, more precisely to the limited ability for learning from past experiences. This conclusion may surprise scholars in the field of teacher education, because of the central notion of 'feed-back' in training procedures. It is quite evident to teacher educators to expect behavioral changes in student teachers, using information from the past. The question is, however, whether (student-)teachers use the appropriate information.

McKay & Marland (1978) use the term "reflection" as a category of interactive thoughts, meaning "units in which the teacher is thinking about past aspects of, or events in, the lesson other than what he has done". These authors limit reflection to that cognitive activities of teachers that concern their not realized teaching behaviors. This interpretation seems too narrow for a understanding fully what is meant by reflection. The definition of Clark & Peterson (1985) is more neutral and efficient, speaking about "postactive thoughts". Peters (1984) points to the same interpretation when referring to "post-reflection".

We will use the term "post-interactive reflection" as a descriptive category for the information processing activities of the teacher after a lesson or a broader unit of time. If teachers use some explicit criteria for determining the quality of the information we will speak, then, about evaluation.

An important problem in the conceptualization of post-interactive reflection is the unit of analysis. Yinger (1978) distinguishes the following five units of planning : year, term, unit, week and day. Although this time schedule was very useful for the study of pre-interactive teaching, it nevertheless seems not precise enough for our study. We therefore added two smaller units (lesson moment, lesson) as well as a larger one (career).

Each post-interactive reflection can be conceived of as a moment in the teacher's professional life. Eisner (1979) distinguished four dimensions within curriculum decisions, namely the molar and the molecular decisions on the one hand and the time at which (present) and for which (future) curriculum decisions are made on the other. Post-interactive reflection can be seen as the (present) activity of a teacher at a very precise moment in his professional career, with reference to some moment in the past. These reflections can bear on some activity or event in the future. (see Figure 1)

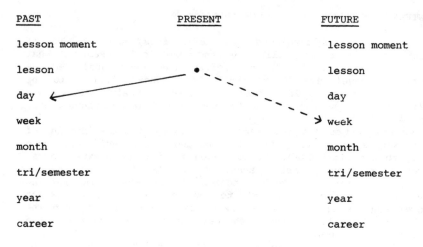

POST-INTERACTIVE REFLECTION

PAST	PRESENT	FUTURE
lesson moment		lesson moment
lesson		lesson
day		day
week		week
month		month
tri/semester		tri/semester
year		year
career		career

Fig. 1. Unit of analysis of the (present) post-interactive reflection, referring to the past and the future.

AN EXPLORATORY STUDY

Due to the lack of empirical studies on the subject at hand, we explored teachers' post-interactive reflections in a descriptive-empirical way. The results will contribute to a better understanding of teachers' complex functioning as well as to some methodological refinement.

Subjects

As in earlier studies (Lowyck, 1980; 1983) we worked with elementary school teachers. Some similarity of the sample guarantees at least a better comparability of the results from the different projects. Twelve teachers participated (nine females and three males). Their teaching experience was spread between 3 and 32 years, with a mean score of 18,75 years.

Method

In order to focus the attention of the teachers on the study object, a short letter with instructions has been presented to each of them. They were informed that we were interested in the post-interactive phase of teaching. Moreover, some orienting questions were asked, like

: do you think about past teaching events, what is the content of the
thoughts, when do you reflect, does it often happens. Then, they were
invited to illustrate some thoughts with very concrete instances.
Last, the question was asked if their after-lesson thoughts had some
impact on their future teaching behavior.
During november 1983, the retrospections of the twelve teachers were
organized in the schools. They lasted between thirty and fourty-five
minutes. The researcher asked at regular intervals for concrete
instances of the reported thoughts. The retrospection was recorded on
tape and later on transcribed. This formed, together with both the
written answers on the questions and the elaborated lesson plans, the
material for the data-analysis.

Analysis of the material

The material was scrutinized in a recurrent, cyclical way. Each
protocol was examined successively. After the analysis of the
information from the first teacher, a provisional classification of
the content was tried out, using rough categories. When inspecting the
data of the second teacher, the usefulness of the categories was
checked and new categories were generated in order to cover the
content of the retrospection. This procedure was repeated with each
teacher. At the end, the material was grouped into two kinds of data :
the results from the broad retrospection on the one hand, and the
information from the concrete instances on the other. In a second
cycle, the whole material has been controlled again, in order to
assure a maximal integration of all the relevant information into the
descriptive categories.

Data from the retrospection

Most teachers experienced it as difficult to distinguish clearly
between past and future events, because a lot of thoughts indeed are
connected and not ordered chronologically. In our opinion, this has to
do with the function of the thought process, namely to gather
information from past lessons or periods which is functional for the
future.
We categorized the data from the broad retrospection into three main
categories : (a) the formal aspects of reflection
(systematic/spontaneous, frequent/sporadic, way of recording the
thoughts), (b) the content of the reflection (individual pupil, group,
teaching behavior, management, lesson content, colleagues, parents and
extra-scolar institutes) and (c) the consequences of the reflection.
    With regard to the more formal aspects of post-interactive
reflection, differences between teachers in the frequency and
consciousness of their thoughts was apparent. Teachers can be placed
in two categories : never looking at the past or almost always
reflecting in a systematic way. That teachers are reflecting
systematically is not a function of the frequency but of their
habitual way of behaving. If there is some problem with the planning
of future lessons and/or with experiences during the past, teachers
tend to use short reflections and quickly search for some indicators
in the past in order to avoid negative experiences in the future. Here

again, the planning and post-interactive reflections are tied together. In the case of negative experiences in the past, teachers try to store that information, together with strategies for some improvement next time. The more clear the problems are, the more teachers will focus on it. For example, when correcting exams, they see the effects of their teaching and reflect on possible causes for the failure of some individual pupils or of the classgroup.

When asked to report how they fix their post-interactive thoughts, only three teachers mentioned one or another way of laying down the ideas in written form to have at least some lasting support for a reflection in the long run. Most of the thoughts of teachers are, thus, very volatile. Maybe, this is one of the reasons why it is difficult to distinguish between planning and post-interactive reflection : the ideas or thoughts are clustered around one topic, without concern about the exact time the ideas were generated.

As to the content of post-interactive reflections, the following results are of interest. Teachers often retrospect on the behavior and/or emotions of individual pupils, mainly in the case of difficulties or problems, both in the personal and interactional aspects of functioning. They think about the class as a group, mainly when the lesson was disappointing, at least in the perception of the teacher. Problems with the lesson seem to focus the attention of the teacher to their teaching behaviors, to the timing and to the subject matter. Sometimes, teachers refer to contacts with parents or colleagues who influence their thinking about lessons or events.

About the question if and to what extent post-interactive thoughts influence future behaviors, the results indicate a very broad unit of analysis. Teachers tend to generalize the very concrete experiences into a higher level of abstraction and use these thoughts as a guide for future activities. This finding lays in the line of previous research data (Lowyck, 1980), where teachers report the gradual condensation of lesson content as well as the cumulative integration of pupil reactions as orientations for their planning.

As to the retrospection, the following conclusions are noteworthy. Teachers seldom reflect systematically about past events, although they store selectively some information. Next, the clear dissection between planning and thinking afterwards is non existing. Teachers very often think in terms of problems or tasks and are not able to use a definite chronological segmentation of the reality. Lastly, the interview as a technique seems not so relevant for exploring the broader aspects of post-interactive reflection, because most teachers reported quite precisely their ideas in the written preparation of the interview. On the contrary : sometimes the verbal interaction seemed to disturb the train of thought, given the tendency of the interviewer to create an atmosphere of mutual talk.

Data from concrete instances

In contrast with the retrospection, teachers are very explicit here, so that the data gathered are richer than in the retrospection. We will use the same classification as for the retrospection, in order to allow the comparison of both techniques.

The analysis of the concrete examples delivers no information about the more formal aspects of post-interactive reflection, as was the case during the retrospection. Only results about both the content and some consequences are available.

After a recurrent, cyclical analysis of all the instances, twenty-two subcategories seemed to cover the whole content of the reflection. Each statement referring to the content has been put into one of the 22 categories. Figure 2 represents the different categories in a reduced form.

1. INDIVIDUAL PUPIL	Reaction of one child	unsatisfactory performance	(1a)
		need for diagnosis	(1b)
		unexpected (positive) performance interesting statement	(1c)
		disciplinary problem	(1d)
	Personality characteristics		(1e)
2. CLASSGROUP	Characteristics of the group		(2a)
	Gognitive achievement	evaluation (general)	(2b)
		unsatisfactory results	(2c)
		satisfactory results	(2d)
	Classroom behavior and attitudes		(2e)
3. TEACHING BEHAVIOR	Method or procedure	content-oriented procedures	(3a)
		affective procedures	(3b)
		behavioral procedures	(3c)
	Feelings and background		3d)
4. OTHER PEOPLE		extrascolar contacts with pupils	(4a)
		parents	(4b)
		colleagues	(4c)
		inspection	(4d)
		non-school contacts	(4e)
5. ORGANIZATION		course of the lesson	(5a)
		timing and amount of content	(5b)
6. LESSON CONTENT			(6)

Fig. 2. Post-interactive reflection : categories of thought content.

The categorization of after-lesson thoughts could suggest some linearity of reflection, as if teachers only reflect upon one aspect at one time. Although they reflect often on one aspect, in some cases, nevertheless, there is a more complex organization of their thinking. We could speak, then, about combined thoughts. In our material, only 5 % of the statements contained more than one aspect. This is possibly not a true sample of reality, because in the wording of their thoughts, teachers could make explicit only a limited part of their thought processes.

Some combinations of categories are situated within the same topic, like individual pupil or classgroup. A stated problem (1a) is combined with some diagnosis (1b). This leads often to the formulation of a procedure for remediation (3a). Negative performances of pupils (2c) lead often to a closer look at the own teaching behavior (3c), while a positive result of a pupil (1c) discharges into a positive feeling of the teacher (3d).

There is a fixed way of direction from one group of categories to another. Reflection on several topics leads often to thoughts on the own teaching behavior, while teachers never reflected about other components, starting from their own teaching behavior thoughts. Nevertheless, a lot of combinations has been found, starting from reflections on management categories.

Another interesting question is whether there is some relationship between the category of reflection and the unit of analysis from the past. In figure 3 the results are showed for a frequency of 361 thoughts.

	1 IND. PUPIL	2 CLASS- GROUP	3 TEACH. BEH.	4 OTHER PEOPLE	5 ORGANI- ZATION	6 * CON- TENT
lesson moment	36	10	10	2	2	3
lesson	43	53	55	2	8	13
day	3	3	2	-	-	-
week	-	-	-	-	-	-
lesson unit	11	6	10	-	1	-
month	-	-	-	-	-	-
tri/semester	1	-	3	-	-	-
year	22	15	8	13	6	1
career	-	8	4	4	2	1

* = main classes of thoughts; see figure 2)

Fig. 3. Number of statements per unit of analysis

Because of the variation of the number of statements in the different cells, it seems not possible to drawn definite conclusions. We will limit the report to some hypotheses which could be studied more intensively in future research.

- Teachers mainly reflect upon the performances of the classgroup and upon the methods they use in relation to the past lesson. In this case, the evaluative aspect of the reflection is dominant.
- Reflection on difficulties from individual pupils refers, more than the thoughts about the classgroup, to restricted lesson moments. - Thoughts about the lesson content are restricted to a specific lesson. On the contrary, reflections upon classroom management are related to broader time units.

- Remarks from parents, colleagues and inspection are incentives for the teacher to reflect upon the own teaching over a very broad period, mainly the year already past.
- Pure chronological units (day, week, month, tri/semester) are far less used as units of analysis than more professional relevant units (lesson moment, lesson, lesson unit, year).

Concerning the effects of post-interactive thoughts on future teaching, it is salient that teachers formulate very often their intended changes of teaching behavior, when reporting some examples. Nevertheless, there is no strict relationship between the entry of the thought (for example the individual pupil) and its consequence (i.c. the classgroup). Teachers often generalize the information gathered from one pupil or a teaching event to broader units in the future. One instance, thus, functions as some point of reference for possible changes in the next professional activity, or, in other terms, as a sufficient representative and valid experience.

The future teaching patterns which are intended as a consequence from the post-interactive reflection, have been grouped into 10 categories. Because of the brief description, it is impossible to show all the entries that influence future teaching. We report only the different classes and some main relations between reflection and future action. The different changes are represented in figure 4.

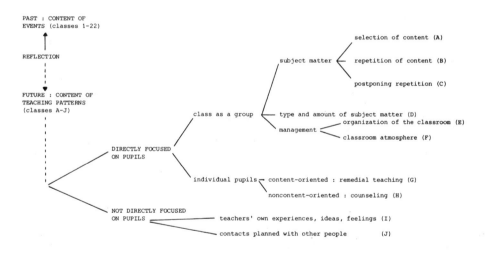

Fig. 4. Categories of intended activities as a consequence of post-interactive reflection.

Conclusions

The data gathered both by means of the retrospection and from the concrete instances, reflect a consistent picture of teachers' functioning during the post-interactive phase of teaching. The main conclusions are the following.

The participating teachers reflect upon striking events, behaviors or situations. Whether something is labeled as striking, depends upon the subjective perception of the teacher. Some teachers, for example, are very irritated by pupil talk when not oriented to the task, while others accept this fact as a normal reaction of children who cannot concentrate during the whole day. Pupils talk is, thus, not always a striking event.

Reflections in the form of post-interactive thoughts will generate in some cases a pattern of problem-solving activities. Reflections on an individual pupil lead often to some kind of diagnosis and this by turns to the search for future remedial behavior. Here we remark the interdependency of the different phases in teaching.

Another observation is that teachers often implicitly work out some naive teaching heuristic, which would sound as follows : "Repeat in the future what has been perceived in the past as powerful and change only what has appeared able of improvement". One could speak rather of rough, sketchy orientations than of precise prescriptions. The adjustment of the teaching activity to coming new situations is not a consequence of the accurate rational planning and reflection. The volatility of thoughts as well as the lack of a systematic control about the reflection content, refer to more intuitive reactions.

Because teaching is a complex activity with different types of behaviors, one cannot restrict the study of teaching to one or another type (Lowyck, 1984). For sure, teachers operate with both explicit thinking and abbreviated behaviors, e.g. routines. The question is now if teachers arrive at the selection of the most important information, in order to direct future behavior. It is until now unclear how teachers reduce gradually the complexity and how often they use relevant criteria.

The teachers do not seem to be the "professional, rational decision-maker" as has been suggested in the literature on teacher thinking. She is in too many cases dependent upon unclear criteria for making adequate decisions. Moreover, the situation is often dominant, so that sometimes there is more field-steered activity than intentionality.

DISCUSSION

If we evaluate the research reported here, we have to consider some limitations. The small sample, the restricted number of research methods, the broad focus of the research questions and the way of reducing the amount of data, result in the impossibility to be conclusive or exhaustive. The findings only can be used as a platform for further refinement.

In this and previous studies, we intended to describe important variables of teaching as a complex activity. We will now appraise more

critically some aspects of (a) the research findings, (b) the methods
and (c) the theoretical framework.

Research findings

An analysis of the findings shows that teachers differ strongly in the
way their teaching is planned and executed. Moreover, the variables
teacher, pupils and subject matter seem to cover most of the teaching
variation. It is striking that teachers who have been confronted with
complex teaching models, relaps into very simple ones. The
insufficiency of teacher training is not a definite argument for
explaining this phenomenon. Maybe the lack of a well elaborated "task
environment" of teaching is one of the main causes for the divergent
conceptions about teaching, for, all a teacher does is called
"teaching".
The results of the research indicate the great difficulty to
discover the essential characteristics of good teaching, only by pure
description. In view of effective teaching, the question remains what
precisely adequate thoughts and behaviors are and in what situation
they are effective. If we cannot find the criteria for good teaching
by description only, other ways must be explored. In our opinion, we
have to set up more "constructive" designs : the precise indication of
the characteristics of a specific teaching task environment, so that
we could control the research input. The integration of the cognitive
approach and the process-product studies, enables us to construct a
well defined task, to describe the teaching processes and to measure
the learning gains. The elaboration of specific curricular segments
could be the platform for such a "constructive" research. We could
call it teaching experiments, if we use this term in a broad sense,
including the descriptive power and qualitative analyses developed by
the recent cognitive paradigm.
Frequently research on teaching parcelled out the complexity of
teaching by making the research-entry more dominant than the teaching
reality. Such a segmentation leads to a centrifugal tendency : research topics escape from the real functioning of teachers into
another reality : that of the researcher.

Methodology

The studies as reported here, mainly use retrospection as a technique,
complemented by concrete examples and written materials, such as the
lesson plans and the information from diaries. The use of self-reports
is a very problematic one, as has been pointed out in recent years
(see : Ericsson & Simon, 1980; Calderhead, 1981; Lowyck & Broeckmans,
1985).
When starting our research, the expectation was that a broad
approach was the most interesting one to explore the key features of
teachers' cognitive processes. Self-reports seemed to be at least
necessary to understand what teachers think. In addition, we expected
that this broad exploration would indicate the critical cues in expert
behavior. Indeed, the self-reports from experienced teachers could
deliver information concerning "good" teaching. The data from our
explorative design however, have shown that the term "experienced"

teachers is too vague a concept, and to some degree irrelevant as an indication for "good teaching".

In our study, attention has been paid to the ecological validity of the research situation. Nevertheless, the intended external validity has not been realized in all its aspects. That teachers collaborate on the base of voluntariness is a very specific way of sampling. Moreover, their collaboration with a researcher entails some changes in the teaching situation and in their way of behaving. As such, a teacher is very sensible for suggestions or demands from the researcher. Written instructions, video registrations, interview questions, all reflect some standpoint of the researcher and the teacher. The hidden influences are numerous.

As to the reliability of the retrospection, we observed the difficulty for teachers to situate exactly their cognitive processes on a time line. The fact that retrospection always takes place after the planning or the interactive phase may very well confuse the distinction between different moments of teacher thoughts. If retrospection is replaced by thinking aloud or anticipation of reality, the interactive teaching is affected, then, by the emphasis laid on the objects of thought during the pre-interactive phase. If the retrospection takes place immediately after the lesson, another problem comes to light : teachers are too involved in their activity, so that they do not seem to be able to take some distance from the past lesson, as has been reported in the study of post-interactive thoughts.

An important methodological refinement is realized when confronting the retrospective data with some external information, like lesson protocols or written textes. The use of examples of the thoughts is usable too, because there are possibilities to compare the information both from the broad retrospection and the other materials. In the reported study, we remarked a great difference between the broad retrospection and the concrete illustrations in their quality of reported thoughts. Teachers can better word their teaching in the form of examples, because they use a non-professional language, as Jackson (1968) already observed.

Although the concrete examples are interesting entries to teachers' after lesson thoughts, there nevertheless remains an important restriction. The data refer to discrete moments of the teaching activity, with the consequence that it seems rather impossible to reconstruct the whole process of the interactive phase. Whereas it was quite easy to realize a process analysis of the planning phase, because the teacher had a chronological way of reporting the planning, it was not the case for the interactive and post-interactive phase. Using some associations, the teacher organizes his thoughts not on the basis of a chronological principle, so that the data reflect more the content than the exact timing of thoughts.

The use of retrospection as a self-reporting technique is, among others, responsible for the high degree of rationality as suggested by the data. The whole research context expresses the outlook from the researcher and/or the teacher that it should be possible to give some information about the "why" of the event. Teachers seldom indicate behavior as "routine", but formulate negative statements such as "I don't know exactly why I do this". The problem with this kind of information is to know whether the behavior is so far routinized, that it is impossible to introspect about it, or if other factors account for this fact.

The problems, mentioned above, refer to the necessity of a broad-spectrum of research methods. Due to the refinement of retrospective methods, it seems nowadays possible to combine the external observation with the self-reports of teachers. Whereas the former indicate the realized behavior, which is the point of reference for the pupils, the latter may contribute to a better understanding of why an how this external behavior originated. By this way, some cyclical research process appears, in which the acquisitions of different traditions could be combined. It is the time now, for example within studies on academic learning time, to complement the quantitative measures of the real time on task, with qualitative data from teachers and pupils.

Theory building

The research projects as reported earlier, had no well elaborated theoretical bases. The aim was rather to explore some characteristics of the complexity of teaching in order to contribute, on the long run, to some models and theories of teaching.

Teaching has been described in a nearly axiomatic way as the intentional activity of a teacher within a complex environment. The search for cognitive processes as well as the process analysis, brought important features to light. The teacher is an information processor : he perceives, selects and interpretes bits of reality on the ground of his ideas and naive models. Observable behavior is only fully understandable if the researcher gains access to the hidden world of thinking and feeling. It is the teacher only who can deliver the important information about the determinants of his behavior. When organizing groupwork in the class, the observer cannot know why a teacher chooses this method : are the reasons pragmatic ones, or based on didactical or social considerations ? On the other hand, this does not mean that an external observer is unable to add some meaning to the observed behavior. A lot of unconscious rules, unknown by the teacher, can be revealed by an observer who can offer his interpretation for falsification by the teacher.

Another remarkable fact is the importance of the specific environment in which the teacher functions. Some behaviors are directly conditioned by situational characteristics, without a high degree of rationality and intentionality. These behaviors are, then, field-steered (van Parreren, 1979).

The contribution to an adequate model of teaching will depend upon the expertness of the scholars in the field to analyse the teaching activity and to structure it along the most relevant features or variables. Although the cognitive approach of teaching is a relatively recent one, there is some danger for a splitting force within the research already done. One of the main shortcomings of the process-product studies has been the lack of conceptualization of the used variables. In a critical analysis of the output of the many studies on teacher effectiveness, Heath & Nielson (1974) already pointed out the main problems in this tradition. The lack of a consistent conceptualization as well as of methodological accuracy were the main reasons for the lack of productivity.

When looking at the cognitive paradigm, it is not easy to avoid the same shortcomings. We do not have a well elaborated conceptual framework, nor a hard and qualitative methodology. We almost exclusevely focus on teacher thoughts, with omission of observable behaviors. We divide the complex teaching activity into a chronological dissection without attention for more meaningful categories. We emphasize the isolated variables within the pre-, interactive and post-interactive phase without great concern for the interrelations between the phases.

Now it seems to be the time to focus on the integration of the research work already done. The number of studies has grown steadily, but they only can become surveyable if we collaborate for an acceptable conceptual framework as well as for the precise analysis of the models. This work will furnish a platform for further research as an entry to the construction of empirical proved theoretical models, in which intentionality, complexity and situational variables are represented in a meaningful way. In the long run, a consistent theory of teaching is the ultimate aim.

REFERENCES

Bromme, R. (1980). Die alltägliche Unterrichtsvorbereitung von Mathematiklehrern : zu einigen Methoden und Ergebnissen einer Untersuchung des Denkprozesses. *Unterrichtswissenschaft,4* 142-156.

Calderhead, J. (1981). Stimulated recall : a method for research on teaching. *British Journal of Educational Psychology, 51,*180-190.

Clark, C.M. & Peterson, P.L. (1985). Teachers' Thoudht Processes. In M.C. Wittrock (Ed.), *Handbook for research on teaching.* New York, Macmillan.

Dunkin, M.J. & Biddle, B.J. (1974). *The study of teaching.*New York, Holt, Rinehart & Winston.

Eisner, W.E.(1979). *The educational imagination.* New York, Macmillan.

Ericsson, K.A. & Simon, H.A. (1980). Verbal reports as data. *Psychological Review, 87,*215,251.

Fets, B. (1984). *De reflectie bij leerkrachten over het eigen onderwijzen.* Leuven, Afdeling Didactiek (niet gepubliceerde licentiaatsverhandeling).

Heath, R.W. & Nielson, M.A. (1974). The research basis for performance-based teacher education.*Review of Educational Research, 44,* 463-484.

Jackson, P.W. (1964). The conceptualization of teaching. *Psychology in the schools,* 232-243.

Jackson, P.W. (1968). *Life in classrooms.* New York, Bolt, Rinehart & Winston.

Lowyck, J. (1980). *A process analysis of teaching.* Leuven, Afdeling Didactiek. Report no. 21 (EDRS-ED 190513).

Lowyck, J. (1984). Teacher thinking and teacher routines : a bifurcation? In R.Halkes & J.K. Olson (Eds.). *Teacher thinking : a new perspective on persisting problems in education.*Lisse, Swets & Zeitlinger, 7-18.

Lowyck, J. (1983). De leerkracht als probleemoplosser : een kritische analyse. In E. De Corte & P. Span, *Studies over onderwijsleer-processen*. Leuven, Helicon.

Lowyck, J. (1984). Reflectie van leerkrachten na afloop van de les. Negatieve leservaringen stemmen tot nadenken. *Didacktief, 14*, 20-24.

Lowyck, J. & Broeckmans, J. (1985). Technieken voor zelfrapportering in het onderzoek van onderwijzen. In R. Halkes & R.G.M. Wolbert (Eds.), *Docent en methode*. Lisse, Swets & Zeitlinger.

MacKay, D.A. & Marland, P. (1978). *Thought processes of teachers*. (EDRS-ED 151328).

Morine, G. (1973). Planning skills : paradox and parodies. *Journal of Teacher Education, 24*, 135-143.

Peters, J.J. (1984). Teaching : intentionality, reflection and routines. In R. Halkes & J.K. Olson (Eds.), *Teacher thinking : a new perspective on persisting problems in education*. Lisse, Swets & Zeitlinger, 19-34.

Shavelson, R.J. & Stern, P. (1981). Research on teacher's pedagogical thoughts, judgments, decisions and behavior. *Review of Educational Research, 51*, 455-498.

Stolurow, L.M. (1965). Model the master teacher or master the teaching model. In J.D. Krumboltz (Ed.), *Learning and the educational process*. Chicago, Rand McNally.

Van Parreren, C.F. (1979). *Het handelingsmodel in de leerpsychologie*. Brussel, V.U.B.

Yinger, R.J. (1977). *A study of teacher planning : description and theory development using ethnographic and information processing methods*. East Lansing, Michigan State University (doctoral dissertation).

Yinger, R.J. (1978). *A study of teacher planning : description and a model of preactive decision making*. East Lansing, Michigan State University, (Research Series no. 18).

Zahorik, J.A. (1970). The effect of planning on teaching. *The elementary School Journal, 71*, 143-151.

DOES A TENDENCY TO GROUP PUPILS OR ATTRIBUTES EXIST WITHIN TEACHERS' COGNITIONS/JUDGEMENTS?

Hartmut-A. Oldenbürger
Universität Göttingen
Fed. Rep. of Germany

SUMMARY

There seems to be a tacit agreement among researchers that teachers structure their cognitions of pupils and/or attributes by grouping. In studies in the framework of theories on 'Implicit Personality Theory' and 'Prototypes' this becomes obvious in three respects:
- the use of data collecting methods that force subjects (teachers) to construct groups of pupils and/or attributes, or to assign them to given categories or (proto)types.
- the use of data analysis procedures, i.e. cluster analysis, which must result in groups of subjects, thus leading to clusters per fiat,
- the interpretation of results of data analysis procedures, e.g. factor analysis, in terms of groups of pupils and/or attributes.

As methodological tools were lacking till now, no explicit and systematic attempt has been made to test this presumption of a grouping tendency in teachers' cognitions/judgments. In addition most studies in this area suffer from misinterpretations by confounding inter- and intraindividual sources of variation of judgments.

This paper presents methodological and empirical contributions:
(a) The rationale for a randomization-test which allows a statistical evaluation of the structural grouping hypothesis without using any special method of cluster analysis,
(b) the results of the application of this test on the data of each individual teacher (N=36, different types of schools). In total 810 pupils were rated on 25 bipolar rating scales.

The striking results are discussed in methodological and theoretical terms as they should lead to a changed perspective in educational research which tries to reconstruct teachers' cognitions on pupils and/or attributes.

186

INTRODUCING REMARKS

The main purpose of this paper is to establish a methodological tool in order to test a widely held and important structural hypothesis on human cognitions, i.e. people tend to organize their concepts of objects, persons, attributes, situations, etc. in categories, or classes. They build (proto)types, construct systems of clusters, e.g. sequences of partitions (hierarchies), and the like.

At first glance it seems plausible that 'grouping things' is a fundamental and simple mean to facilitate structure in the subjects' cognitions, for example, for the perception of people and events, or the planning and performance of action (Cantor/Mischel 1979).

This contribution especially investigates the validity of the structural grouping hypothesis for teachers' cognitions on pupils and assigned attributes (For a discussion see Hofer 1986, p. 139ff).

Though this topic lies well in the domain of theories on theories on subjects' 'implicit personality theory' (IPT), I have to neglect the important problems related to the conception of the theoretical term 'IPT' (Asch 1946, Heider 1958), its embedding in the framework of 'subjective theories' (Mandl/Huber 1983, Oldenbürger 1984), its function, genesis, and effects (Dusek/Gail 1983, Brophy 1983), and its role for teachers' actions in teaching-learning-processes (Hofer 1975, Wahl/Schlee/Krauth/Murek 1983).

For this presentation it must be sufficient to conceptualize the teacher's IPT on pupils as an open, dynamic, active, interrelated system of the teacher's cognitions on pupils, situations, their attributes, his goals, planned actions, and the anticipated results for the pupil(s).

If one studies the investigations on IPT, one finds that the common belief in the grouping tendency always works as a mere presupposition, and not as a hypothesis to be tested. Research in the area seems to be based on this assumption which is thus protected from refutation. This is done in various ways:
- data collection;
  Subjects are forced to sort objects (pupils, or attributes) into piles (Morine-Dershimer 1978, Rosenberg 1982, Powell/Juhnke 1983), or subjects are required to assign pupils or attributes to given categories (Höhn 1967, Silberman 1969), or
  subjects are asked to estimate the 'nearness' of pupils or attributes to given prototypical names (Hofer 1969, Schneider/Blankmeyer 1983).
- data analysis;
  Various kinds of cluster analytical procedures are applied, which guarantee the representation of pupils or attributes by groups (Tscherner 1974, Hofer 1981) or
  if factors or principal components are extracted, rotation to simple structure - which is also a group-concept - is almost always performed automatically. In so doing a general factor is destroyed,
  which very often is present in the IPT-domain (evaluation). (See

Gigerenzer/Strube, 1978, for an elaborated criticism of dimensional decomposition in this area of research.)
- interpretation of results;
  The assignment of typical names to groups of pupils, or lineair combinations of variables by the researcher supports the impression of 'existing' grouping tendencies in judgments given by subjects.
The demonstration of the effects of the researchers' prejudices is then often added by a 'conclusion', which incorrectly states the empirical confirmation of the structural grouping-hypothesis.

The present investigation should at least in principle be able to falsify this fundamental hypothesis on teachers' cognitions. To do so, the format of the data and its collection procedure have to meet the following demands: Each of several teachers (1) should judge a sufficiently large number of real pupils (2), using the same set (3) of relevant and representative attributes (4) for each pupil. Fortunately such data have already been gathered by Tscherner (1974). (I am very grateful to F. Masendorf and M. Hofer for providing the material.) Tscherner used Hofer's (1969) set of bipolar (7-point) rating scales to collect data of 36 teachers from different types of schools. Each of these teachers was asked to judge each pupil of his/her class. Thus, 810 pupils in total were rated according to the 25 scales. (See Tscherner/Masendorf 1974, Hofer 1975, 1981 for former analyses of these data.)

To avoid confounding inter- and intraindividual sources of variation, this study investigates the clusterability of pupils and attributes (rating-scales) for each individual teacher. Therefor, 36 data matrices, with columns corresponding to scales/attributes, and rows corresponding to the pupils of the respective classes, have to be analysed separately.

Before reporting the results of this reanalysis, however the main line of argument which lies at the basis of the methodological strategy, will be introduced below.

RATIONALE FOR A TEST OF CLUSTERABILITY

Beside other approaches, the usual standard application of cluster-analysis methods proceeds as follows (see Anderberg 1973, Hartigan 1975, Oldenbürger 1983):
(a) Construct a data-matrix $\left[x_{ij} \right]$, whose rows i contain cases (e.g. pupils), and whose columns j contain variables (e.g. attributes/ rating).
(b) Choose a modality (rows/cases or columns/variables), the elements of which will be grouped.
(c) Calculate proximities for all pairs of elements (e.g. distances, covariances, correlations).
(d) Apply a partitioning or hierarchical clustering algorithm on the symmetric matrix of proximities. (These methods construct groups of elements with high similarities or low distances within clusters and low similarities or large distances between clusters.)

(e) Check the result for plausibility and interpret it in theoretical terms.

Clearly, this kind of standard procedure is quite uncritical due to the grouping-hypothesis. Under all circumstances, it must produce cluster-results simply by pure application of the method. Because this is a degenerate form of modelling, it should be called 'clustering per fiat'. Even if one samples random data from the continuous interval of real numbers, e.g. between 0 and 1, the above method will create "reasonable clusters", although the source of the data has no grouping-structure at all.

To test the central grouping-hypothesis and to prevent cluster analysis from the creation of artefacts, a criterion-referenced decision-procedure is needed. Such a procedure must be able to test the validity of the cluster-analytical model by thoroughly investigating the structural properties of the proximity-matrix between elements (e.g. pupils, Step c, above) <u>before</u> a clustering algorithm (step d) will be applied.
The following part of this contribution presents in three steps an <u>a-priori-test</u> <u>of</u> <u>clusterability</u> of objects <u>without</u> <u>using</u> <u>any</u> specific <u>cluster-analytical</u> <u>method</u> at all. (For more details and illustrations, see Oldenbürger/Becker 1976.)

Step 1: Definition of a Measure of Clusterability

As the literature provides the appropriate transformations of the most common proximity-measures (e.g. set differences, covariances, correlations) into distances (see Anderberg 1973, p. 72 ff., Example: $\text{Dist}_{ij} = \text{SQR} (2(1-\text{Corr}_{ij}))$), it is sufficient to investigate proximity-matrices of distances.

These are conventionally characterized als follows:
A function d: O x O → $\mathbb{R}$ is called distance(-measure), iff

$\forall i,j,k$: (D.1) $d(O_i, O_j) \geqslant \emptyset$
       (D.2) $d(O_i, O_j) = d(O_j, O_i)$
       (D.3) $d(O_i, O_k) \leqslant d(O_i, O_j) + d(O_j, O_k)$

The pair (O,d) is called the 'metric space'.
Iff the triangle inequality (D.3) is tightened to

$\forall i,j,k$: (D.4) $d(O_i, O_k) \leqslant \max \{d(O_i, O_j), d(O_j, O_k)\}$

d is called an 'ultrametric'.

It was ultrametric inequality (D.4), that several authors almost independently identified as the common characteristic of the large variety of non-overlapping cluster-analytical methods (Hartigan 1967, Jardine/Jardine/Sibson 1967, Johnson 1967): These procedures transform a given empirical proximity-matrix into a matrix, which satisfies the ultrametric inequality for all triples of points. Even though different partitioning or hierarchical clustering procedures may produce different results, they share this structural property. Therefore a global, but exact characterization of the 'grouping' - or 'cluster'concept is available using (D.4).

To get a more concrete impression of an <u>ultrametric space</u>, one should note, that all triples of points form triangles, which are isosceles with a small basis. The connection to the concept of grouping is readily apparent. If one imagines a space with, say, two cleary separated clouds of points, there are many triangles present, which are similar to such isosceles - with the two long sides bridging the gap between the clouds. Within only one cloud, in comparison, the triangles can take arbitrary forms.

Whilst the exact definition of the concept 'grouping-structure' by the ultrametric inequality (D.4) is pure, in the case of an empirical investigation - for example, on the structure of pupils in the judgments of a teacher - the given data, after a suitable transformation into a distance matrix, will exhibit the properties (D.1) to (D.3), but that of (D.4) only to a less specific extent. Therefore a <u>measure</u> of clusterability has to be defined. Regarding the above arguments, this should be directly based on the ultrametric inequality, and for n elements/points in a multidimensional space, all single triples of points should be inspected.

<u>Departure from ultrametric inequality</u>:

$$\text{Depfui1} = \sqrt[t]{\frac{\binom{n}{2}\sum_{i<j<k}/d'_{ijk} - d''_{ijk}/^t}{\binom{n}{3}\sum_{i<j}/d_{ij}/^t}} \quad ; t \geq 1$$

$$\text{Depfui2} = \sqrt[t]{\frac{1}{\binom{n}{3}}\sum_{i<j<k}\frac{/d'_{ijk} - d''_{ijk}/^t}{/d'_{ijk}/^t}} \quad ; t \geq 1$$

These measure simply calculate for all triangles i,j,k, the mean of the comparisons (differences) of the largest side d'_{ijk} with the second largest side d''_{ijk}, either in relation to the mean of all distances (Depfui 1), or individually in relation to the largest side d'_{ijk} of the triangle (Depfui2).)See Oldenbürger/Becker 1967, p.606 f for a number of illustrative examples.) The exponent t governs the influence of lager against smaller discrepancies. (To fix t=2 would be the usual choice, though t=1 seems better in terms of robustness and resistence. Therefore the latter value is used in this paper.)

So far two measures for <u>non</u>-clusterability of elements in an empirical proximity-matrix of distances are given in a precise way. (See figure 1 for artificial configurations and their respective measures.)

190

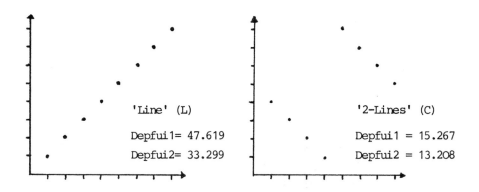

Figure 1: Two artificial configurations and their measures for depar-
          ture from ultrametric inequality

But there is no foundation for the evaluation of clusterability. -
It is one of the general, basic ideas of this approach, that elements
under consideration should be better clusterable than random configurations of points. The comparison of the empirically gathered multivariate distribution of elements with appropriately chosen random scatters
of the same order (number of points and dimensions) therefore provides
a tool for the evaluation of the structural grouping hypothesis.

Step 2: Defenition of an Appropriate Basis for a Randomization-Test

The randomization-basis of this test is the set of all independently
combined permutations within the columns of the data matrix. It is
called 'appropriate', because this basis preserves the empirical distributions for all variables, i.e. all means, variances, etc. remain
the same.

*Step 3: Execution of an approximate Randomization-Test of
         Clusterability*

As the number of possible configurations for the above defined randomization basis usually is too large, it is not managable to calculate
the Depfui-measure(s) for all configurations, so 'only' a random
sample can be considered. The total distribution(s) of the statistic(s)
therefore has to be estimated, and an approximate randomization-test
has to be constructed, consisting of the following steps:
(a) Formulate scientific and statistical hypotheses (one-/two-sided,
    level of significance, etc.),
(b) collect data,
(c) Calculate 'Departure from ultrametric inequality' for empirical
    data-matrix: empDepfui,
(d) Construct random-data-matrix by shuffling within columns,
(e) Calculate 'Departure from ultrametric inequality' for random
    data-matrix: ranDepfui,

```
Depth      Stem * Leaves    for  Depfui1
                 *
   6        21 * 588999
  10        22 * 4567
  11        23 * 0
  16        24 * 34449
  23        25 E 1333567
  38        26 * 003555566677889
  47        27 Q 013467889
  65        28 * 001112223334455588
+ 18        29 M 0000111344556668888
  75        30 * 011233555557788899
  57        31 * 0222334455667778
  41        32 Q 01233457889
  30        33 E 001222233344566899
  12        34 * 000113
   6        35 * 02
   4        36 *
   4        37 * 25
   2        38 * 36
                 *
Depth      Stem * Leaves
                 *

Mean     =     29.579
St.Dev.  =      3.527
Minimum  =     21.572     -    Depfui1(C) =    15.267
Maximum  =     38.657     -    Depfui1(L) =    47.619
 Count   =    158
-------------------------------------------------------
Depth      Stem * Leaves    for  Depfui2
                 *
   4        16 * 3569
  12        17 * 00222247
  18        18 * 336789
  34        19 E 1122477888899999
  54        20 Q 11333344456777888999
+ 31        21 M 000001122333445566777788888889
  73        22 * 00112222334566678888888888999
  46        23 Q 122223344455788999
  28        24 E 000001234444456678
  10        25 * 00112233
   2        26 * 24
                 *
Depth      Stem * Leaves
                 *

Mean     =     21.887
St.Dev.  =      2.216
Minimum  =     16.323     -    Depfui2(C) =    13.208
Maximum  =     26.498     -    Depfui2(L) =    33.299
 Count   =    158
-------------------------------------------------------
```

Table 1: Results of Test-Examples for Depfui1 and Depfui2:
The simulated distributions lie between
the values for the constructed configurations.

(f) Sample Distribution-Function of 'Depfui' by repetition of 'd' and
'e'
(g) Estimate probability according to (a), for example: $\hat{p}$ (empDepfui
< ranDepfui),
(h) Decide on H_o and H_1 (or goto (d)).
A stopping-rule, which serves as a control-structure for the repetition of components (d) to (h) has to be constructed (sequential
binomial, Wald, etc. - I have omitted the discussion of this issue
since it has no importance for this contribution.)

Example

Table 1 illustrates the approximate randomization distribution of
clusterability for the two 8-point configurations of figure 1.

For both measures the distribution of random departure measures lie
very clearly between the measures for the constructed configurations:
As the '2-Lines' (C) depart much less from clusterability than any of
the random configurations, this pattern is diagnosed by the procedure
as having a grouping-structure. The regular 'Line' (L) departs very
far from clusterability and is to be characterized as non-grouping-
structure. Of course, there can be very different grouping- and non-
grouping patterns, not only lines.

Thus the procedure does what we want it to do, and the two measures
lead to the same results. (The hard work to investigate the power of
this statistical test still remains. But this example, and the results
of its further application shown in this paper lead to the impression
that the test is highly sensitive.)

RESULTS ON TEACHERS' JUDSMENTS

Table 2 shows the results of the investigation on clusterability of
pupils within teachers' judgments. (For the calculation of distances
between pupils the variables have been standardized.)

For both measures the empirically gained response patterns in the
judgments depart much more from the ultrametric inequality than the
respective random configurations do. The Z-values indicate the distances of the empirical Depfui-values from the means of the corresponding
sampling distributions, measured in units of their standard deviations
(unbiased estimates). These high Z-values show how far the empirical
values of the Depfui-statistic lie on the "wrong sides" of their
respective distributions. (For the purpose of testing significance,
one could even use the very conservative Tchebychef- and Cantelli-
inequalities ($1/z^2$ and $1/Z^2+1$)) to estimate probabilities.) Moreover
for each teacher, each of the 60 appropriately constructed random-configurations had a lower value for non-clusterability than the empirical original.

This result not only indicates a lack of support for the structural
hypothesis, which states tendencies to group pupils in teachers'
judgment, but it definitely contradicts this assumption.

Tea-cher	100 x Depfui1			100 x Depfui2		
	Emp. Value	Mean (Ran)	Z	Emp. Value	Mean (Ran)	Z
1	13.51	9.10	4.53	11.10	8.08	3.85
2	15.07	9.28	5.36	12.36	8.24	4.80
3	17.20	9.23	10.59	13.59	8.21	9.07
4	18.57	8.90	9.03	14.26	7.94	7.31
5	14.96	8.56	10.36	12.26	7.67	9.14
6	13.84	8.34	5.20	11.34	7.50	4.41
7	15.54	8.77	11.77	12.69	7.84	10.32
8	16.10	8.92	8.79	12.82	7.95	7.37
9	13.81	8.61	7.13	11.47	7.71	6.31
10	14.83	9.44	6.03	11.89	8.38	4.89
11	17.73	9.36	12.36	13.84	8.30	10.41
12	18.85	8.94	11.17	14.88	7.98	9.77
13	18.26	8.70	14.90	14.62	7.77	13.53
14	19.29	8.78	10.33	15.31	7.84	9.02
15	14.95	8.65	12.08	12.44	7.74	11.19
16	17.13	9.30	13.82	13.71	8.25	12.40
17	16.60	9.74	10.31	13.23	8.58	8.84
18	15.20	9.23	10.50	12.41	8.20	9.28
19	17.52	9.69	15.62	13.60	8.57	12.74
20	16.74	9.33	13.15	13.47	8.28	11.68
21	17.10	9.02	23.32	13.60	8.04	19.47
22	17.39	9.01	24.91	13.93	8.01	22.32
23	16.75	8.70	18.19	13.37	7.79	15.53
24	13.93	9.23	7.11	11.46	8.19	6.31
25	17.43	8.89	17.72	13.96	7.94	15.54
26	19.22	9.98	14.13	14.58	8.80	11.10
27	16.52	9.23	11.06	13.56	8.21	10.09
28	17.19	9.20	22.28	13.81	8.18	20.04
29	13.64	8.82	11.45	11.53	7.87	10.98
30	16.72	9.47	17.66	13.31	8.39	15.45
31	18.16	9.81	18.44	14.21	8.65	15.76
32	17.09	9.54	12.36	13.70	8.45	11.01
33	15.10	9.09	15.87	12.45	8.09	14.24
34	17.33	8.86	17.89	13.39	7.91	14.35
35	17.92	9.21	20.62	14.19	8.16	18.23
36	17.51	9.04	15.64	13.79	8.05	13.28

Table 2: Results of the approximate randomization tests for clusterability of PUPILS in teachers' judgments

	100 x Depfui1			100 x Depfui2		
Tea-cher	Emp. Value	Mean (Ran)	Z	Emp. Value	Mean (Ran)	Z
1	13.00	11.04	5.15	10.85	9.63	4.17
2	11.62	10.22	3.87	9.97	8.98	3.48
3	11.18	9.03	6.30	9.53	8.06	5.38
4	12.97	10.19	6.88	10.84	8.97	5.97
5	12.48	9.28	8.53	10.55	8.25	7.62
6	12.90	11.97	1.70	10.69	10.32	0.89
7	13.39	9.81	8.88	11.28	8.67	8.19
8	11.86	9.98	4.88	10.01	8.80	3.99
9	13.96	10.22	8.20	11.47	8.99	7.47
10	13.25	10.00	8.18	11.07	8.82	7.12
11	14.10	8.00	16.66	11.69	7.21	14.94
12	13.41	10.64	6.52	11.13	9.32	5.49
13	14.32	9.54	12.81	11.92	8.46	11.63
14	14.78	10.60	9.77	12.14	9.28	8.64
15	11.98	9.01	8.20	10.19	8.03	7.48
16	11.75	7.61	12.50	9.95	6.89	11.07
17	10.89	7.81	10.32	9.24	7.06	8.89
18	12.45	8.00	12.76	10.47	7.22	11.32
19	11.69	7.23	15.63	10.04	6.58	14.50
20	12.02	8.25	12.27	10.17	7.42	10.82
21	10.81	6.50	16.46	9.19	5.98	14.26
22	11.65	6.53	15.14	9.87	6.00	13.48
23	11.37	7.77	10.37	9.61	7.03	9.06
24	12.97	8.45	12.33	10.84	7.59	10.87
25	14.14	8.13	18.97	11.77	7.32	17.08
26	11.71	8.28	8.81	9.80	7.45	7.46
27	12.08	8.30	10.47	10.27	7.47	9.45
28	12.48	6.42	25.09	10.48	5.90	22.38
29	12.03	7.78	14.64	10.27	7.03	13.64
30	11.06	6.46	15.20	9.48	5.94	13.85
31	12.40	7.10	16.76	10.48	6.48	15.09
32	13.03	8.43	12.94	10.91	7.57	11.43
33	10.90	6.64	17.28	9.34	6.09	15.57
34	12.07	7.52	17.33	10.13	6.83	15.25
35	11.82	7.18	14.85	9.98	6.54	13.08
36	12.58	7.44	15.61	10.62	6.75	14.23

Table 3: Results of the approximate randomization tests for clusterability of ATTRIBUTES in teachers' judgments

Table 3 shows that the same holds true for the clusterability of attributes. (Teacher 6 rated only 10 pupils. This reduces the power of the test.)

According to the testing strategy presented here, there is clear evidence concerning both pupils and attributes, for a strong and highly, significant tendency against clustering within each teacher's judgments.

METHODOLOGICAL REMARKS

To comment on this impressive result some methodological considerations are appropriate:
- It is improbable that 'hidden' groups of pupils exist in attribute spaces at a lower dimension. In this case one would expect empirical values of the Depfui-statistics near the mean and on the "other side" of the simulated sampling distributions.
- An additional application of the randomization test on the variables weighted according to their variation (by omitting standardization) led to the same results.
- The procedure does not detect clusterability created by gaps in distributions related to single attributes/variables. But if clusters in single variables are supported by covariations of the variables with others, again the method should exhibit empirical Depfui-statistics which lie near the mean and/or on the "other side" of the randomization distributions.
- The appropriateness of the randomization-basis might be questionable because the random permutation of entries within columns destroyes the dependencies between variables (Step 2, see above). This is not critical for the investigation of the attributes, but specifically for the cases/pupils.
The construction of a randomization basis that preserves all intercorrelations between variables is a difficult problem for further methodological work.
But this criticism does not alter the main results: Almost all random-configurations departed less from clusterability than their empirical parents, which is in sharp contrast with the structural grouping hypothesis.

Therefore, provisionally, a conclusion of substantial content can be drawn: Teachers' cognitions/judgments on pupils and their attributes are not organized like 'clouds in the sky', but seem to show a pattern characterized by high regularity. Which kind of structure these interrelated nets possess is an open question to be answered by further investigations.

INTERPRETATION

Speculating on an explanation for these strong tendencies against clustering one should consider the task situation: Each teacher was asked to judge each pupil of his/her class using the whole set of 25 bipolar rating scales. On the one hand this task can strengthen the teachers' tendencies to avoid grouping pupils by regularly spacing covariational judgments, on the other hand satiation effects mau occur (average number of judgments = (810x25)/36 = 562.5).

Furthermore all teachers in the present study can be regarded as being fairly familiar with their classes, because they already had assigned marks to their pupils before data collection took place (see Tscherner 1974, p.48f). But probably categorizing things, persons, or attributes is only a simple and powerful preliminary means to gain structure in cognitions on complex situational aspects. Therefore in further research it is necessary to study the structural properties of developing cognitive systems of teachers.

In any case, the teaching situation apparently differs in fundamental aspects from the situation considered here. For example, the teachers' focus of attention and its content, and the varying necessity to act for the support of pupils' learning processes makes things incomparable. Therefore the findings presented here cannot be transferred to teachers' actions in the classroom. Further investigations are necessary to study tendencies to group pupils in teaching behavior. But the methodological criticism presented in this paper remains valid for such research on teaching interactions.

In general, studies on structural and systemic properties of teachers' cognitions, feelings, goals, actions, and their interconnections in relation to its systemic context and development obviously are indispensable. This widens the view for embedding the present study.

CONSEQUENCES FOR FURTHER RESEARCH ON TEACHERS' COGNITIONS

As the subjective and/or implicit theories of teachers are conceptualized as open, dynamic, interrelated nets of systems (see above), this should have its real counterparts in all components of research on this topic:
- It is necessary to perform individualized data collection and analysis (modelling and testing). Summarizing results has to take place afterwards. This avoids the usual confounding of different sources of variation: The reconstruction of intraindividual structural relationships for an 'average person' by using averaged interindividual variation in general has no bases. (See Gara/Rosenberg 1981, and Gigerenzer 1981 for a supplementary discussion).
- It is necessary to gain genuine structural data from each individuum in the data collection phase. For example, simple assignments of attributes - as in the present investigation - do not suffice. It only gives a basis to reconstruct relationships between attributes computationally (e.g. by correlations). In my view this might be interpreted as a modelling of an 'implicit personality theory' but not as a reconstruction of a 'subjective theory', because for the latter the interconnections between attributes or pupils at least in part can be conciously actualized by the subject.
- Teachers' thinking connects various implicit and/or subjective theoretical systems: IPT on pupils and their attributes, knowledge on teaching objects and objectives, goal structures, prototypical views of situations. theories on the effects of actions, and the like.

197

Research should also represent these systems and their _systemic interplay_.
- As subjective and implicit theories are regarded as open and dynamic systems, their _genesis_ and _development_ has to be considered (see above). - In addition teachers themselves know that things change, e.g. frame-conditions of teaching, pupils, knowledge on teaching objects, interaction situations etc., and they theoretize on their ability to exert influence on these, which probably governs their actions. - Thus research should reflect perspectives of teachers and their change.

Though different cultural, sociological, and paedagogical contexts are complex intervening systems, which should also be incorporated in research on teachers' cognitions, and though different perspectives on the applicational, technological role of this research have been given at least the above mentioned aspects can form its common basis.

It seems obvious that traditional empirical research procedures (e.g. gather observations, questionaires, or tests; calculate correlations; perform factor- or cluster-analysis, etc.) are sometimes necessary but generally not sufficient, because the system-perspective is disregarded.

Therefore several parallel theoretical, methodological, and empirical advances are necessary which gradually rise complexity in research on teachers' thinking.

REFERENCES

Anderberg, M.R. (1973). _Cluster analysis for application_. New York, Wiley.
Asch, S.E. (1956). Forming impressions of personality. _Journal of Abnormal and Social Psychology_,41, 258-290.
Brophy, J.E. (1983). Research on the self-Fulfilling Prophecy and Teacher Expectations. _Journal of Educational Psychology_,75, 631-661.
Cantor, N & Mischel, W. (1979). Prototypes in person perception. In: L. Berkowitz (ed), _Advances in experimental social psychology_, vol. 12, New York: Academic Press, p. 3-52.
Conte, H.R. & Plutchik, R. (1981). A circumplex Model of Interpersonal Personality Traits. _Journal of Personality and Social Psychology_, 40, 701-711.
Dusek, J.B. & Gail, J. (1983). The Bases of Teacher Expectancies: A Meta-Analysis. _Journal of Educational Psychology_, 75, 327-346.
Gara, M.A. & Rosenberg, S. (1981). Linguistic Factors in Implicit Personality Theory. _Journal of Personality and Social Psychology_, 41, 450-457.
Gigerenzer, G. (1981). Implizite Persönlichkeitstheorien oder Quasi-implizite Persönlichkeitstheorien. _Zeitschrift für Sozialpsychologie_, 12, 65-80.
Gigerenzer, G. & Strube, R. (1978). Zur Revision der Üblichen Anwendung deminsionsanalytischer Verfahren. _Zeitschrift für Entwicklungspsychologie und Pädagogische Psychologie_,10, 75-86

Hartigan, J.A. (1967). Representation of similarity matrices by trees. *Journal of the American Statistical Association*, 62, 1140-1158.

Hartigan, J.A. (1975). *Clustering Algorithms*. New York, Wiley.

Heider, F. (1958). *The psychology of interpersonal relations*. New York, Wiley.

Höhn, E. (1967). *Der schlechte Schüler*. München, Piper. 7. Augl. 1976.

Hofer, M. (1969). *Die Schülerpersönlichkeit im Urteil des Lehrers*. Weinheim, Beltz. 2. Aufl. 1970, 3. Aufl. 1974.

Hofer, M. (1975). Die Validität der impliziten Persönlichkeitstheorie von Lehrern. *Unterrichtswissenschaft*, 3, 5-18.

Hofer, M. (1981). Schülergruppierungen im Urteil und Verhalten des Lehrers. In: Hofer, M. (Ed.), *Informationsverarbeitung und Entscheidungsverhalten von Lehrern*. München, Urban & Schwarzenberg.

Hofer, M. (1986). *Sozialpsychologie erzieherischen Handelns*. Göttingen: Hogrefe.

Jardine, C.J., Jardine, N. & Sibson, R. (1967). The structure and construction of taxonomic hierarchies. *Mathematical Biosciences*. 1, 173-179.

Jardine, N. & Sibson, R. (1971) *Mathematical Taxonomy*. New York, Wiley.

Johnson, S.C. (1967). Hierarchical Clustering Schemes. *Psychometrika*, 32, 241-254.

Mandl, H. & Huber, G.L. (1983). Subjektive Theorien von Lehrern. *Psychologie in Erziehung und Unterricht*, 30, 98-112.

Morine-Dershimer, G. (1978). *Teacher conceptions of pupils*. Paper presented at the meeting of the Amer. Educ. Res. Assoc., Toronto.

Oldenbürger, H.-A. (1983). Clusteranalyse. In: Bredenkamp, J. & Feger, H. (Eds.), *Strukturierung und Reduzierung von Daten* (Band 4) Forschungsmethoden der Psychologie (Serie I), *Enzyklopädie der Psychologie*, Göttingen: Hogrefe.

Oldenbürger, H.-A. (1984). *Subjektive Theorien in Lern-Lehr-Prozessen* - Mittelfristige Lösungsansätze für einige Überbrückungsprobleme. Unpublished Paper, Göttingen.

Oldenbürger, H.-A. & Becker, D. (1976). Are there clusters of frequencies in powerspectra of EEG? How to find and prove them statistically. In: Matejcek, M. & Schenk, G.K. (Eds.), *Quantitative analysis of the EEG*. Proceedings of the 2nd Symposium of the Study for EEG-Methodology, Jongny sur Vevey, May 1975. Konstanz AEG-Telefunken.

Powell, R.S. & Juhnke, R.G. (1983). Statistical Models of Implicit Personality Theory: A comparison. *Journal of Personality and Social Psychology*, 44, 911-922.

Rosenberg, S. (1982). The Method of Sorting in Multivariate Research with Applications Selected from Cognitive Psychology and Person Perception. In: Hirschberg, N. & Humphreys, L.G. (Eds.), *Multivariate Applications in the Social Science*. Hillsdale, New Yersey, Lawrence Erlbaum Ass.

Schneider, D.J. (1973) Implicit Personality Theory: A review. *Psychological Bulletin*, 79, 294-319.

Schneider, D.J. & Blankmeyer, B.L. (1983). Prototype Salience and Implicit Personality Theories. *Journal of Personality and Social Psychology*, 44, 712-722.

Silberman, M. (1969). Behavioral expression of teachers attitudes toward elementary school students. *Journal of Educational Psychology*, 60, 402-407.

Tscherner, K. (1974). *Untersuchungen zur Schülerbeurteilung in Abhängigkeit von Impliziten Persönlichkeitsmodellen bei Lehrern.* Dissertation Pädagogische Hochschule Ruhr, Dortmund.

Tscherner, K. & Masendorf, F. (1974). Analyse von Schülerbeurteilungen und Zeugnisnoten bei einzelnen Lehrern. *Psychologie in Erziehung und Unterricht,* 21, 135-149.

Wahl, D., Schlee, J., Krauth, J. & Murek, J. (1983). *Naive Verhaltenstheorie von Lehrern.* Universität Oldenburg, Zentrum für Pädagogische Berufspraxis.

ADDRESSES OF THE AUTHORS

Ben-Peretz, M.
University of Haifa
Mount Carmel
Haifa 31 999
Israel

Bromme, R.
Universität Bielefeld
Institut für Didaktik der
Mathematik
Postfach 8640
4800 Bielefeld 1
Western-Germany

Brown, A.F.
The Ontario Institute for
Studies in Education
252 Bloor Street West
Toronto, Ontario M5S 1V6
Canada

Brown, S.
University of Stirling
Department of Education
Stirling FK9 4LA
Scotland

Buchmann, M.
Michigan State University
Institute for Research on Teaching
East Lansing, Michigan 48824
USA

Chayot, R.
Ben Gurion University of the Negev
Department of Education
P.O.B. 653
Beer-Sheva 84 105
Israel

Clandinin, J.
University of Calgary
Faculty of Education
2500 University NW
Calgary, Alberta T2N 1N4
Canada

Clark, C.M.
Institute for Research on Teaching
Michigan State University
East Lansing, Michigan 48824
USA

Connelly, F.M.
The Ontario Institute for
Studies in Education
252 Bloor Street West
Toronto, Ontario M5S 1V6
Canada

Dobslaw, G.
Universität Bielefeld
Facultät Psychologie
Postfach 8640
4800 Bielefeld 1
Western Germany

201

Elbaz, F.
Ben Gurion University of the Negev
Department of education
P.O. Box 653
Beer-Sheva 84 105
Israel

Halkes, R.
Tilburg University
P.O.B. 90153
5000 LE Tilburg
The Netherlands

Hofer, M.
Universität Mannheim
Lehrstuhl für Erziehungs-
wissenschaft II
Schloss
6800 Mannheim
Western Germany

Hoz, R.
Ben Gurion University of the Negev
Department of Education
P.O.B. 653
Beer-Sheva 84 105
Israel

Krause, F.
Universität Konstanz
Sozialwissenschaftliche
Fakultät
Postfach 5560
D 7750 Konstanz 1
Western Germany

Kremer-Hayon, L.
University of Haifa
Centre for Educational
Administration
Haifa 31223
Israel

Lampert, M.
Michigan State University
Faculty of Teacher Education
East Lansing, Michigan 48824
USA

Lowyck, J.
University of Leuven
Department of Education
Vesaliusstraat 2
B 3000 Leuven
Belgium

Mahler, S.
Ben Gurion University of the
Negev
Department of Education
P.O.B. 653
Beer-Sheva 84 105
Israel

McIntyre, D.
University of Oxford
Department of Educational Studies
Wellington Square
Oxford OX1 2JD
England

Oldenbürger, H.A.
Seminar für Wirtschaftspädagogik
der Georg-August-Universität
Göttingen
Nikolausbergerweg 9b
D 3400 Göttingen
Western Germany

Olson, J.K.
Queen's University
Faculty of Education
Duncan McArthur Hall
Kingston, Ontario K7L 3N6
Canada

Rapaille, J.P.
16, Rue de Bruyeres Hubertfays
4651 Bruyeres Herve
Belgium

Tabachnik, B.R.
Mucia
World Bank Education IX Project
Tromolpos 3285-JKT
Djakarta 10002
Indonesia

Tomer, Y.
Ben Gurion University of the Negev
Department of Education
P.O.B. 653
Beer-Sheva 84 105
Israel

Yeheskel, N.
Ben Gurion University of the Negev
Department of Education
P.O.B. 653
Beer-Sheva 84 105
Israel

Zeichner, K.M.
University of Wisconsin-Madison
Department of Curriculum and Instruction
225 N.Mills Street
Madison, Wisconsin 53706
USA